THE SECRET LIFE OF THE SAVOY

Also by Olivia Williams:

GIN GLORIOUS GIN:
How Mother's Ruin Became the Spirit of London

THE
SECRET LIFE
OF THE

SAVOY

OLIVIA WILLIAMS

PEGASUS BOOKS
NEW YORK LONDON

THE SECRET LIFE OF THE SAVOY

Pegasus Books, Ltd.
148 West 37th Street, 13th Floor
New York, NY 10018

Copyright © 2021 by Olivia Williams

First Pegasus Books paperback edition May 2022
First Pegasus Books cloth edition June 2021

ISBN: 978-1-63936-208-0

10 9 8 7 6 5 4 3 2

Printed in the United States of America
Distributed by Simon & Schuster
www.pegasusbooks.com

For my late father,
and my late friend, Georgie

'The function of the Savoy is to make people happy, to get rid of the problems of life. We all have them.'

Sir Hugh Wontner,
chairman of the Savoy Hotel (1948–84)
and of the Savoy Theatre (1948–92)

CONTENTS

ACT TWO – RUPERT

ACT THREE – BRIDGET

INTRODUCTION

Fantasy worlds were the stock in trade of the D'Oyly Carte family. They were, at their height, the greatest impresarios and hoteliers in the world. With their Savoy Theatre and Savoy Hotel, which take up nearly an acre of central London, they pioneered a luxurious form of escapist socialising. Their name became a household term, at first as the impresarios behind Gilbert and Sullivan. Starting in the 1870s, they took these unprecedently popular light operas on tours to America, Europe, Asia and Africa, year-in, year-out, from their base on the Strand. On stage they conjured early modern Venice in *The Gondoliers*, commissioned a real Arcadian babbling brook for *Patience*, and the tiny bulbs that they embedded in fairies' costumes for *Iolanthe* gave us the term 'fairy lights'. They then applied this stagecraft to creating one of the world's earliest luxury hotels, next door to the theatre, putting it together with the same flair and glossy precision as their theatrical productions.

Their Savoy Hotel became a microcosm of a newly diverse local and international elite, who came to be wined and dined and entertained, and, as the D'Oyly Cartes grasped intuitively, to see and be seen. Wherever guests had arrived from, the aim was to create a sense of belonging and excitement for them. I gravitated towards the family not only because I liked that they made the city a more romantic, sociable place, but also because I liked *them*. They were not successful in a detached, failsafe way; they were a little eccentric and too emotional to be truly businesslike. I became as curious about the things that went wrong for them as the things that went right.

During a century of almost surreal change and upheaval, from the 1880s, when their theatre and hotel opened, to the 1980s, when their line ended, their resistance to any kind of standardisation served them well. The Savoy was a 'city in itself', staff liked to say – they did things differently there.

Following on from the family's Victorian patriarch, Richard D'Oyly Carte, his son and then his granddaughter took up the mantle. As though casting for one of their productions, they thought about how to keep a cosmopolitan mix of illustrious people coming back again and again to the hotel. Ailing aristocrats were offered cheaper rooms to keep them in the game, artistic types could come for the *prix fixe* rather than the full-blown restaurant menu, while the super rich could book out whole floors and make outlandish banqueting demands as they saw fit. Tycoons were kept in touch with Wall Street with a ticker tape charting the movement of the markets, couples seeking discretion were offered private entrances, and the hotel press office organised photo shoots and interviews for celebrities in the comfort of their suites. All sorts of needs were catered for, in the hope of keeping all sorts of guests happy.

So, if the Savoy and its creators are so special, why has no one written their story before? It has only really become possible with the passage of time. During the D'Oyly Cartes' reign at the Savoy, the hotel board worried that the family's personal lives would not reflect well on the business, so they repeatedly brushed off biography offers. For their part, the family themselves were content to operate behind the scenes without recognition. Their name has accordingly lost the resonance it once had as they fade further and further into the past.

Introduction

Whether privately troubled or not, high achievers often yearn to have their lives recorded, however. Aristotle Onassis, a Savoy regular, who makes an appearance in this book, is a case in point. He enthusiastically commissioned his own biography, despite his often dubious behaviour. For nearly a year he had a journalist listening to his self-aggrandising anecdotes, plying him with champagne, not letting him go to bed, and then dragging him to breakfast at Claridge's, the Savoy's smaller sister hotel, to carry on talking about himself – having spent all night doing exactly that.

The D'Oyly Cartes took the opposite approach. They gave only a handful of interviews in over a century of prominence. Beyond their most immediate confidantes and friends, few people knew them well. Among a small group, they were generous and trusting. They wrote blank cheques for certain employees to use while they were abroad, left others money in their wills, and invited household staff to make use of their houses in their absence. Outside that circle, however, most found them secretive, and wondered what they had to hide. It resulted in persistent rumours, including the suggestion that the hotel laundry was being used as a place to squirrel away personal documents, far from the rest of the management, where no one would think to look.

Towards the end of her life, the last D'Oyly Carte, Bridget, started burning papers herself, and had others unceremoniously emptied into skips. Perhaps the staff theory about secrets had some truth – or perhaps, if she had been in a happier state of mind by then, and more confident about her legacy, she may not have wanted to clear some of it away. The only reason we have some documents now is that staff found their disposal a shame and fished them out of the skips again.

Introduction

Taking their lead from the family, staff across the various D'Oyly Carte enterprises took their work admirably seriously, which drew me into the wider story of the hotel and theatre.

Paolo Contarini, the Savoy's former head of banqueting, who worked there from 1945 until his retirement in 1971, wrote an elegiac book about his time there. In his memoir, *The Savoy was my Oyster*, he brought his learned reading to bear on his hotel work, quoting Dante, Shakespeare and gastronome Jean Anthelme Brillat-Savarin, but, in this intellectual approach, he was not unusual among his colleagues. The Savoy management speeches at shareholders' meetings were peppered with Biblical and classical references, Latin phrases and word play, while front-of-house staff were expected to read the daily newspapers to understand their guests' lives better, ensuring they would be ready to hold informed conversations with anyone who walked in through the polished doors.

Contarini opened his autobiography by quoting *Julius Caesar*, as he recalled arriving at the Savoy when peace came to Europe. I would like to follow his lead, but to re-frame it for the D'Oyly Cartes:

> There is a tide in the affairs of men,
> Which, taken at the flood, leads on to fortune;
> Omitted, all the voyage of their life
> Is bound in shallows and in miseries.
> On such a full sea are we now afloat,
> And we must take the current when it serves
>
> (Brutus to Cassius, *Julius Caesar*, Act IV, Scene iii)

The D'Oyly Cartes took the current when it served. This is where it carried them.

PREFACE

9 July 1923
The Savoy, London

Parisian courtesan Marguerite Fahmy slept with a pistol under her pillow every night of her honeymoon at the Savoy. Her husband was twenty-three-year-old Prince Ali Kamel Fahmy, a playboy ten years her junior whom she had met through her work. They had started the extended trip in his native Egypt, where he had coerced her into posing for photographs in a pharaoh's sarcophagus and kept her a virtual prisoner on his yacht, she later claimed. The marriage, characterised by violence and material excess, had been a disaster so far.

Nevertheless, Marguerite and Ali continued on to London, intending to stay for a month. With their luggage, staff and yapping dog, they took up residence on the fourth floor of the Savoy Court, the furnished apartments attached to the hotel. Richard D'Oyly Carte, the mastermind behind Gilbert and Sullivan, had built the hotel, theatre and the set of lanes around it from scratch, starting in the 1870s. They were his lasting treasures, financed with his profits from *The Pirates of Penzance* and *The Mikado*. It was all now the domain of his younger son, Rupert D'Oyly Carte, and covered nearly an acre of central London. Rupert was charged with upholding his father's grand ambition for the Savoy, that it be not only the finest hotel in London, but the world.

With this in mind, one of Rupert's many innovations had been putting together the Savoy Havana Band as in-house musicians, mainly with his American guests' taste in mind. Popularising the Band's jazz through nightly BBC broadcasts and record deals, he believed, with some pride, that there was no more famous band in all of Europe. They had been entertaining Marguerite and Ali in the hotel's Louis Quatorze-style ballroom nightly during their stay. The couple also made regular use of the Restaurant, with its soothing view of the River Thames, and Hungarian quartet playing 'melodies of melancholy sweetness'.[1]

As with many younger guests, Marguerite and Ali also did the rounds of local nightclubs before bedtime. Around the hotspots of London they made a spectacle of themselves with their loud rows. At the Riviera Club on Grosvenor Road, patrons heard Ali shouting that he had a good mind to throw Marguerite in the river. A few days later, they were visiting Hampton Court Palace one afternoon, where the Savoy kept punts for guests, and exchanged blows next to their chauffeur-driven car before being separated by friends.

On 9 July, a hot and humid day, they had been out for another drive, then back for lunch at the Savoy, followed by shopping at Selfridges. For the theatre, Ali changed into full evening dress: a tailcoat, bow-tie, starched shirtfront and waistcoat. Marguerite chose a beaded white-satin cocktail dress, designed for her by Coco Chanel. In their finery, they went to Leicester Square to see the operetta *The Merry Widow*, which turned out to be an appropriate choice.

Relations became more strained than ever during the interval, when Marguerite insisted that she would return to the couple's house in Paris alone the next day. Unable to persuade her to stay, Ali had telegrams sent to her favourite shops to pre-empt one of her sprees. They read: 'Nothing to be delivered to my wife on my account during my absence. Fahmy.'[2] They were sent to Louis Vuitton on the Avenue des Champs-Élysées, Cartier on the Rue de la Paix and Van Cleef & Arples on the Place Vendôme.

Back at the Savoy after *The Merry Widow*, the pair fought again. Marguerite brandished a wine bottle during their late supper in the Restaurant, threatening to smash it over his head. In bad humour, they made their way to the ballroom. Marguerite stayed until 1 a.m., at which point she left Ali to brood over whether their marriage was already finished.

He turned up at their suite of rooms at 2 a.m., where Marguerite was still in her satin dress, writing letters, and they had another fight. In distress, Ali came rushing out into the corridor in the white silk djellaba that he wore for bed and ran into the night porter, John Paul Beattie. 'Look at my face,' he pleaded, and pointed to marks on his cheek where Marguerite had hit him.[3] Ali wanted to speak to the night manager, Arthur Marini. Beattie told the lift attendant to pass on the message, while he proceeded to attend to some newly arrived guests.

After walking a few paces down the corridor with the guests' luggage, Beattie heard three shots over the storm that was in full force outside. He ran back to see that Marguerite had thrown her Browning semi-automatic down on the carpet. Next to the pistol was Ali, slumped on the floor against the wall. Brain tissue and fragmented bone were protruding from his temple. Further wounds were found in his back and his neck. A pool of blood was spreading out around him.

Beattie held on to Marguerite with one hand, while calling the telephonist for the hotel doctor and an ambulance with the other. Marini came up from the night service office and instructed Beattie to fetch the police. The Savoy's managing director, George Reeves-Smith, who had held the position since 1900, would be informed at a more civilised hour. He was known for being elegant and handsome and resolutely unflappable. He lived ten minutes' drive away in a penthouse suite at Claridge's, the Savoy's smaller sister hotel in Mayfair. Rupert lived nearby in a townhouse on Derby Street, just behind Park Lane.

Ali meanwhile was taken to the Charing Cross Hospital, just down the road from the Savoy, by Trafalgar Square. He was already unconscious and would die at 3.25 a.m. In the meantime, Beattie set to work scrubbing the corridor walls and the carpet. His overzealous cleaning destroyed forensic material that the prosecution would later want for the trial.

Rupert and Reeves-Smith, the top of the Savoy hierarchy, would be informed of the crime at their usual daily meeting at 10.05 a.m. Like Reeves-Smith, Rupert himself had decades of experience by now. He had worked at his father's hotel since 1893, when he had started as his father's assistant, aged seventeen. Richard D'Oyly Carte had taught his son all that he knew about running his hotel and the adjoining Savoy Theatre, and Rupert paid close attention. By now, aged forty-seven, he had seen plenty of overdoses, affairs and scandals among his guests. Deaths were discreetly dealt with and bodies removed surreptitiously[4] – but a murder was a first.

By lunchtime, Rupert's clockwork routine was over. Many second-edition newspapers carried the murder in their STOP PRESS column. His hotel and its infamous guests were splashed around London on billboards for the *Evening Standard*, *Evening News*, *Star* and *Pall Mall Gazette*, and journalists were jostling outside in search of more details. Marguerite was not just a source of horror and embarrassment for the Savoy, however. When the Prince of Wales, the future Edward VIII, had been a seventeen-year-old in Paris, he had met Marguerite at the Hôtel de Crillon and she had become his wartime lover. The Palace sprang into action to avoid the calamity of their association becoming public, and the judge agreed that her previous relationships would not be discussed at the trial, which was vital for the prince. 'His name is to be kept out', the relieved foreign secretary, Lord Curzon, wrote to his wife.[5] Ill-advisedly, the prince had committed his feelings for Marguerite to paper, which created an extra headache. After some horse trading, a then-junior member of the Foreign Office, Archie Clark Kerr, retrieved the cache of incriminating letters.[6] The prince postponed a planned tour of British cities and abruptly left for Canada.

As Marguerite's trial at the Old Bailey unfolded, what the coroner referred to as 'a sordid, unsavoury and unpleasant story' of married life was relayed to an intrigued public.[7] Marguerite's barrister, Edward Marshall Hall, seemed to be borrowing heavily from *Othello* for his characterisations of the couple. He described Ali as 'a monster of Eastern depravity and decadence, whose sexual tastes were indicative of an amoral sadism' and Marguerite as a 'helpless European wife', driven to despair by the lasciviousness of her North African brute of a husband.[8] Marguerite made but one grave mistake in life, Marshall Hall argued, and that was being 'a woman of the West' married to 'an Oriental'.[9]

Rupert feared that the case's lurid descriptions would put off respectable guests. He should, however, have adopted the attitude of Savoy regular Oscar Wilde: the only thing worse than being talked about was not being talked about. Money could not have bought publicity on this scale. To add to the perverse glamour of the case, Marguerite turned up to court glinting with jewellery: pearl earrings, a pearl necklace, her marquise-diamond engagement ring, another, even heftier emerald ring, and a three-tier diamond-and-sapphire bracelet. The risqué details of the murder and of the life of Marguerite Fahmy did no harm to the Savoy – quite the opposite. The flurry of attention, with the photographs and newspapers' breathless insights into the high life, gave the hotel an even greater magnetism. Coco Chanel, designer of Marguerite's now infamous bloodied white dress, would start coming to stay herself the following year.

As for Marguerite, sensationally, she was acquitted. She spent the rest of her days in legal wrangles with her murdered husband's family, who, unsurprisingly, did not agree with the British court's verdict. She lived well into old age on the Place Vendôme, opposite The Ritz in Paris. When she died, it turned out that, calculating character that she was, she had kept back a few letters from the Prince of Wales – just in case.[10]

ACT ONE

RICHARD

ONE

Curtain up

'l'espoir de mieux me fortient'
['The hope of better gives me strength']
D'Oyly family motto

On the banks of the Thames a ruined medieval palace was left for over a century to crumble down to its foundations. The Savoy, as the grand residence of John of Gaunt, had dominated the skyline of the Thames between Temple Church and Westminster Hall – but none of its finery survived the Peasants' Revolt of 1381. As the embodiment of princely luxury, 'the fayrest manor in Europe'[1] was burned and pulled apart, its contents stolen, destroyed or hurled into the water by the mob. It was not until Henry VII paid for a military hospital that this corner of London was occupied once again. The hospital too fell into dilapidation, its two stately quadrangles 'misused by loiterers, vagabonds and strumpets'.[2] It became a barracks, then a makeshift prison. A fire eventually put it out of its misery, and its charred remains were cleared to make way for the first Waterloo Bridge in 1809.

The empty former palace's grounds became a muddy, sloping rubbish dump. Instead of vagabonds and strumpets, it was home to rats and stray dogs. At one end of the plot came wafts from Monsieur Rimmel, manufacturing perfumes, which mixed nauseatingly with the output of 'Burgess' Noted Fish-Sauce Shop' at the other, and all the refuse in between.[3] Stranded in the middle was the Tudor Savoy Chapel, left standing out of respect for its godly purpose.

In 1878, an ambitious young Londoner set his heart on buying this sorry mess. Richard D'Oyly Carte was then a thirty-four-year-old theatre impresario whose career had taken off stratospherically, after a decade of frustration. D'Oyly, as everyone called him, revelled in striding the streets of Theatreland in his sable-lined coat with its voluminous fur collar and cuffs, and his cane, spats and top hat, on the look-out for talent and money spinners. He had enough energy to watch as many as a hundred auditions in a day, playing accompaniments himself at the piano.[4] He carried on working into the evening until he was 'giddy'.[5] His charisma and cunning coaxed people into supporting him, even when the chances of success were dubious. Contemporaries found him crafty-looking, with his watchful expression and meditative cigar-smoking. Whenever one of his schemes fell flat, he proved endlessly resourceful, and his persuasiveness had earned him the nickname 'Oily Carte'.

After hits and misses in the West End and London's suburban music halls, he had put together his own D'Oyly Carte Opera Company. The premise was to pioneer an original form of entertainment, the English light opera – which became the staging post between highbrow Continental opera and the twentieth-century musical. Italian opera had been a touchstone for elite culture in London since it was introduced in the eighteenth century. It was expensive to attend and, to most English ears, incomprehensible. D'Oyly wanted to take the genre, inject a lightness of touch and comic elements, and popularise it for an English-speaking audience. He did not want opera to be 'monopolised by a fashionable aristocracy' any longer, but opened up to Victorian Britain's burgeoning and increasingly sophisticated, wealthier middle classes – in other words, people like him.[6] With this in mind, he was commissioning and producing his own light operas, with lyrics by a former barrister, William Gilbert, and music by a young classical composer, Arthur Sullivan. The combination was proving thrillingly popular among both Londoners and Americans. With only two full-length operas to perform so far, *The Sorcerer* and *HMS Pinafore*, his touring Opera Company was already the entertainment sensation of the age. D'Oyly dreamed of building his own theatre to give it a home. Unable to afford the site he had in mind quite yet, he could not resist engaging an architect to explore the possibilities all the same, and pored over plans for the next three years.

While daydreaming of his own theatre, D'Oyly was cooped up down the road with his two assistants, using a rented room in a courtyard behind Trafalgar Square as his office. His operas were being staged at the Opera Comique, a fleapit of ill-repute on the Aldwych, which would later be demolished in a round of slum clearances. D'Oyly often walked past the rubbish dump by the Thames between the Opera Comique and his office, and the blank canvas filled him with lofty ideas. The romance and history of the plot was not lost on him. He would call his little fiefdom 'the Savoy'.

There were green shoots of improvement to spur D'Oyly's fantasy on. The Thames had been embanked recently in a vast engineering project by Joseph Bazalgette, who fashioned for the first time a riverside esplanade in central London, with a broad tree-lined avenue for horses and carriages. Thanks to Bazalgette's sewage system, the Thames itself was no longer noxious, and, through the new gas lamps and manicured

Victoria Embankment gardens, there was a pastoral view across to the south bank's expansive greenery. The gardens' focal point was the newly delivered Cleopatra's Needle, an obelisk from Alexandria, donated by a governor of Egypt to commemorate the British victories at the Battles of the Nile and of Alexandria. The British government had rather ungraciously been reluctant to bear the cost of transport, so the gift had languished for decades before arriving in London in 1878.

The apparent smartness of D'Oyly's name was the result of embellishments that could mislead about his beginnings. He was born a ten-minute walk from the Savoy site, in a shared rented house on Greek Street in Soho. He was his parents' first surviving child, born on 3 May 1844, five years into their marriage. Richard senior and Eliza had married at nearby St Martin-in-the-Fields on Trafalgar Square on 2 January 1839, under its soaring vaults of stone and marble. The stormy winter weather, the harshest in living memory, had been howling outside. Richard was thirty-two, a flute-player, recently returned from touring the provinces. Twenty-five-year-old Eliza Jones was the highly educated daughter of the widowed vicar of the Chapel Royal on Whitehall. Reverend Jones did not give the wedding his blessing, nor lend his financial support, nor did he attend.

Reverend Jones surely rued the day that he had allowed Eliza out to the summer garden party where she had been beguiled by this tall, blue-eyed flautist, who was there to entertain the guests. As the 'base born'[7] illegitimate son of a quartermaster stationed in Welshpool, Richard had been raised in rural poverty in Hampshire by his mother. He did not represent a catch to Reverend Jones. The moment of Richard and Eliza's meeting had come when one of the party guests had asked him for an encore, but he demurred. Eliza whipped away his plate of strawberries and cream, refusing to give it back until he conceded to play. This little flirtation sparked the clandestine courtship that, in a matter of months, had ended in elopement.

They set up home at 61 Greek Street, then a dirty, crowded thoroughfare, in the decrepit mansion with 'an unhappy countenance of gloom', which had provided a backdrop to Thomas De Quincey's *Confessions of an English Opium-Eater*. As the infamous town house where De Quincey had camped out while in the depths of his addiction and destitution, it was probably no one's first choice of marital home.[8] It had been renumbered and divided into rental accommodation, with Richard and Eliza's rooms at the top, bearing the brunt of the elements, and another household living below. The building has long been demolished, but its view in the 1840s was of Soho Square to the left, while the House of St Barnabas, soon to become a homeless shelter, now a members' club, was opposite, and down the street were five pubs and an infamous whorehouse.[9] Out of one window, the family could see a statue of Charles II, the focal point of Soho Square. As with the surrounding streets, Charles II had fallen into 'a most wretched mutilated state'.[10] The house backed on to the Royalty Theatre, which was not conducive to a sound night's sleep.

As in much of 1840s central London, Greek Street's inhabitants came from disparate walks of life; the desperately poor and the destitute, bohemians and the fairly respectable all lived cheek by jowl. Eating and drinking places run by a recent influx of Greek and Italian immigrants kept the area humming with activity until late. Less innocently, it was a hub of London's sex industry. At the garish brothel the White House on Soho Square, customers could choose from women dressed to match the gold, silver or bronze-decorated rooms: it was one way to stand out in a crowded marketplace.

When Eliza took thirteen-day-old D'Oyly along to be signed into the parish register two streets away at St Anne's Church, in May 1844, he suffered the early indignity of having his unusual middle name misspelled. D'Oyly, or D'Olyly as the registrar noted down, was a Norman name from Eliza's more illustrious side, of which she was keen to remind everyone.[11] She was told that her lineage on one side was traceable to the Norman Conquest, to the baronial D'Oyly family. Although a pain to spell, it would come in handy, in providing her son with a distinctive name for his theatre career. Richard senior had already added an 'e' to his surname, to distinguish himself from a flute-player with a similar name, giving it some Gallic flair. All in all, little D'Oyly had a far more exciting name than the plain 'Richard Cart' he should have been.

While D'Oyly was a toddler, Richard senior juggled moonlighting in theatre orchestras with flute teaching and recitals. He was back on tour a year after his son was born, as favourable reviews recorded. In Manchester, 'the talented flautist was loudly encored [. . .] At Liverpool subsequently Mr Carte's efforts were crowned with a success still more brilliant'.[12] After a few years, he gave up balancing jobs and joined his childhood flute mentor George Rudall's musical-instrument manufacturing business at 20 Charing Cross, by Trafalgar Square, instead.[13] Rudall's firm produced simple-system flutes until Richard persuaded them to buy the British rights to Theobald Boehm's 1847 cylindrical model from Bavaria, the one that most players use to this day, and to import concertinas, accordions and Aeolian harps. The firm was renamed Rudall, Carte & Company, to reflect his new prominence.[14]

As the Cartes were on the up in the 1850s, they left Greek Street behind in time to miss the cholera outbreak of 1854. They had a lucky escape, given that the Broadwick Street pump in Soho, which they had relied on, was identified as the source. By the time that D'Oyly and his parents moved to leafy north London, he had younger sisters, Blanche, Viola, Rose and Lizzie, and a baby brother, Henry. Richard's snowballing wealth afforded the purchase of a Georgian villa by Hampstead Heath for them all. One of the prettiest houses on the eastern side of the Heath, 2 Dartmouth Park Road was surrounded by greenery all year round, both from its own garden and from the gardens beyond. The Heath, a few houses away, was then wild with hares, and popular for the foraging of horseradish, sorrel and garlic.

There was plenty to stimulate D'Oyly's mind in his spacious new stucco-fronted home and, as his sister Lizzie remembered, he was 'always up to something'.[15] He spent many hours in his parents' drawing room, choreographing productions in his toy theatre. Here he could picture his grand plans in miniature: in his mind there were tour-de-force performances, enraptured audiences and beautiful scenery. Studiously learning favourite roles by heart, D'Oyly would perform for his parents and siblings. A formidable, tubby little boy with rich dark hair, he harnessed his ursine features – his soft round face and wide brown eyes – to express the most dramatic of Shakespeare's speeches. Blanche recalled that on occasion they made her cry.

Richard and Eliza spotted D'Oyly's talent early on, and presided over a middle-class hothouse of self-improvement: with Richard, he learned the flute, violin and piano, and with Eliza he spoke French for two days a week.[16] Nurturing his interest in performance, he was taken to plays, most often Shakespeare's tragedies, and recitals in the West End, and grew up listening to Beethoven and Mendelssohn. Family legend has it that he tackled his first Beethoven sonata aged four. Alongside all of his diligent solo practice, he attempted to corral his sisters into chamber recitals – no small undertaking, given that they were all under eight at the time. Dartmouth

Park Road became part family home, part conservatoire. All of this grooming paid dividends: D'Oyly's parents would live long enough to see him become one of Victorian Britain's biggest success stories – and he never forgot his French.

The only drawback to the bucolic new home for D'Oyly was a four-mile daily journey into Bloomsbury to the progressive new University College School. It would have been a curious choice for the daughter of a chaplain, as it did not offer the standard Church-of-England education, which was also a prerequisite for Oxbridge entrance. Disparaged as 'that godless institution on Gower Street',[17] University College School was secular. Given his schooling and the grand house in which he spent his teenage years, the 'self-made' accolade that D'Oyly is sometimes accorded is not quite the full picture. Life had begun unpromisingly, in that insalubrious flat in Soho, but his prospects had picked up rapidly.

Although he lived a long distance from school, being characteristically sociable, D'Oyly invited friends back to participate in his amateur productions. Lizzie remembered him as a teenager being 'good-looking, affectionate, generous, hot-tempered and full of fun'.[18] He was singled out to be doted on by his father, resulting in fishing trips to Wales and the Lake District, from where he sent letters with action-filled ink cartoons to his siblings, and flowery descriptions of the countryside that parodied the stilted formal guidebooks of the day.

Thanks to his first-class grade in the matriculation exam, he earned a place at University College London when he was seventeen. Eliza the tiger mother was vindicated, and clearly Richard had an intelligent heir to follow him into business. In deference to his father, although D'Oyly matriculated, he did not start his degree, and started work instead.[19] By now the other partners, Rose and Rudall, had died, leaving Richard as sole owner. He would surely have been pleased to see that his new employee had a hawk eye for money. When the company messenger stole two shillings (£20), D'Oyly not only spotted it, but gathered all the evidence for a court case, resulting in a sentence of six months' hard labour.[20] This appears to have been D'Oyly's earliest litigation. Over the coming years, he would prove a valuable customer for any solicitor looking for a steady flow of work.

In his idle moments away from his father's business, D'Oyly was drawn to his love of theatre, acting in amateur farces around Soho and north London, and composing one-act operettas, both the scores and the lyrics. His first performed composition, the staging of which he financed from his salary and organised himself, was an English-language opera, *Dr. Ambrosias, his Secret*, at St George's Hall, off Regent Street, in 1868, when he was twenty-four. The 'secret' was the identity of a child left in the care of schoolmaster Dr Ambrosias. In the manner of Shakespeare's *Twelfth Night*, the young boy is in fact a girl, who felt it necessary to disguise herself. None of *Dr. Ambrosias'* score survives, but a few parlour songs, which were middlebrow easy pieces for amateurs, written by D'Oyly, were published by Rudall, Carte & Co., and still exist. They had whimsical titles, such as 'Wake, sweet bird' and 'Stars of the summer night'.

Working in the West End, D'Oyly was well-placed to spend his evenings exploring London's mixed bag of live entertainment. A lifelong boulevardier, he strolled for miles, turning ideas over in his mind and smoking cheap cigars in the day and expensive ones in the evening. It was on his forays into London's live music that he became a fan of a fellow composer his own age, Arthur Sullivan. He had eagerly sent Sullivan a letter inviting him to *Dr. Ambrosias*. With no inkling of the vital role that this hopeful stranger, Richard D'Oyly

Carte, would play in his fortunes, Sullivan had written a short, polite note back, wishing him success, but regretting that he was out of town. After awaiting a reply for weeks, D'Oyly no doubt felt a little flat.

He followed up *Dr. Ambrosias* with *Marie*, in 1871, which introduced him to working at the Opera Comique, where he would one day stage Gilbert and Sullivan far more successfully than his own compositions. As with *Dr Ambrosias*, his second light opera, *Marie*, was was staged for one night only in the graveyard slot of high summer, when theatres had the lowest box-office expectations of the year. Yet he received some, if rather backhanded, compliments. One reviewer posited, 'there were evidences that the composer might, with a little more experience, produce something much superior'.[21]

One of his few surviving complete songs is 'Come back to me', the lyrics of which suggested an emotional young man. He wrote plaintively of his heart 'toss'd like the waters wide':

> The strong waves roll'd against the shore,
> The wind sough'd over the waste
> And scurrying o'er, the dark clouds bore,
> And the moon show'd not her face.
> My heart was toss'd like the waters wide,
> Darkling clouds of doubt blew free,
> Yet my thought wing'd thro mist and gale
> And it cried 'Come back to me'.
> The light waves ripple on the shore,
> The breeze laps the foam with glee,
> One snow-white cloud skims across the blue,
> And the sun shines gloriously.
> My heart is clear like the blue above.
> And it flies across the sea,
> One white cloud floats across its sky,

And it cries 'Come back to me'.[22]

Back at his managerial day job with his father, life was not quite so dramatic. D'Oyly stuck at musical-instrument retail until later that year, in 1870, when he was twenty-six. Having not enjoyed quite the acclaim that he was hoping for as a composer and librettist himself, he pivoted to set himself up as a theatre agent in the back room of his father's shop. He was ready to receive clients and prospective clients between 11 a.m. and 4 p.m. daily, and he daydreamed and composed in the time around it. As with most fledgling enterprises, no job was too small. He took on bookings for a whole manner of live performances – even scouting for church choir singers. Two years later, he was still auditioning choir boys to get by. More commonly, though, his search was for performers. One advertisement gave an idea of what he spent his days hoping to see. The bar was not especially high:

> 'YOUNG LADIES with Good Voices and Good Appearance can be Engaged on salaries. No previous knowledge necessary if the above requirements are fulfilled. Apply personally, between Eleven and One, to R. D'Oyly Carte, 20 Charing-cross, London'.[23]

As he elaborated in a later advertisement, having perhaps not even found many 'good voices', he was prepared to nurture anyone promising, and would refer them to two singing teachers and an elocution coach. In the manner of a Victorian Simon Cowell, he was looking not only for people who could sing, but who would charm the public. Whenever there was a choice to be made between a more technically able singer and a charming one, the charmer always won.

His first big client was superficially a coup, but tricky

to manage. Giovanni Matteo de Candia, famous enough to be known to audiences simply as 'Mario', was the era's most celebrated tenor. He had been performing in Britain since before D'Oyly was born. He entrusted D'Oyly with the arrangements for his farewell tour in 1870, before he retired home to Sardinia.

The tenor, although much-loved, found his elderly voice faltering. It resulted in an unplanned fortnight-long break between engagements. One review described him as a 'wreck of his former self'.[24] To make matters worse for D'Oyly personally, he was berated by Mario's manager. Working within the confines of a nascent national public transport system, moving a veteran tenor, his grand piano and his retinue around the towns of Great Britain required far more thought than D'Oyly gave it. Mario's manager was not impressed:

> 'The arrangements of the tour were placed in the hands of an agent then learning his business, and whose inexperience caused all concerned the greatest inconvenience. The distances we had to travel were unreasonable and increased the expenses considerably. In one instance a concert was announced to be given on Friday at Cardiff, another the next day morning at Aberystwyth and on the Monday following at Newton Abbot in Devonshire. A glance at the map will show the travelling such arrangements involved'.[25]

Mario's reedy warbling was not D'Oyly's fault, but the geographically ignorant bookings were. Having snubbed his father's business, D'Oyly had everything to prove with this solo undertaking – and so far he had not. The tour was rescued at the very end by a gratifying wave of adoration, thanks to Mario's impassioned performance as Fernand in Donizetti's *La Favorita* at the Royal Opera House in Covent Garden. *La*

Favorita lived on in the memory of those who attended. The rest of the patchy four-month tour was forgotten.

Fitful tours and bookings made his agency's income precarious, and D'Oyly often could not pay his assistants on time. Meanwhile, at Rudall, Carte & Co., Richard would rope in his youngest son, Henry, to take D'Oyly's place. Despite his mental health problems, which contemporary doctors referred to as 'melancholia', Henry did indeed run the business in the end. Richard was determined to have at least one of his two sons involved, it seemed.

D'Oyly moved his theatre agency out of his father's back room in Charing Cross to nearby Craig's Court, a narrow yard by Trafalgar Square.[26] There he and his assistants presided over a growing mass of paperwork: the diary of engagements, addresses of venues, managers and performers, travel and accommodation bookings, contracts, fees and accounts. As one assistant recalled, D'Oyly was 'a man of ideas and impulse, of violent fits of work and ardent periods of enjoyment – and rather untidy'.[27]

One of D'Oyly's 'very bossy' aunts, impatient for him to settle down, took matters into her own hands and arranged a marriage.[28] Her bride of choice was seventeen-year-old Blanche Prowse. D'Oyly knew Blanche from their having acted together four years earlier in an amateur farce, *Ici On Parle Français*, when he was twenty-two, and she had been thirteen, playing a parlour maid. The match had two benefits for his family. Firstly, it stopped twenty-six-year-old D'Oyly galivanting around London unattached, as his aunt so disapproved of, and, secondly, it forged a link within the industry for Rudall, Carte & Co., as Blanche was the daughter of a music publisher with whom the company did business occasionally. On the marriage certificate, D'Oyly was listed as a 'musician'.[29] Although he was already a theatre agent, in the summer of 1870 he perhaps harboured hopes that he would yet be known for his own works. But, as he wistfully wrote of his music career, 'wiser counsels prevailed', and he knuckled down to his new agenting business.[30]

For the first few years of marriage, D'Oyly and Blanche would trail around rooms in Covent Garden. As he had started life, he found himself in multiple-occupancy tenancies, renting either the attic or the basement of various decrepit houses. Eventually they left for the suburbs, to South Norwood, where their first child, Lucas, was born in 1872. They may have moved so far out partly in the hope of easing Blanche's lung problems, but she remained sickly. Before their second child, Rupert, they moved round the corner from D'Oyly's childhood home, to a cottage backing on to Hampstead Heath.

With his one illustrious client on his final tour and a new family to support, D'Oyly needed fresh talent post-Mario, and quickly. His admiration for Sullivan undampened, he went along to watch an obscure two-act burlesque, *Thespis, or the Gods Grown Old*, for which Sullivan had written the score. The lyrics were written by W. S. Gilbert, who was a part-time journalist, having given up on a lacklustre legal career. *Thespis* started in the traditional Christmas pantomime slot of Boxing Day at the Gaiety Theatre on the Strand, in 1871. It was poorly received. Critics pounced on the underprepared actors, a plot that was too highbrow for the audience, the leading lady who was half a tone off, and the second act that was far too long, ending in a 'yawning audience', who were hissing by the time the curtain fell after midnight.[31] It was not a performance in working order.

Sitting in the audience, D'Oyly, through the amateurish chaos, perceived potential. This Gilbert and Sullivan had something special. What they were missing was him.

TWO

Entertainment of a higher order

D'Oyly would have to wait a while to graduate from a struggling agent to an impresario. However, he made a start by saving up over the next three years to lease the Opera Comique for a whole season to put on his choice of productions. The playhouse and its adjoining neighbour, The Globe, had been hurriedly built in the hope that the site would soon be redeveloped, and handsome compensation would therefore be paid to knock them down, which did eventually happen. The theatres were known as 'The Rickety Twins'. Overlooking a row of pornographic booksellers and 'dwellings of a dubious nature', they were so flimsy that performers could hear each other through the common wall.[1]

D'Oyly optimistically booked to take it over from June to October of 1874. In the hot, uncomfortable dive, he showcased his vision of how theatre could be. He presented adaptations of two French-language operettas, *La Branche Cassée,* and *Giroflé-Girofla,* translated into English for their British premiere. They were incongruously refined for the setting. Most managers might have been embarrassed to present such highbrow work at the Opera Comique of all places. D'Oyly ploughed on as though he were at the Royal Opera House. Other than the actual writing of a work, he now partly or entirely did everything else: he was the equivalent of a modern casting director, producer and director rolled into one. *The Observer* judged it an early critical success, 'Mr D'Oyly Carte is not only a skilful manager, but a trained musician [. . .] he appears to have grasped the fact that the public are ready to welcome a musical entertainment of a higher order'.[2] This desire to create 'entertainment of a higher order' was his driving force.

Throughout his lifetime, Victorian London had been swelling rapidly. It had prompted an explosion of music halls that offered cheap, raucous entertainment. They were often the scenes of violence, casual sex (among both spectators and performers) and drunkenness. D'Oyly wanted to offer an altogether different experience. He sought to appeal to the flourishing urban middle classes, of which he was a member. He pitched his entertainment somewhere between the music hall and the opera house – intelligent but not intellectual, tasteful but not pretentious.[3] He announced his aspiration in public on the front of his programme for *La Branche Cassée*: 'It is my desire to establish in London a permanent abode for light Opera',[4] and he repeated his wish so often over the coming years, he almost seemed to be willing it into existence. Already, before he even had the chance to commission Gilbert and Sullivan or to see one whole season through at the West End, he was speaking publicly about having his own theatre with its own distinct work.

English light opera, which began with *The Beggar's Opera* (1728) by John Gay, was, by now, a century and a half later, devoid of its former satirical bite and musical merit. Eighteenth-century tragedy, comedy and satire had been replaced by melodrama, burlesque and pantomime. Light operas that did make it to the London stage were imported, mostly the works of Jacques Offenbach and Johann Strauss. They were poorly translated, the music badly performed and the productions vulgar. D'Oyly rightly believed that he could do better, and hoped to prove it with his debut season at the Opera Comique.

Less sophisticated productions in Theatreland were, at this time, matched by less sophisticated customers. Beyond the opera, it was by now primarily frequented by people who paid little and expected little. Theatre managers' livings were precarious, as were those of composers and lyricists, who often moonlighted as actors or journalists, while actresses were considered little better than prostitutes.[5] Unsurprisingly, the middle classes had more or less withdrawn from theatre-going altogether. D'Oyly determined to win them back.

Having realised that, much as he would have loved to be, he was not the man to compose successful English light operas for the Opera Comique himself, he thought back to *Thespis,* the Christmas entertainment of 1871 that he had seen. *Thespis* had improved from its bad start, but still only managed a run of sixty-three performances. D'Oyly was tempted to bring together Gilbert and Sullivan to try again, under his guidance at the Opera Comique. He approached Gilbert, when he came came in one night as a spectator, and asked him to write a 'bright little one-act trifle', to which Gilbert agreed.[6] However, *La Branche Cassée* would only survive a fortnight. So D'Oyly had to abandon the rest of the season. This meant losing the chance to commission an original Gilbert and Sullivan piece, as he so longed to do. As he wrote to them both in disappointment, 'it fell through because I was short of money'.[7]

Despite the small audiences at the Opera Comique, one of D'Oyly's clients, an actress called Selina Dolaro, offered him the chance to dust himself off. Dolaro invited him to manage the theatre that she owned in Soho, the Royalty, which backed

on to the house where he was born. Her ramshackle establishment was pulled down in 1955, but, at the time, it occupied
73 and 74 Dean Street. Poky, dank, obscurely sited, perilously
combustible and seldom prosperous, the theatre was the opposite of what D'Oyly fantasised about owning himself. Still, it
gave him a second chance at a West End theatre season.

Dolaro brought him in when the Royalty was already
suffering low attendance, as it often did, between fleeting successes. Falling into this pattern of short-running productions
was the theatre manager's nightmare scenario. It involved
casting around for ideas constantly, the hassle of getting new
productions in working order, and also made the least money.
A theatre's greatest expense is changing the bill – the longer
running its productions, the more can be spared on commissioning scenery, costumes and writing. Having been stung
already with a critically acclaimed but sparsely attended programme, D'Oyly was aware of the risks of the business.

As a result, from early in his career, he had a very active
sympathy for actors down on their luck, and gave and raised
money to help. One of his earliest fundraisers was a benefit
performance for stranded French actors, who had opened
to enthusiastic reviews, but had soon been left stranded in
London without pay. The Princess Theatre, where they were
booked for a show, had closed without warning shortly after
they arrived, and D'Oyly raised enough for them to get home.
Alongside the misfortune of actors, there were plenty of worrying examples of fellow managers who were riding high one
season and desperate the next. Actor-turned-manager Charles
Hawtrey went bankrupt several times between hits. He had
one big money spinner, a farce called *The Private Secretary*.
It opened to disparaging reviews, dismissed by *The Observer*
as 'a purposeless romp', but Hawtrey had persisted.[8] He
tweaked the script, changed theatre, and recast the principal

roles. Suddenly it took off, and he made £9,000 (£920,000) – an enormous sum for a manager in those days.[9] However, Hawtrey staged over a hundred plays, and the peaks and troughs wreaked havoc with his finances. At one point he managed to clear his debts in a game of Baccarat, but he was only lucky that once.

Obvious as it may be to identify a new group in society with money to spend, and give them somewhere to spend it, D'Oyly was short of rivals in his pursuit of a mass middle-class audience. The nearest was John Hollingshead, a journalist-turned-manager. It was he who had tried out *Thespis*, the Christmas production of Gilbert and Sullivan at the Gaiety. Luckily for D'Oyly, Hollingshead had presided over one of the greatest false starts in cultural history.

Having taken on the headache of turning the Royalty's fortunes around, D'Oyly chose a tasteful French light opera, Offenbach's *La Périchole*, about an impoverished couple of Peruvian street-singers who cannot afford a marriage licence, as a safe bet. *La Périchole* started well, but before long ticket sales were flagging. One theatregoer was overheard grumbling, 'this is the sort of thing you could take your grandmother to see'.[10] That grumble would be where D'Oyly made his fortune – respectable, middlebrow entertainment, artfully done. Victorian live entertainment had already proved the maxim that sex sells; D'Oyly was convinced that modesty could sell too. It was going to be high necklines, long hemlines, no cheap laughs, no innuendo, and no playing to the gallery and this prim production of *La Périchole* was a chance to try it all out. D'Oyly outlined his rationale: 'I believe many will come who have long stayed away from fear of having to sit through hours of dull and unwholesome frivolity'.[11]

It was, of course, not good news for D'Oyly that *La Périchole* was stuttering. However, it did give him the chance to persuade Dolaro to pay for a warm-up act to entice more customers in through the door. It allowed him to pair up Gilbert and Sullivan without having to bank on them as the main event. Audiences expected one or two warm-ups to offer value for money, and managers often used them as inducements to a well-worn main event. A short opener by Gilbert and Sullivan, *Trial by Jury*, a satirical depiction of a court case about a breach of promise to marry, would be D'Oyly's 'more bang for your buck' addition to *La Périchole*. Sullivan rapidly wrote a score to fit Gilbert's lyrics, and the piece was first performed in March 1875, with Fred Sullivan, Arthur's brother, as the comic lead.

Trial by Jury proved a far greater draw than *La Périchole* itself, and it had served to bring together Gilbert, Sullivan, and D'Oyly, who acted as their 'catalyst business genius'.[12] While the next twenty-five years witnessed the three men's spectacular professional chemistry, Dolaro did not benefit from her theatre's only historic hit for long. D'Oyly made sure to capitalise fully, now that he had the composer and librettist, to make the 'scheme of his life' a reality.[13]

He persuaded Gilbert and Sullivan to work together again under his management. In light of *Trial by Jury*'s popularity, this should have been easy. There being little to suggest their personal compatibility, however, it initially looked unpromising. Gilbert and Sullivan's personalities and backgrounds proved jarring. Sullivan was a highly strung *bon viveur* from an Irish family who lived in the slums of Lambeth. As D'Oyly's own father had managed, Sullivan had harnessed his musical talent to improve his prospects from a young age, starting when, aged fourteen, he won the Mendelssohn Scholarship at the Royal Academy of Music. Although professionally well-respected since his teens, in private Sullivan drank and gambled his way into numerous scrapes. He and D'Oyly shared a love of opera and feasting and an aspiration for Continental travel, and together they were going to make the money to finance the lives they wanted.

However, D'Oyly's ability to turn his raw talent into cash aggravated Sullivan's reckless spending, which continued, whether he was running low or not. He would visit gentlemen's clubs, sometimes twice in a day, to play cards for high stakes. In the summer he would rent a country house for entertaining, and at home at 1 Queen's Mansions on Victoria Street, his hospitality was bountiful. No sooner did D'Oyly pay out from their profits than the money would be earmarked for one destructive pastime or other. Trying as they often found each other, however, Sullivan and D'Oyly soon became best friends.

Gilbert was tricky to manage in a different way. A curmudgeonly former barrister from a well-established upper-middle-class family of surgeons, he shared neither the parvenu background nor temperament of the other two. He was born at 17 Southampton Street in Covent Garden, just across the road from where D'Oyly would one day build the Savoy Theatre as a home for his work. At school Gilbert was, by his own admission, unpopular and lazy, but still went on to university at King's College, London. Temperamental in the extreme, he veered from genial to tetchy in an instant. His landlady, from the boarding house in Pimlico where he lived in his twenties, remembered him as a practical joker with a sharp tongue. By the time that he teamed up with D'Oyly and Sullivan in 1875, they were thirty-one and thirty-four respectively and Gilbert was nearly forty, with a personal life grounded in an enduring marriage. His wife, Lucy, whom he called Kitty, as a diminutive of kitten, was the Victorian ideal of an 'angel in the home', to use the phrase of the time, providing a soothing sanctuary for her hard-working husband. Sullivan and D'Oyly, meanwhile, chose to spend a lot of their free time out and about together, rather than being mollycoddled at home.

Gilbert's private life was a world apart from Sullivan's in particular, who had numerous relationships, often overlapping, without ever marrying. Liaisons were recorded in his diary with the woman's initials followed by the number of sexual acts in brackets. His most significant relationship lasted for almost thirty years, with a married, but separated, American living in London, Mary Frances Ronalds, generally known in society as Mrs Ronalds. She was a good friend of Lady Randolph Churchill, the mother of Winston, and of Queen Victoria. Her relationship with Sullivan was not publicly acknowledged, and she had at least two abortions as a result. And Sullivan's interest in other women remained prodigious. Even when Sullivan and Mrs Ronalds went on holiday together to Paris, he stopped by brothels most days.

While Sullivan spent his entire adult life using his musical talent, Gilbert, in the same spirit as D'Oyly, who had busily composed while plodding through Rudall, Carte & Co., had written comic verse for *Punch* and *Fun*, *Punch*'s rival comic weekly, to amuse himself while practising the law and trying his hand at journalism. He had been an undistinguished barrister at the Middle Temple, with an unsustainable average of five clients a year. Restless and unhappy, he then went briefly to Paris as *The Observer*'s correspondent to the Franco–Prussian War. As a child, he had been nicknamed Bab, for 'baby', and he used the name for his verses and drawings. He was able to rework many of them to create the lyrics for their early operas, including *Trial by Jury*.

While Sullivan displayed little of Gilbert's pique and was generally amenable to D'Oyly's requests, he was wayward and often abroad, where D'Oyly could not badger him so easily to get to work. Sullivan's efforts to finish music in time for rehearsals would be hampered by his long spells in the south of France. As he admitted in a letter from Nice: 'Occasionally I try to find a new idea [. . .] but my natural indolence, aided by the sunshine, prevents my doing any real work. I enjoy myself in the "*dolce far niente* [pleasant idleness]".'[14] When Sullivan arrived back in London, he would knuckle down, burning the midnight oil in his music room. However, bringing him to heel often involved D'Oyly turning up on his holidays or persuading him to break off to meet him in Paris or Monte Carlo, with a view to cajoling his friend into composing.

They were an uneasy, combustible trio. Even as their triumphs became dizzying over the coming years, success occasionally eased the tension, but never dispelled it. They were locked in a struggle for money, acclaim and creative control. However, out of that tension emerged a unique new British style of comic opera – the one of which D'Oyly had dreamed for so long. As *The Sunday Times'* music critic, Herman Klein, would enthuse of D'Oyly's Opera Company: 'For until then no living soul had seen upon the stage such weird, eccentric, yet intensely human beings . . . [They] conjured into existence a hitherto unknown comic world of sheer delight.'[15]

During *Trial by Jury*, D'Oyly had gained their broad agreement to work together again, but he did not yet have the money to stage any full-length productions on his own. Instead, he had formed a small syndicate with four investors. This formally became the Comedy Opera Company in 1876. He installed himself as the manager and as a company director, alongside the other four.[16] Even with his fellow company directors investing, it was still a strain. D'Oyly provided £250 (£28,000) himself. His secretary worried about the talent agency, from which he was drawing the funds. She wrote home, simply saying, 'there is no money in the office'.[17]

Unlike the later, enduring triumph of the D'Oyly Carte Opera Company, in which Gilbert and Sullivan were D'Oyly's partners, splitting the profits equally after expenses,[18] for its forerunner, the Comedy Opera Company, the pair simply worked on commission and were paid royalties. D'Oyly took £15 (£1,700) a week as his managerial salary, plus 10 per cent of any profits.[19] He obtained the lease for the Opera Comique once more in his own name, and sublet it to the Comedy Opera Company. This would become a significant detail when their arrangement turned sour.

Their first show together at the Opera Comique was *The Sorcerer*, in November 1877. It was a classic topsy-turvy Gilbert story, in which a love potion stirred into a teapot scrambles the romantic relationships of the characters. The Company agreed the payment of 200 guineas (£22,000) on delivery of the words and music, and a further six guineas (£700) for every performance during the run in London.[20] Gilbert and Sullivan requested George Grossmith, an actor who performed one-man sketches, for the lead. D'Oyly's investors feared the expense. They telegrammed D'Oyly as a matter of urgency: 'Whatever you do, don't engage Grossmith'.[21] D'Oyly invited Grossmith out to lunch and gave him the job. Many of the other parts in *The Sorcerer* went to his agency clients.[22] It 'achieved a genuine success', according to *The Times*, and 'moreover, a success in every respect deserved'.[23] It ran for 175 nights.

By January 1878, things were going so swimmingly that, while Sullivan was on holiday on the French Riviera, Gilbert was already drafting ideas for the next opera. He read the plot outline to D'Oyly on the 17th, then to the other investors five days later. It was the tale of a captain's daughter falling for a sailor when her father intends her to marry the First Lord of the Admiralty. The investors were nervous about the expense after *The Sorcerer*, but were coaxed into it. The meeting minutes record:

> 'Mssrs Gilbert and Sullivan further agree to write a new two-act opera and deliver the same to the Comedy Opera Company by 31st of March 1878, on the following terms: a nightly royalty of eight guineas, with a guaranteed run of 100 nights.'[24]

This new two-act opera would become *HMS Pinafore*, opening in May 1878. In January, when *Pinafore* was commissioned, *The Sorcerer* was selling well. It was lucky timing for Gilbert, Sullivan and D'Oyly. By March, full houses were less reliable for the show. It would doubtless have made the investors even more reluctant to pay for another had they pitched *Pinafore* then. At the end of the month, Gilbert came to D'Oyly's new office, now right by the rubbish dump where the Savoy Theatre would eventually be, to discuss *Pinafore*'s casting. Later in the day he came to find D'Oyly again at the Opera Comique, to secure his agreement not to pull the plug on *The Sorcerer* in the meantime.

As would become D'Oyly's modus operandi, the schedule was punishing. *The Sorcerer* drew to a close in May, and day-times were spent on stage rehearsing *Pinafore* in time to open on the 25th. After the curtain came down on *The Sorcerer* for the last time, most of the same cast were kept behind for an emergency *Pinafore* full dress rehearsal. It did not finish until 4 a.m., with plenty of frayed nerves and vocal criticisms from the investors throughout.

It looked as though D'Oyly's confidence had been misplaced. As any manager dreaded, it proved a hot summer.[25] The prospect of a baking, poorly ventilated, gaslit theatre was not all that tempting. The jittery investors put up closing notices several times. One proposed closing until the hot spell had passed, which would have saved on the theatre staff, performers and royalties. As a result, the cast did not know whether they could expect payment from one week to the next. D'Oyly lobbied to keep it open through the losses of June and July. The reviews were 'generally kind, except the *Daily Telegraph*', as Sullivan noted, which dismissed *Pinafore* as 'frothy'.[26] However, the heat was putting audiences off.

Eventually, after the heat of summer, *Pinafore* became immensely popular, running for 700 nights.[27] This was such a rare achievement that it became the second-longest-running musical piece ever at the time. In the first two and a half months, even with the lean patches and the cost of the authentic naval costumes and fine replica of Lord Nelson's HMS *Victory* for the set, the profit was roughly £200 (£22,000) a week.[28]

D'Oyly had firstly broken away from his father's business, then from Selina Dolaro's Royalty Theatre. Now he was ready to shake off the Comedy Opera Company. That September, with *Pinafore* going record-breakingly well, he had invited Gilbert and Sullivan to meet him in Covent Garden and proposed they all walk down to the river together. Standing by the sloping muddy plot, he wanted them to imagine the Savoy Theatre. There was not much to show them, other than a pretty view in the distance of the other side of the river, but D'Oyly could picture how to seize on the Thames' new attractiveness. A year later he would make enough with Gilbert and Sullivan to buy up the freehold of the plot for £11,000 (£1.2m).[29] He was, he told them, planning a future without fair-weather investors, who put a damper on all that they wanted to achieve. It would be just the three of them. He wanted to know if Gilbert and Sullivan were on board. They were.

D'Oyly started to prepare for their future as a standalone trio. He resigned as a company director in November to become an ordinary theatre manager. Rather unflatteringly, no one challenged his resignation. Finding him extravagant and demanding, the investors were surely relieved to have him off the board. D'Oyly later said that he had been sparked into action because he discovered that they were 'endeavouring to get rid of me'.[30] With a sure hint of pride, he told the reporter, 'I turned the tables on them completely. I told Gilbert and Sullivan that they had the opportunity of choosing between the director of the Comedy Opera Company and myself, and they at once decided to stand by me'.[31]

By December, D'Oyly had aligned everything for their independent venture. It was important that he, personally, was the lessee of the Opera Comique, rather than the Company, as it allowed him to close it over Christmas until 1 February 1879. He said that this was necessary due to pungent odours from the drains and that the theatre would be renovated. This closure was all too useful. D'Oyly's new lease would run from 1 February to 31 July 1879, the day that he planned to leave at the end of his contract, taking Gilbert and Sullivan with him. It all passed by under the investors' noses. Had they been more alert, they might have noticed that D'Oyly was already cheekily referring to the British touring version of *Pinafore* as being presented by 'Mr D'Oyly Carte's Opera Companies' rather than by their Company.[32]

With everything falling into place for July, D'Oyly arranged his first business foray to America. *Pinafore* was so popular in Britain that unauthorised performances were springing up over there. Perhaps a good indication of how rare this popularity was, there was no international agreement to prevent American theatre managers staging works by British authors and composers without paying. With no legal remedy available, D'Oyly planned to stage his own American productions to tackle the piracy, as he saw it, and to split the profits between just himself, Gilbert and Sullivan. The three of them were already discussing their first American tour for October. D'Oyly sailed from Liverpool to New York on the new steam liner, *Gallia*, arriving after an eight-day journey in July 1879 to set it all up.

Meanwhile, Sullivan's solicitor informed the other company directors that they could not use the music after 31 July – the end of D'Oyly's contract, and of the Opera Comique lease. The next day the directors responded that they would mount their own *Pinafore* production at another theatre. Sullivan's solicitor was too slow in securing an injunction, so this threat gathered pace. While D'Oyly was in New York, he had left his friend from Dublin, theatre manager Michael Gunn, in charge. Gunn telegrammed to inform him of the legal wrangling at home, and that a boat had capsized on the British *Pinafore* tour. D'Oyly was not too preoccupied with work to offer to pay for, and organise, the funeral of the American chorus member who had drowned and had no family in Britain.

Seizing the advantage of having D'Oyly a week's journey away, the investors tried to sack him and Gunn for unsatisfactory management. They instructed all theatre staff and the cast to ignore any of Gunn's orders. They came unstuck when the Master of the Rolls, the second highest judge in the country, looked into the matter and saw no grounds for dismissal. Rather than rushing back to sort the messy business of leaving the Comedy Opera Company, D'Oyly ploughed on with protracted negotiations for the American autumnal debut. He secured a season at the prestigious air-conditioned 1,500-seater Fifth Avenue Theater on Broadway. He felt the theatre befitting of his own, yet to be created, opera company. He started back for Britain on 30 July.

The following day, when the curtain fell on *Pinafore*, the Comedy Opera Company became a theatre company with no manager, no work to perform, and no place in which to perform it. Having failed the legal, formal route to block D'Oyly, Gilbert and Sullivan, the incensed investors stormed the final show. One thing that they did still own, they reasoned, were the sets and costumes. They arrived backstage with a gang of thugs and a solicitor during Little Buttercup's confessional song to reclaim them by force. The stage hands and cast fought them off in a scuffle that spilled over on to the stage and into the auditorium. Audience members fled while the performers sang over the chaos. Alfred Cellier, a conductor and Sullivan's assistant, and Grossmith, the lead, tried to keep everyone calm. Backstage, the Opera Comique's manager, Richard Barker, was injured in the fracas.[33] Within two weeks the investors appeared at Bow Street Police Court, where they expressed their regret at the violence and agreed to compensate Barker.

The investors had left empty-handed, but still set up a production around the corner, while D'Oyly once again became the lessee of the Opera Comique. This time Gilbert took out an injunction. This was then lifted, as a different judge agreed that, as the Comedy Opera Company had commissioned *Pinafore*, they were free to perform it. To Gilbert, Sullivan and D'Oyly's disappointment, the judge did not recognise the break in the initial run, for which the Comedy Opera Company held the rights. On the wrangling went.

Not that he had waited, but from the day after 31 July, D'Oyly could proudly advertise his own *Pinafore*, as presented by Mr D'Oyly Carte's Opera Company. His 'official' production at the Opera Comique, endorsed by Gilbert and Sullivan, with the original cast, and the Comedy Opera Company's new version at the Olympic Theatre, ran in competition, streets away from each other. In the attempt to derail D'Oyly's production, his old investors threatened to fine each performer of his company £2 (£220) per show if they went to work, but found that they could not enforce the threat.[34] In October, the Comedy Opera Company gave up on their *Pinafore*.

This ongoing legal nightmare did not hold D'Oyly back in any of his other work, however. His agency clients naturally expected their tours, events and lectures to be running as normal, and he organised back-to-back auditions in the hunt for performers to take to America for *The Sorcerer* and *Pinafore* for October. In the back of his mind were thoughts of his own theatre behind the Strand, the building of which was now coming together. Sullivan did not handle the stress and intense activity quite so well. He felt ill from all of the offstage drama and took to the hills near Pontresina, in the Alps just outside St Moritz, for an operation and an extended rest at the remote Hotel Roseg.

D'Oyly had no such holiday. He was busy drilling his cast to deliver dialogue at a slower pace that Americans, who were unaccustomed to their accents, would understand – or so he hoped. Peppering his language with French, as he often did, he described this style as 'prononcé'. He wrote to Sullivan after his reconnaissance mission to New York: 'they [Americans] like "emotional" singing and acting. The placid English style won't do and I assure you that if we took out such a company as at the Opera Comique we should make a big failure as likely as not'.[35]

D'Oyly was keen to find himself a strong principal soprano to make a splash, and wondered whether to cast an American. His first choice was Hélène Crosmond, a Londoner whom he had noticed in her debut two years earlier. He offered her £20 (£2,200) a week. She wanted £100 (£11,000).[36] Given her greed, as he saw it, he did not continue the negotiation. He moved on immediately to his second choice, Blanche Roosevelt, an opera singer from Ohio who became a journalist in France on retirement and the lover of author Guy de

Maupassant. Sullivan had met her in the south of France. Perhaps a little swayed by her beauty, which was widely reported, and the holiday atmosphere, Sullivan became very keen to give her a part. D'Oyly allowed her a trial run in his London *Pinafore*, despite one reviewer noting that, in her debut a few years earlier, she was 'met with a great deal of applause and many bouquets [. . .] for whatever cause they were presented to her, it could not have been because she sang in tune'.[37] Audiences warmed to her again in *Pinafore*, whatever her vocal limitations, and she got the job.

Their own *Pinafore* having closed, the Comedy Opera investors tried to prevent D'Oyly setting off for his American debut in the autumn. They claimed that he owed them £150 (£17,000). Their legal papers had been ready on 30 October, when he was in London, but, to push him into a corner, they were served at the docks in Liverpool. Sheriff's officers detained him under the 1869 Debtor's Act as he was boarding the liner. Because of the alleged debt, if he was leaving the country, he had to pay £250 (£28,000) as security.[38] Having little choice, D'Oyly paid up with minutes to spare. He was disappointed that he could not recover the full amount later, arguing that he had only paid for his freedom, not as an acknowledgement of debt.

Having paid his way out of trouble in Liverpool, arrangements did not run smoothly in New York either. D'Oyly was joined by Sullivan and Gilbert in November, when they planned to present their own *Pinafore*, and then to premier *The Pirates of Penzance* in December.[39] Aggrieved by the unauthorised American *Pinafore*s, they hoped to head off any copies of *The Pirates of Penzance*. By staging it for the first time simultaneously in Britain and America, D'Oyly thought it might secure copyright in both places. However, the American one was nearly derailed by Sullivan, who realised on arrival that he had left Act One at home. He had to start afresh, and nearly had a breakdown in the process. On New Year's Eve, the day of the premiere, he managed to get up for a haircut in the morning. He then went back to bed until 5.30 p.m. to calm his nerves. After twelve oysters and a glass of champagne before the show, he took to the rostrum to conduct 'feeling more dead than alive'.[40]

As an additional headache, the New York orchestra pushed for higher pay, because orchestras in the city were paid more for operas than for other productions. D'Oyly made the slightly pedantic argument that they were playing in a light opera, not an opera. After the disagreement was resolved with a compromise amount, *Pinafore* went ahead on 1 December and *Pirates* on New Year's Eve, to fashionable, appreciative audiences on Broadway. Following the reception in New York, D'Oyly put together another four touring companies to cover America between them. Performing *Pirates* at the same time were his companies in New York, Philadelphia, the north west and Canada, New Orleans, and the South.

The British *Pirates* premiere was a very different affair. It was a one-off matinee at the Royal Bijou Theatre in the little seaside town of Paignton in Devon. D'Oyly's company was appearing at nearby Torquay when they were instructed to break off to perform the new piece, which they had never seen before. The performance was chaotic, with the music sent from America in two shipments. The second act arrived before the first, and only one complete rehearsal was possible. The quality did not matter, however, as it was only staged in the hope of establishing transatlantic copyright. In the region of 150 pirate productions of *Pirates* appeared in America in any case.[41] Gilbert was particularly incensed – not only financially but artistically. For all of the effort, D'Oyly's simultaneous premiere plan had not quite worked out.

In the end, it would be up to Gilbert and Sullivan themselves to take the Comedy Opera Company to the High Court in 1881 to clarify once and for all that performance rights no longer belonged to the previous investors. It all hinged on D'Oyly ending the 'initial run' with his canny break for repairs. This judge was satisfied that the Comedy Opera Company could not make claims after that date, and he granted an injunction.[42] The Comedy Opera Company soon folded, after allegations of a director misappropriating its funds, while D'Oyly became the sole producer of the works of Gilbert and Sullivan. He held the right to authorise and charge a fee for amateur productions too, and his enthusiastic licensing made him largely responsible for the late Victorian craze for amateur operatics in the country's village halls. His Gilbert and Sullivan monopoly would turn out to be a rare, transformative coup.

THREE

'Light of the future'

By 10 October that year, the Savoy Theatre was ready. Waiting behind the immense gold satin curtain that night, D'Oyly could hear his auditorium buzzing with life for the first time. The boy with the toy theatre had managed to build himself a real one. A carnival atmosphere animated the 1,300 spectators while his orchestra tuned up. On the other side of the curtain was a lively High Society gathering of supporters, including his latest agency client, Oscar Wilde; the Prince of Wales, with his spirited aristocratic circle; Sullivan's mistress, Mrs Ronalds; and London's press. Although an evening of high anticipation for D'Oyly, the only hint of nerves was the dainty pink carnation tucked into his lapel for luck.

Contemporary cartoons depicted D'Oyly as stylish and supremely confident. The most famous, in *Vanity Fair,* picked up on his love of grand designs, showing him with bulging rolls of architectural plans under his arm, his chest puffed out and his gaze fixed on the middle distance, as though watching his vision materialising before his eyes. Following Gilbert's lead, he became a customer of the tailor Henry Poole of Savile Row. He truly looked the part of an impresario in his white gloves and his tails, a gold monogrammed pocket watch clipped to his waistcoat.

After enough suspense had built up in the auditorium, from the wings D'Oyly walked out in front of the satin curtain, flanked by two other tailcoated men. Affectionate applause, amplified for the first time by the cutting-edge acoustics, greeted them. Beady eyes from the distinguished audience of friends, family, strangers and critics peered through their opera glasses for a closer look. Those hoping to see the D'Oyly Carte triumvirate, however, would have been disappointed.

Alongside D'Oyly was indeed his friend Sullivan. But they were joined by the architect Charles Phipps, who took a bow for his design of London's finest new theatre. Gilbert, however, tended to avoid the socialising and left public appearances to the other two. Too agitated to enjoy opening nights, he would pace the Embankment outside until it was safe to appear after the curtain call. Tonight, he had made excuses to stay home altogether, begging leave to work on with their next opera, which would become *Iolanthe*, in his gloomy study in The Boltons in South Kensington. Here he wrote many of the lyrics that financed an even larger mansion at 39 Harrington Gardens, also in Kensington, two years later. He decorated the new house with comic mottoes and fanciful embellishments. Negotiations with the builders were typical of Gilbert, who informed them that he would be moving in on his chosen date, come what may.

Getting Gilbert to work was no trouble, it was managing his temper. With Sullivan, the problem was, as ever, reversed, and this year was a good example. While Gilbert drafted ideas for *Iolanthe* in his study, Sullivan was off on HMS *Hercules* with the Duke of Edinburgh, Queen Victoria's second son, staying in the admiral's quarters. On the extended trip, they were entertained at Copenhagen by the King of Denmark, at St Petersburg by the Tsar, and at Kiel by the future Kaiser Wilhelm II, who greeted him by singing a tune from *Pinafore*.

Sullivan was a restless traveller, to Paris and Switzerland from his early years, and, later, further afield to Italy, Germany, Austria and Egypt. While in the United States in 1879–80, he had found time for a visit up to Niagara Falls and to Ottawa as a house guest of Canada's governor-general. On the French Riviera, where he liked to rent a house, ostensibly for a period of sustained work away from casual callers, the gaming tables of Monte Carlo were a perennial temptation.

For all the pleasure of his eponymous Opera Company, the opening night of the Savoy Theatre gave D'Oyly an even firmer new grip on the future, and the 'permanent abode' he had wanted for so long. His sturdy red-brick and Portland-stone theatre on the Strand was a source of great personal satisfaction. The building was his independent financial venture, and it tipped the balance of power from Gilbert and Sullivan in his direction. The fact that Gilbert had not appeared this evening at all, followed by many bad-tempered letters, hinted that he begrudged it. D'Oyly's plan was to let his theatre to their partnership, but Gilbert had immediately made a caustic remark about the rent of £4,000 (£40,000) a year, which D'Oyly insisted was well below the market rate. D'Oyly confided to Sullivan that he was 'boiling over' with Gilbert's ingratitude after he had built a home for his work: 'Money is not everything to me, and I feel more about this tone he has taken than I care to say'.[1] He rarely told Gilbert anything personal, but often shared his emotions with Sullivan: 'I have worked like a slave for four or five years [in the run-up to opening the theatre]. The overwork and worry have tired me out physically and mentally'.[2]

The balance of their partnership was a problem even from the beginning. D'Oyly did not think it meant a partnership when it came to decision-making. Gilbert and Sullivan had veto power over casting and free rein during rehearsals, and to D'Oyly that was enough. After a contract that the three signed for *Patience*, this eventually led to Gilbert's complaint that he felt like a 'hack author' at D'Oyly's commissioning beck and call, there to provide lyrics to order. Sullivan, who only wanted to write one more after *Patience*, had a similar complaint towards the end: 'I shall never consider myself anything more than a paid piecework composer'.[3]

D'Oyly had his own unhappiness within the trio. As he wrote to Gilbert, over a decade later: 'If I could be an author like you, I would certainly not be a manager. I am simply the tradesman who sells your works of art'.[4] All three were uneasy about their status in the partnership: Gilbert and Sullivan had the nagging feeling that they were there to serve D'Oyly's light opera ambitions, and D'Oyly had the nagging feeling that the others did not appreciate his work. He was regularly hurt by Gilbert's dismissive attitude, as he felt it, towards him. He felt compelled to point out to Gilbert during one argument that he had 'devoted the greater portion of my time and energies during the best years of my life' to their venture. Two days later he was still upset enough to send an addendum: 'if you do not know – or have forgotten – what I have done, the first passerby in the street could probably tell you.'[5] The relationship between D'Oyly and Gilbert was the most fraught. He wrote to Sullivan that Gilbert was 'almost impossible' during their flare-up over the Savoy Theatre rent.[6] He then crossed it out. The crossed-out phrase encapsulated how frustrated but co-dependent they were. Dealing with Gilbert was hard, but D'Oyly could not quite bring himself to say that it was impossible.

Whether or not D'Oyly enjoyed a disproportionate amount of profit, as Gilbert often felt, there was no doubt that the theatre was his pet project. To modern eyes it would no doubt look *de trop,* but it was complimented by contemporaries as a sumptuous but restrained homage to the Italian Renaissance. D'Oyly was keen to claim credit in the programme for having discarded the standard motifs of 'cherubim, muses, angels, and mythical deities',[7] and the change was received with relief by critics. As *Reynolds's Newspaper* reflected, it was: 'spacious, and with a noble depth and frontage [. . .] a wonderful improvement on those antiquated, fusty, and most uncomfortable portions of the older theatres.'[8] Unusually, windows were discreetly embedded at the back of the auditorium for natural light and traditional heavy colours were avoided. D'Oyly loved black-and-white marble chequered floors, which he used for the box office and would use again in his hotels. He lauded his own taste as 'rich, but not in the least garish or vulgar'.[9]

A fine building was not enough for D'Oyly – he wanted to refine the entire experience. Following close observation of where other proprietors were falling short, he did away with badly paid attendants angling for tips or charging for services, as he felt it 'a fertile source of annoyance to the public'[10] and paid them properly himself. His programmes were artistically presented mementos, often printed on silk, rather than the standard cheap playbills, and were free of charge, as were the cloakrooms. His 'refreshment-saloons' were not sublet to a contractor in whose interest it was, D'Oyly pointed out, to get every possible penny out of the public. He ran his bars himself, to give 'the most careful attention to procuring everything of the very best quality'.[11] As a whisky connoisseur, he chose unadulterated malts, and instead of the standard acrid chicory, there was proper coffee. He placed great emphasis on showing customers that nothing was spared when it came to hosting them.

The hurly burly outside other theatres for the best seats upset his sensibilities, so he instigated a now-familiar 'queue' system, with tea and cake for the wait.[12] Tickets were printed with seating plans on the back to encourage order. One of his programmes explained that 'disgraceful scenes of battle and hooliganism were to be witnessed all over the West-End'. The Savoy would be different.

Inside, the auditorium was cool and airy. This negated the need for ladies to carry fans. However, he saw them as a way to catch the attention of potential theatregoers, so he gave away souvenir Japanese-style fans to celebrate an anniversary of *The Mikado*, long after they would have offered practical use. The programme details, printed on fine paper, were attached to the Liberty fabric of the fans, which matched that on stage.

He left the auditorium spacious, rather than packing in seats for the highest returns. The embossed peacock-blue velvet armchairs left plenty of room for 'promenading between rows',[13] as one critic appreciated. Most theatres used hard-wearing, easy-to-clean wooden or leather-covered seats, but the atmosphere was so cool, compared to normal theatres, that the audience could sit in velvet chairs without overheating. D'Oyly cut out and kept advice from a trade magazine, which warned: 'do not crowd or crush them [the audience] in their places; remember they have to occupy them for three or four hours and if they go away suffering from cramped limbs, they will not be likely to come again'.[14] The article also noted contemporary audiences' regular grumbles about having their chair kicked because of the pokiness of the rows, and there being nowhere for smart patrons to keep hats and coats uncrumpled.[15] D'Oyly took care of these annoyances too.

Theatres were noisy, and stages and auditoriums were lit from one great chandelier, making the audience as visible as the performers throughout. Audiences would chat, walk around and play games, leaving the performers competing for their attention. Aisles in the pit were known as 'Fops Alley', as young men would cruise up and down, flirting with women. In the Savoy there would be stillness and silence. Although keen to encourage the theatre as a place to socialise, the Savoy's dark auditorium, once a show began, was a statement of intent that the performances themselves were to receive undivided attention. One critic, unused to such reverence, likened it to being in church.

For refined socialising, at an appropriate time and away from the performances, there were the 'refreshment-saloons', where D'Oyly displayed portraits and busts of actors, the smoking room, and retiring and cloak rooms. D'Oyly was keen to attract unchaperoned women out to respectable matinees, which was helped along by a 'boudoir lounge' for ladies.

On the brand-new stage, once D'Oyly, Sullivan and Phipps had enjoyed their fill of attention, the satin curtain rippled back to reveal the entire Opera Company in luxurious new sashes, velvet breeches and ruffled shirts. Sullivan was cheered on his way to the rostrum below, from where he conducted the Opera Company in 'God Save the Queen', the three verses of which he arranged to have a dramatic cumulative climax, starting with sopranos and rising to a *tutti*.

As applause subsided, expectation turned to D'Oyly's big moment. He had promised that the opening night would be the first time that a building anywhere in the world would be entirely lit by electricity. Since he had beheld electric street lights outside the Paris Opera House some years earlier, he had wanted to recreate the magic on a larger scale.

To this end, while planning his four-storey theatre over the course of four years, he had had a more modest building in progress. London would have to wait until the Edwardian era for electricity companies. For now, D'Oyly's power would come from early steam engines in his own shuddering shed on the Strand, which acted as a prototype power station. However, the scale of his ambition had flummoxed his engineers. After months of trying, they could not light the stage and the auditorium simultaneously without incident.

Undeterred, D'Oyly had taken adverts in *The Times* over the past three weeks to announce the opening on 3 October. This was revised to the 6th, then the 10th. The latest advertisement explained that the first night was 'unavoidably postponed' in order to complete 'very complicated work and experiments'. D'Oyly expressed the hope, increasingly desperate by now, that 'the novelty of the undertaking will be an excuse for the delay'.[16]

He had the awkward task of announcing that, even now, this novelty was not quite ready. To head off disappointment, there would be an attempt to illuminate the auditorium only with the 'incandescent lamps'. He reassured the audience that, should any glitches occur, the theatre would instantly be flooded with reserve gaslight from the 'great central sun-burner'.[17] He was acutely aware, as *The Times* wrote the week before, that the new light: 'is an experiment, and may succeed or fail'.[18] The pressure was on from the Prince of Wales in particular, who had told his friend Sullivan that he was longing to see the dazzling spectacle.

The lamps could have been on when the audience walked in, but that would not have meant quite so much fun for D'Oyly. Instead, he disappeared behind the curtain and, as if by magic, a few moments later, the pear-shaped bulbs flicked into action. The auditorium filled with a brilliant blaze that proclaimed 'the light of the future', as he liked to call it. For many it was the first time that they had seen the bright light that rendered the night as clear as day. The audience regarded each other and their surroundings with fresh interest, and ladies observed their evening dresses popping with colour.

Its efficacy was not appreciated by everyone, however: one newspaper complained that it gave a 'ghastly look' to the less fortunate, as the many 'plastered dames' attempted to conceal the 'ravages of time in the fierce light'.[19]

There was little that D'Oyly could do about the 'plastered dames', but he had thought ahead to the stage. As a satire on ostentatious Victorian fashion, his latest opera, *Patience*, was an ideal moment in which to bring the theatre into technicolour. The set was painted afresh in finer detail, in particular the Arcadian forest glade backdrop for the second act. Costumes were tested from every angle in front of electric light by his designer, Henry Emden. He hoped that the Savoy would 'open up fresh fields of ambition to those who look beyond mere work-producing and money-making'.[20] D'Oyly could not have found a set designer with a more similar attitude to his own.

Flickering light bulbs aside, it was remarkable that the theatre had managed to open at all in October. After several costly delays, many of which were caused by D'Oyly's pursuit of electrical glory, it had opened at the very latest date that it could without disrupting *Patience*'s run. Even in *Patience*'s final week at the Opera Comique, he had put the transfer back once more, thanks to Sullivan's last-minute insistence on a larger pit for his twenty-seven-piece orchestra. By the time of the press preview on the Saturday, three days before opening, the 1,200 light bulbs were being fitted as the journalists were arriving. As an unforeseen hiccup on the day itself, Rutland Barrington, starring as one of *Patience*'s poets, started a heavy cold, for which D'Oyly was suitably apologetic to the audience. As supremely successful as D'Oyly was to become, his ambitions rarely came to fruition without incident: although remembered as an achievement, opening the Savoy Theatre had hardly gone to plan.

As much as he loved the thrill of a first night, the performance was an anxious one, as, backstage, he willed the electricity to remain constant. There was no technology to provide back-up power and, as *The Times* noted, 'occasional sudden changes from light to darkness showed that the machinery was not as yet under perfect control'.[21] At one point a vital band slipped off entirely, putting the theatre into near pitch black. The electrical hitches seemed to do D'Oyly no harm, however. Goodwill towards the venture meant that few critics wrote them up. After all, as the reviewers wrote the following day, there was no need to appraise *Patience* itself, on its 170th performance, as it was already a classic.

Just after Christmas, on 28 December 1881, D'Oyly's power station on the Strand was ready to light every bulb. He took the opportunity to host what was, in name, a 'safety demonstration', but was, in reality, pure theatre. He telegrammed journalists, fellow stage managers and actors to gather for a spectacle.

At first his demonstration looked so alarming that it caused 'a visible movement towards the exits' among the more nervous theatregoers. As there had been several fatal fires in recent memory, a trip to the theatre was already a dangerous prospect, but D'Oyly devised a way to reassure the audience. He appeared on stage holding a lit Swan lamp, around which he had wrapped a highly flammable cotton gauze. He smashed the lamp with the single stroke of a hammer. With a muffled crunch, it splintered; its glow immediately extinguished. Had it been gaslight, the fabric would have been up in flames. With a magician's flourish, D'Oyly held up the muslin to reveal that it was a perfect white.

In the auditorium, anxious quiet gave way to applause. The audience would 'willingly have seen a few more lamp glasses broken for their edification', as they appreciated this 'success of a most emphatic kind'.[22] D'Oyly took two curtain calls of prolonged cheers, before calling spectators up on stage to satisfy themselves that there had been no deception. The party trick captured the imagination to the extent that smashing a bulb was appropriated by the Edison Company, one of the pioneers of the light bulb, to persuade the public of its safety.

D'Oyly was now the first man in the world to light a whole public building with electricity. Better still, he had scored a publicity coup in pipping inventor Thomas Edison himself to his first display in London by a few weeks. Having ironed out the initial problems, D'Oyly's Strand Power Company generated so much energy that it allowed that little corner of the city to stay off-grid well into the twentieth century.

The contented colossus of Victorian entertainment took several bows and swept off stage to allow Act Two of *Patience* to begin.

FOUR

Off on tour

'The man who can dominate the London dinner party
can dominate the world'

Oscar Wilde

Patience was a satire of the aesthetic movement, which
encompassed poets, artists and devotees of fashion, and many
such people were D'Oyly's friends and associates. The front
runners to have inspired the main character, arch-aesthete
Reginald Bunthorne, were two of his agency's clients: the
American artist James MacNeill Whistler, and Oscar Wilde.
The poet who struck classical poses and mooned over sun-
flowers is now generally assumed to be Wilde, but both men
were in the running at the time. Whistler wrote fan mail to
George Grossmith, who played Bunthorne: '*Je te savais brave
– mais je ne te savais plus brave que moi*' ['I knew you were
amazing – but I did not know you were more amazing than
me']. There was already rivalry between Whistler and Wilde.
D'Oyly's assistant recalled that, at a party, Whistler uttered
'a *bon mot* before an admiring audience and Mr Wilde, who
was lolling on a couch close by, could not help exclaiming –
"I wish I had said that". Turning towards Wilde, Whistler
replied – "Never mind, Oscar, you will".'[1]

As one who managed every situation to his best advantage, D'Oyly persuaded the twenty-six-year-old Wilde, whom he had signed up after the publication of only one slim volume of poetry, to be a 'poster boy' for the satire. As D'Oyly wanted to send his touring companies to America with *Patience*, he arranged a lecture tour there first for Wilde, to make sure that audiences were primed for the joke. D'Oyly realised that he had to proceed delicately – after all, the opera's main object of fun was a 'fleshy poet' and Wilde could easily take offence. D'Oyly had started gently, by convincing him to attend the first night. Attend, he did. As one reporter noticed, 'there with the sacred daffodil stood the exponent of uncut hair'.[2]

D'Oyly's plan proved a good example of how he earned his 'Oily Carte' nickname. Who else could get away with dispatching London's most celebrated new poet to America to be a potential laughing stock for the benefit of another venture? D'Oyly was aware of the risk, but decided to take it anyway. He had sent his invaluable assistant, Helen Lenoir, ahead to New York on a semi-permanent basis to manage American tours. She travelled to America roughly twice a year for D'Oyly, and stayed for extended periods. He wrote to her advisedly: 'Wilde is slightly sensitive, although I don't think appallingly so [. . .] I told him he must not mind my using a little bunkum to push him in America. You must deal with it when he arrives.'[3]

Wilde appeared not to mind 'a little bunkum', if it meant being the centre of attention. Bankrolled by D'Oyly, in January 1882 he launched into lecturing on 'The English Renaissance of Art – The decorative arts', 'The house beautiful', and 'Irish poets and poetry in the nineteenth century'. D'Oyly made sure that he had publicity shots of Wilde looking as dandyish as possible, posing with flowers. He was resplendent in green velvet knee-breeches, patent leather shoes with silver buckles, black silk stockings, great bow-ties and ornate hats.[4]

Wilde was embraced. New Yorkers loved being told that the Niagara Falls was 'nothing but a vast, unnecessary amount of water going the wrong way'. He threw in remarks about Renaissance painting that delighted them: 'I described to them the pictures of Botticelli and the name seemed to them like a new drink.' The tour made £1,000 (£116,000) in appearance fees for Wilde.[5]

D'Oyly was interviewed straight off the liner when he arrived to check on the tour, a few weeks after his light-bulb-smashing demonstration. 'I thought that he would make a stir,' he enthused. 'He's a clever young man and has lots to say to the people [. . .] He's an æsthete – but, come to think of it, I believe he doesn't like that word – he's an art critic; that's better, you know. I don't consider it anything out of the way bringing Wilde over here. *Patience* is only a good-natured satire.'[6]

Despite D'Oyly's breezy confidence, Wilde's first lecture had not been entirely well-received. The audience was confused by his accent and bored by his lecture's rambling length. Fortunately, Wilde was soon into his stride. As it was now going so well, D'Oyly told the journalist that he intended to take Wilde around the country:

'He's to have a reception in Philadelphia on Monday, and lectures there on Tuesday. He's going to Baltimore, Washington and Chicago. He will probably be here two or three months [. . .] *Patience* is having an immense run. Sullivan is wintering in Cairo, Egypt. He's there for his health and to amuse himself, but is working on the new opera.'

'Do you expect to stay here in New York some time?' the journalist persisted.

'No; I haven't had a holiday for five years. I'm going to take one now.'

'*Patience* has been a great success, has it not?'

'Yes; we are playing in London to $9,000 houses every week, and it's being [sic] running since September 22. I've got fifteen companies playing now in Europe, America, and Australia – including, of course, Oscar Wilde and Archibald Forbes'.[7]

In this quickfire dockside exchange, D'Oyly managed to convey what a hard-working man he was, to get a plug in for a new opera, and another for his other client touring America at the same time, war correspondent Archibald Forbes. Forbes, who had made his name reporting from the Franco–Prussian war of 1870, took himself seriously, and it was important for D'Oyly to promote him as he was getting jealous of the attention that Wilde was attracting. America, it seemed, was not big enough for two of D'Oyly's clients. Forbes' tour had started some months earlier, and had not captured the public imagination in quite the same way. Given that Wilde announced on arrival: 'I have nothing to declare but my genius', if it was attention that he wanted, Forbes had formidable competition.

Unfortunately, D'Oyly had the two men booked on the same train from New York to Baltimore and they proved uncomfortable travelling companions. D'Oyly had co-opted Wilde to attend Forbes' forthcoming lecture, to drum up a larger audience. A little ungraciously, Wilde snubbed it to travel on ahead to Washington, DC, instead. Forbes started to make unflattering remarks about Wilde in public to journalists, but D'Oyly did not rouse himself from his long-awaited holiday in Florida to reprimand him.

D'Oyly had travelled extensively for work since his first

American tour, but it was only now that he started to take holidays abroad – not that he was entirely relaxing even then. As he described in his correspondence with Sullivan, Florida was a 'semi-holiday'. He was still thinking about work, albeit without his usual London backdrop. He had in mind, not a fully-fledged hotel as yet, but a world-class restaurant next to his new theatre. It would act as a public 'green room', where performers and audiences could eat and drink before and after the show.

While D'Oyly was planning his dream restaurant in the Florida sunshine, as a self-professed 'dweller in the high places of feeling', Wilde had taken Forbes' snipes to heart. He complained to his solicitor, who telegrammed Forbes himself: 'like a good fellow don't attack Wilde. I ask this personal favour to me'. After Forbes learned to ignore Wilde's popularity, he became pleased with the 'great success' of his own tour, or so he wrote to tell D'Oyly when he arrived home in March. Wilde, too, would eventually acknowledge the great success of his tour, having grumbled at the beginning. But while the bickering with Forbes was ongoing, to make matters worse for Wilde, the young underling whom D'Oyly had booked to chaperone him everywhere abandoned his post early on, and he was upset to be left unattended.

Wilde, as with so many of D'Oyly's clients and performers, complained about the intensity of the work. D'Oyly himself was buzzing with activity from the moment he woke up, and expected the same from everyone around him. He would be jogging around Bloomsbury near his new house in Russell Square first thing in the morning, a peculiar sight for the time, then he was at work in his messy office, multitasking, writing with a new gadget, the fountain pen, as it was faster than a quill, and ploughing on late into the night. On D'Oyly's schedule, Wilde had never seen work like it. As Sullivan had also complained, writing home to 'dearest mum', when D'Oyly had brought him to New York for *The Pirates of Penzance* premiere, that D'Oyly put him into a state of 'penal servitude'.[8] 'I have had the usual tremendous strain upon me,' Sullivan told her.[9] Even after years of working together, he was unused to it.

D'Oyly considered travelling in style and making a great deal of money to be a trade-off for hard work, but Wilde was punch drunk. The slant given by D'Oyly's American road manager, a retired military man called Colonel Morse, was that 'nothing was spared to make the journeys comfortable and to supply every need and luxury. The arrangements made by Mr Carte were liberal,' he said in D'Oyly's defence.[10] By mid-February, however, Wilde was a wreck, at one point collapsing on stage from apparent exhaustion. His journey covered thirty states, from the Atlantic to the Pacific, and from Canada to the Gulf of Mexico. He clocked up 15,000 miles by rail. 'I don't know where I am. Somewhere in the middle of coyotes and canyons,' he wrote to a friend in London.[11]

He acclimatised to both the timetable and the lack of company in the end, especially when D'Oyly's publicity machine was in full throttle. He was thrilled to be selling autographed photographs of himself in the halls and theatres where he spoke, attending 'immense receptions and wonder-ful dinners',[12] and having his likeness used to advertise cigars and kitchen stoves. Attired in his florid costume and fur coat, he endorsed two quack products: 'Madame Marie Fontaine's Bosom Beautifier for beautifying & enlarging the bust' and 'Madame Fontaine's Freckle Cure'. The tour generated over 500 articles and profiles. Crowds waited for his carriage. 'I wave a gloved hand and an ivory cane and they cheer,' he wrote.[13] He ended up staying far beyond D'Oyly's original plan, until 27 December, arriving back in Liverpool, after a whole year of delighting Americans, in January 1883.

A retired barrister, Serjeant-at-law William Ballantine, whom D'Oyly sent on an American lecture tour in the same year, found him a gentler taskmaster. Ballantine wanted money for his retirement, so he embarked on D'Oyly's breakneck schedule. He had a two-week break in New York before starting. He had plenty of anecdotes for the lectures but did not prove popular. Ballantine had court-case tales of murderers, philanderers, and of the deposed maharajah who plotted to poison Lord Salisbury, Secretary of State for India. He had been involved in juicy trials including the divorce of Lady Mordaunt, which dragged in the Prince of Wales, later Edward VII, with whom Lady Mordaunt confessed adultery. However, his stories did not excite the audiences. Feeling disappointed and embarrassed, Ballantine asked D'Oyly to be relieved of his contractual obligations so that he could go on holiday to Utah with his friends. He found that D'Oyly 'behaved with the greatest liberality and gentlemanly feeling' and let him off the hook.[14] An alternative reading might be that D'Oyly did not mind the old man quitting if he was unlikely to improve. By this time, D'Oyly had taken on more risk for a bigger cut. With Forbes, one of his earliest tours, he took only 10 per cent of the net profit. In that scenario, if there were poor sales, the burden fell on the venue. After the success of Wilde, D'Oyly started to pay for the venues and split ticket sales fifty-fifty with clients.[15] Letting Ballantine go may have been more calculation than kindness.

The poet Matthew Arnold had heard that D'Oyly was 'very capable and trustworthy' and asked him to plan a tour in the summer of 1883.[16] He had a week in New York before getting started at the Chickering Hall, an auditorium in Boston. D'Oyly booked him into Ivy League universities, as he had with Wilde, including Yale and Dartmouth, and another upmarket Massachusetts establishment, Amherst. The tour was going well, and Arnold was able to relax and socialise with his family in between engagements, and had plenty of dinners and receptions thrown in his honour. However, he felt that D'Oyly's publicity machine was geared towards D'Oyly's own ends, and that, again, D'Oyly himself was doing far too well out of the deal. Arnold wrote to his publisher, Alexander Macmillan: 'I do not know whether to laugh or cry when I hear the rumours from England as to what I am making.'[17] Though Arnold was paying to take his family around with him, he still made £1,200 (£138,000) in four months.[18] He did admit that, although he was tempted to ponder how much he would have made without D'Oyly's cut: 'I shall still make a sum which I could have got in no other way'.[19]

It was little wonder, perhaps, that D'Oyly's attention span was a recurring complaint. Helped only by two assistants at his agency, he reached the milestone of 200 clients, now including two of his favourite French composers, Charles Gounod and Jacques Offenbach, and the explorer Sir Henry Morton Stanley. It is a common misconception that one of his clients was the highest paid opera star of her generation, Adelina Patti. The Diva, as she was known, had her $5,000 fee paid before a performance, her name top of the bill in larger type than other performers, and she was not contractually obliged to rehearse. According to opera promoter James Henry Mapleson, she kept a parrot that she trained to shriek 'cash! cash!' whenever a theatre manager walked into the room.[20] D'Oyly did indeed work with her often, and she would become a regular at his Savoy Hotel, but he represented The Diva's substantially less famous, limping elder sister, Carlotta. Unsurprisingly, he described her as the 'sister of Adelina Patti' on bills and adverts. Also unsurprisingly, Carlotta resented it. When she saw the description on the programmes, adverts and posters for a concert at Birmingham Town Hall, she turned on her heel for London, leaving him to explain her absence.

*

After D'Oyly's holiday to Florida in 1882, it was plain sailing until a hot summer in 1884 brought the run of the latest Gilbert and Sullivan opera, *Princess Ida*, to an untimely end. When he commissioned a fresh work for six months' time, the world's most successful creators of light opera were racked by doubt and discontent. Sullivan longed to escape D'Oyly's middle-brow embrace to write something serious, which added to frustrations as the fractious pair set to work.

The tension over who deferred to whom creatively was never settled between them. Gilbert generally started and then his words were set to music. Sullivan resented having to write music to fit the words and not the other way around. For the new opera, Gilbert proposed a plot about a magic lozenge that would change the characters' behaviour. Sullivan shot it down as lacking in 'human interest and probability', as well as being too similar to *The Sorcerer* with its magic love potion.[21] They were at an impasse until Gilbert dropped the idea of the magic lozenge. In his study one day, a Japanese sword crashed on to the floor from its place on the wall. It was enough to spark his imagination to write *The Mikado*. He wrote to Sullivan, expressing the hope that it might tempt him back to the Savoy.

What started as a moment of artistic crisis turned into one of the most performed musical theatre works in history, and the rapturous reception revitalised them. It opened at the Savoy in April 1885. Rutland Barrington, the lead, recalled that: 'From the moment the curtain rose on the Court swells [. . .] to its final fall it was one long succession of uproarious laughter at the libretto and overwhelming applause for the

music.'[22] Sullivan noted in his diary: 'Tremendous reception
[. . .] Seven encores taken – might have taken twelve.'[23]

By this time of popularity, D'Oyly was running seven
touring companies simultaneously. His Opera Company
troupes would travel Britain, Europe, North America and the
Commonwealth almost every single year for the next century,
performing Gilbert and Sullivan operas six days a week, for-
ty-eight weeks a year. As Gilbert would enthuse to Sullivan:
'We are world-known, and as much an institution as Westminster Abbey'.[24]

With *The Mikado* such a runaway hit, it made little sense
for D'Oyly to keep up his lecture tours. They were small fry,
financially and artistically. He explained in 1885, after a lecture
series for his friend Whistler, 'I now confine myself almost
entirely to operatic performances and am obliged to decline
all other undertakings.'[25] But even then he could not entirely
resist leaving the possibility open for later: 'I shall have to leave
this branch alone for the next six months at least.'[26]

D'Oyly took one company on tour with *The Mikado* himself, from London to Berlin, and then onto other Continental
cities. Vienna's leading critic, Eduard Hanslick, noted that its
'unparalleled success' was owing not merely to the libretto or
the music but also to 'the wholly original stage performance,
unique of its kind, by Mr D'Oyly Carte's artists [. . .] riveting
the eye and ear with its exotic allurement'.[27]

Whimsical as *The Mikado* itself was, its staging brought out
the most ferocious side of D'Oyly's character. An American
manager, James C. Duff, wanted to stage his own *Mikado* in
New York. D'Oyly complained that Duff had 'haggled and
haggled' over terms until D'Oyly no longer wanted him involved, and had chosen to partner up with another American
producer.[28] Duff then tried to put on his own production
anyway. D'Oyly's methods were outlandish in seeing off the

threat. When Duff arrived in London, he found that it was his new rival's town. Liberty, the shop behind Regent Street that provided many of the Opera Company fabrics, would not serve Duff for his own costumes to take back to New York, and he found the same with London's set designers. They all knew whose custom was more important. To make sure that Duff could neither make them nor buy them, D'Oyly bought up all of the Japanese costumes in London and in Paris that he and his staff could find. In New York, he planned to pip Duff to the post by staging his own American *Mikado* without warning. This involved getting himself, his principal performers, and his chorus to New York without Duff finding out. D'Oyly would usually have recruited the less important chorus parts in New York, but any auditions would have alerted Duff, so he brought everyone over from London. All of this expense was worth it to D'Oyly: 'I will spend anything to smash Mr Duff,' he told his American *Mikado* producing partner.[29]

As D'Oyly headed off on a Cunard liner to oversee the New York shows in August 1885, he was full of the 'extraordinary energy' that Sullivan so admired in him.[30] He had heard that Duff was pressing ahead, so he sailed from Liverpool, calling himself Henry Chapman on the crossing. His cast travelled under assumed names too. They arrived on the 18th and opened *The Mikado* the next day, a week ahead of Duff.

It was then that, aged thirty-two, D'Oyly's sickly wife, Blanche, died of pneumonia, after years of ill health.[31] She was thought to have an alcohol problem as well, which must have contributed to her overall frailty. At the time of her death, she was convalescing in a private house by the Thames that D'Oyly had rented for the summer. She was taken to their home at the time, 71 Russell Square in Bloomsbury, before being buried in her family vault at Old Highgate Cemetery. D'Oyly did not change his plans for her funeral, however.

He did not return from New York until mid-October, in the company of Sullivan.

D'Oyly was now a widower at forty-one, with two young sons, twelve-year-old Lucas, and eight-year-old Rupert, who would keep his mother's plain gold wedding band until he himself died. The boys were sent to his sister Lizzie, and to boarding school at Winchester for the rest of the time. From the time they were young teenagers, they were brought up by D'Oyly on a diet of rich food, late nights and sporadic attention in their school holidays. There was a plaintive note when he put off a meeting with Gilbert on his return, because he needed to go to Brighton: 'My children are there and Sunday is my only chance of seeing them.'

Waiting in the wings for D'Oyly after Blanche's death was his assistant, Helen Lenoir. She had been patient a long time. Eight years earlier, in February 1877, Lenoir had taken advantage of the phrase 'no previous knowledge necessary' in his advertisements. She turned up to audition having only been in the chorus of a Christmas pantomime, *Aladdin*. D'Oyly cast her in a small part on a provincial tour of *The Great Divorce Case*. His judgement was perhaps a little clouded by attraction. His assistant, Frank Desprez, met her at the same time, when she walked into the office by the Savoy Theatre site. Desprez remembered 'the large, dreamy depthful eyes of the little lady in a fur lined cloak' who came knocking on the door looking for 'work of some kind'. He concluded that she was 'not of the stuff of which artists are made'. She was not beautiful in any conventional understanding, and Desprez, in his 'youthful insouciance', as he said, took 'no particular notice of her'. D'Oyly, however, did. 'With his Napoleonic estimate of individuals, he was more discerning,' Desprez recalled. 'That's a clever little girl, Desprez,' he said to me; 'a very clever little girl. I shall make something of her'.[32]

He had the knack of surrounding himself with talented assistants and friends, and Helen proved invaluable. She could not attend the University of London, as it did not award degrees to women until 1878. However, she could be examined externally and awarded qualifications that way. One of the first women to persevere with this approach, she received 'Special Certificates' in mathematics, logic and moral philosophy.[33] After her studies, she had taught maths as a private tutor, which she found dull, and had a brief acting career, for which she changed her name from Susan Helen Couper Black to Helen Lenoir. Like D'Oyly, with some tweaking, she had rustled up a more exciting Gallic name.

If D'Oyly was fairly pragmatic and low key when he met Helen, she seems to have been giddily attracted straight away. She turned up again at his office after only a few weeks of touring *The Great Divorce Case*. She abandoned acting altogether and offered to become his secretary,[34] starting with offering to organise his chaotic desk. She was devoted from the outset – and it could not have been D'Oyly's salary that swayed her into abandoning acting. If he was attracted at this stage, it did not move him to put his hand in his pocket. He paid her thirty shillings (£185) a week. Although it did improve years later as his cash flow became less worrying, her family back in Scotland were concerned. Her brother, after she had been working at the agency a few months, pleaded with her to stop wasting her time. He encouraged her to book herself on to a liner bound for Adelaide to join him in moving to Australia. She stuck at her badly paid job in D'Oyly's haphazard office instead, in all likelihood already infatuated with her financially unstable, married boss. She was not known to have any love interest other than D'Oyly for as long as she knew him.

D'Oyly, for his part, did not seem to spend any unnecessary extra time with Helen while he was married to Blanche.

Travel would have been an easy excuse, but he frequently dispatched Helen on her own across the Atlantic to oversee productions and tours from his office at 1267 Broadway. She made at least fifteen visits to promote his interests there before they were married.[35] D'Oyly referred to her as his 'American brain'.[36]

In 1886, a year after Blanche died, D'Oyly raised Helen's salary to £1,000 (£123,000), with an additional 10 per cent on net profits. Even having proved herself over many years, she had humbly demurred. He replied, 'You know very well, and so do all those who know anything about my affairs, that I could not have done the business at all [. . .] without you'.[37] His fondness for her was clear when she asked for a lower sum: 'Knowing your particular disposition as I do, I can quite understand your hesitation in receiving this amount. Probably most outsiders would think your line of conduct absolutely quixotic but I fully appreciate your motives. You object to receive more than you have fairly earned.' He suggested bringing in one of his business acquaintances to help them settle on the figure.[38] All of that intelligence that D'Oyly had spotted the first time they met was finally making Helen wealthy.

Nine years after they had first met, and three after Blanche had died, they married at the Savoy Chapel, with Sullivan as best man, in April 1888. In *Brideshead Revisited*, Evelyn Waugh referred to the Chapel as somewhere that 'divorced couples got married [. . .] a poky little place'.[39] It was a royal peculiar, which meant that it did not answer to any dignitary other than the monarch. The Chapel is now much more regulated and marriage services need a licence granted by the Archbishop of Canterbury. In D'Oyly's day, however, marriages without banns could occur there, which leant itself to furtive, expedient weddings.

In the register, Helen's age was listed as twenty-nine. She

was, in fact, thirty-four. Other than an administrative mistake, a likely explanation is that she perhaps knocked five years off for her audition to present herself as one of the young actresses that D'Oyly was looking for, and never corrected the deceit.

Rupert and Lucas did not have much warning about the new addition to their family. On 11 April 1888, sixteen-year-old Lucas simply wrote in his diary: 'Dinner with HL [Helen], Father, us, Mr Stanley, and Mr Fladgate [D'Oyly's solicitor]. Afterwards Father [told] of his intentions for the following day. Billiards.'[40] D'Oyly and Helen organised a six-week honeymoon on the Italian and French Rivieras. On their return, he made her his business partner, and therefore a rare, eminent female player in Victorian public life, with a salary of £200,000 in today's money. When a journalist came to interview him, he deferred to Helen: 'She's the business woman, and she really can do two things at a time – six, I believe.'[41] While D'Oyly's first wife had little bearing on his professional life, his second was integral.

In his memoir, Opera Company performer Henry Lytton described her in similar terms: 'a born business woman [. . .] No financial statement was too intricate for her, and no contract too abstruse. Once, when I had to put one of her letters to me before my legal adviser [. . .] he declared firmly "this letter must have been written by a solicitor." He would not admit that any woman could draw up a document so cleverly guarded with qualifications.'[42] As the editor of theatre newspaper, *The Era*, reflected: 'She never took advantage of anybody; but I never heard of her letting anybody take advantage of her.'[43]

D'Oyly's newly reconstituted family moved to Adelphi Terrace, a row of Robert Adam neoclassical town houses between the Savoy Theatre and the Thames, overlooking the river. They had six servants: a cook, kitchen maid, two housemaids, a butler and a footman. The street was demolished in 1936, but they were four-storey town houses with architectural flourishes of balustrades, cornices, friezes and ornate ceilings. The back windows looked out over Embankment Gardens to the Thames. D'Oyly had the house decorated in flamboyant fashion by his friend Whistler. He gilded the mouldings in the principal rooms, and mixed the paint himself so the house had a colour scheme that could not be bought in any shop. D'Oyly had a new-fangled lift installed, making him the first person in the country to have one at home.

For weekends, D'Oyly designed a country residence at Weybridge, on an island in the Thames that he spotted on a walk with Rupert and Lucas. When he first saw it, it was little more than a mound in the water. He enlarged it to allow fifty boats to be able to moor up, adding a dash of wit by giving the island the prow shape of an ocean liner. It was known as D'Oyly Carte Island by locals, and as Folly Eyot by the family themselves. The house was an Arts and Crafts-influenced thirteen-bedroom mansion, the centrepiece of which was a forty-foot ballroom, with a library, dining room and wine cellar, and a curved main staircase that was lit by a glass atrium above. Adding to the sense of occasion, visitors would ring a bell on the riverbank and await collection by boat. Surrounding the house were rare trees from Kew Gardens, inhabited by nightingales. Also living among the trees was a small pet crocodile that a staff member brought back from a tour of South Africa as a gift for Lucas.

As with D'Oyly's 'semi-holidays', the island was not entirely a retreat from work, or, at least, it was not originally intended as such. He had initially embarked on building there on such a scale because he had pictured it as a possible countryside annex to the Savoy Hotel and Restaurant that he had taking shape next to his theatre. His future guests might enjoy a day or two out on the island, he had thought. However, local authorities would not grant him an alcohol licence, and unable to imagine guests tolerating such enforced abstinence, he decided to keep the place for himself and his family.

Before the house was finished, he would take Lucas and Rupert to stay there with his butler and cook from Adelphi Terrace. Rutland Barrington was invited along for these luxury camping weekends, and they had 'splendid times', Barrington recalled. D'Oyly's neighbour on Adelphi Terrace, J. M. Barrie, creator of Peter Pan, braved the temporary huts as well.[44] Once the house was ready, Gilbert and Sullivan spent weekends rehearsing with the Opera Company in the ballroom. Sullivan liked it so much that he started to rent a house at nearby Walton-on-Thames, which allowed him to visit D'Oyly more easily.

Despite being only seventeen miles downriver from The Savoy, the island was pastoral and remote. On the weekends, D'Oyly took Rupert and Lucas for golf in Weybridge and to the cricket, and fishing and wild swimming were regular pastimes. All of this was not without incident. At one stage the pet crocodile broke loose. One alarmist local headline read: 'LOST – A CROCODILE. A Terrible Reptilian Now Disporting Itself in the Thames'. It scuttled away unguarded one Whit Sunday from the lawn and jumped into the river. D'Oyly offered a £1 (£120) reward for his missing pet, which he described as 'quite harmless'. Ever sentimental about his animals, when his terrier Trapp, who featured heavily in family photograph albums, died, he had a little mausoleum built for him on the mainland, where it could be seen through the trees from the house.

FIVE

'The Hotel de Luxe of the World'

D'Oyly catapulted himself to a new level of fame in 1889. Adjoining his Savoy Theatre, he unveiled his Savoy Hotel with great pomp and publicity. Despite having no relevant industry experience – other than as a globetrotting regular guest – he built 'the Hotel de Luxe of the World', as he liked to call it, and installed himself as the chairman and managing director, with his friends as investors and board members. After five years of escalating bills and legal wrangles, he had transformed the wasteland next to the theatre into a marvel: the place that kickstarted the modern luxury hotel scene. By August, the elegant shell was furnished and awaiting *le beau monde* to glide in through its revolving doors. He had spent five years promising the best hotel in the world to anyone who would listen. Now it was ready to be judged.

Since he had started travelling with the Opera Company, D'Oyly had been gathering ideas about how to make London more exciting. Compared to what he saw in America and Continental Europe, he lamented that his hometown was lagging behind in entertainment, restaurants and nightlife. London was a mushrooming metropolis of five and a half million people – far bigger than Paris, New York, Berlin, or any other city, for that matter. It was the hub of an empire that encompassed a quarter of the world. Buildings were going up, slums were being cleared and streets were being built. For all that, it was lacking in style, and suffered a reputation for poor hospitality. As Australian opera singer Nellie Melba, who became a Savoy regular, complained before it opened, in London: 'the cooking was execrable, the carpets were dirty, the menu was medieval, the service an insult'.[1]

D'Oyly would have agreed. He was disappointed by how uninspiring the places to stay were. His Savoy was so far ahead that, even in 1932, its managing director was able to mock the competition: 'there still lingers in Great Britain the stoic idea that the absence of central heating [. . .] sparsely furnished bedrooms and primitive bathrooms are in themselves admirable and help us retain those qualities which made the Empire'.[2]

In D'Oyly's day, there were two big, established London hotels, the Langham and the Westminster Palace. They were lacklustre and, of greatest frustration to D'Oyly, did not offer tempting food. In his estimation, the country had two decent restaurants, the Café Royal and Kettner's, both in Soho, but he was not bowled over by either. Dissatisfied that there was not one world-class restaurant, he wanted to create one at the Savoy. His inspirations were the best restaurants of the century: the Café Anglais in Paris, Delmonico's and the Brunswick in New York, the Belle-Vue in Philadelphia, and Pfordte's in Hamburg.[3] He wanted his to be among them, but it had been a while since a newcomer had come close: the Café Anglais opened in 1802, Delmonico's in 1827, and Pfordte's in 1859. They served mostly French food in hushed, wood-panelled rooms. More unusual, D'Oyly thought, would be cosmopolitan food on offer both alfresco and indoors. He wanted an authentic French haute cuisine menu, but peppered with English, Russian, German and Indian dishes for the international guests that he had in mind. A most important addition, as D'Oyly was always thinking of American taste, would be imported terrapins and green corn.

What made London more plausible as a holiday destination by 1889 was the advent of faster, flashier travel. A flourishing trade in shipbuilding made boats fashionable and investment poured in. British ocean liners, chiefly Blue Ribband, held the lead on the fastest transatlantic journeys until the Edwardian era, when they were overtaken by German companies. D'Oyly would permanently post porters at Southampton to greet his guests at the port and collect their luggage, and, back at the hotel, the hall porter kept a large board above his desk of liner arrival times so as to know when to expect an influx. Dressed in their finery, guests would be escorted from the docks to the private train carriage to the horse-drawn carriage to the hotel. The new Calais–Mediterranean Express train, coupled with a ferry ride, connected London to the Riviera overnight.

At the time, the international super rich were on an annual circuit of picturesque Continental towns and cities: Paris, Monaco, Cannes, Baden-Baden, Biarritz. Getting London on to this circuit was going to be tricky. London had uninspiring restaurants, mediocre weather, and no spring waters or dramatic landscape. The draw would have to be culture and history – and service and food, with a bit of work. D'Oyly hoped that the Savoy would pique travellers' interest enough to cross the Channel. As with D'Oyly's Opera Company, trains and liners made his grand ideas and schemes possible on an international scale. For his theatre, trains meant a renewable audience beyond locals, and taking productions on tour was much easier now than it had been during his early forays with Mario. His little Savoy fiefdom was even on the same street as Charing Cross Station. It brought audiences from around Britain to his theatre, and now, hopefully, overseas visitors from Southampton to his hotel.

Developments in the city at the time tended to be functional: transport, infrastructure and housing. D'Oyly was ahead of *fin de siècle* frivolity in turning his attention to flightier improvements. He was primed for the decade in which the phrase 'conspicuous consumption' was coined, by economist Thorstein Veblen. In Veblen's *Theory of the Leisure Class*, he described the characteristics of the nouveau riche at balls, where guests were invited to 'witness the consumption of that excess of good things' owned by the host. 'It is not sufficient merely to possess wealth or power. [It] must be put in evidence', Veblen observed.[4] D'Oyly envisaged the modern luxury hotel as a backdrop against which people could admire each other and be admired in turn, as Veblen described. Starting with his mother's refined ideas about culture and his father's growing wealth during his childhood, D'Oyly had cultivated an intimate understanding of how rich Victorians might want to spend it. His own love of the good life allowed him to dream up a slick operation in which everything from shoeshine to champagne would be taken care of, on the romantic stage set of a palatial purpose-built hotel. As Winston Churchill, whose parents were regulars from the beginning, would nickname it, the Savoy was the *'essence de civilisation'*. It was an apt summation of D'Oyly's guiding principle in all that he did.

At the time of opening, the hotel mimicked the homes of the guests it sought to attract. With the mahogany, gold leaf, mirrors, stucco work and liveried staff, the setting was reminiscent of the English country house, but transplanted to the West End and given an exterior of iridescent white from its matt-glazed tiles, which kept it sparkling in the sooty London air. D'Oyly hoped to coax the rich in through the doors to do something new in Britain: eat, drink, dance, smoke and socialise in public, rather than at each other's houses.

The Savoy offered upmarket guests a form of stylish collective living that was novel in London. His Continental vision was carried through to trying out riverside drinking on a terrace that would be 'warmed in cold weather but open in warm weather', where his guests could drink coffee and smoke al fresco.[5] As well as a courtyard filled with plants and flowers, D'Oyly promised 'the finest and only open air restaurant in London'. It would offer breakfast, dinner and 'dejeuner forchette'. For the uninitiated, he helpfully put in brackets in the advertisement, 'lunch'. D'Oyly wore his ambition on his sleeve, claiming that his 'cuisine and cellars' would 'rival the most famous Continental and American Restaurants'. He made a direct pitch at getting Londoners to relocate their entertaining to his palace for hire, telling them that it was 'specially adapted for private parties and "At Homes"'.[6]

D'Oyly drew inspiration from the theatre to create an immersive experience. From the moment a guest arrived, he wanted them to feel important, starting with a big entrance. Smartly dressed doormen would welcome them in, before they would walk through the expansive marble foyer to find themselves playing a cameo role in the life of the hotel. The Hotel Bar and Restaurant had an unnecessary flight of steps, to create drama on entering, and full evening dress had to be worn. Once guests had finished their preprandial drinks, waiters, dressed for dinner service in red jackets with gold buttons, silk stockings and velvet breeches, escorted them through the glass-and-gilt doors to the Restaurant. D'Oyly set up a printing department to make artistic daily menus. They were lavish productions, featuring sketches and embossing, worthy of keeping as mementos, as though they were one of his theatre programmes.

From one of his holidays in Monte Carlo, he had poached François Rinjoux, a maître d'hôtel, to oversee the Restaurant. For a classically trained French chef, with all the status that conferred, he lured Henri Charpentier away from Mayfair private members' club White's. For a general manager, he poached William Hardwicke from a large country estate. Other front of house staff were formerly D'Oyly's private butlers, housekeeper and footmen from Adelphi Terrace. They received promotions from running his household to running hotel departments. Nicholas Mockett went from being D'Oyly's butler to becoming 'the world's most famous head porter' – a job that he kept until 1933. As a smiling, ever-discreet diplomat, Mockett was well-suited to the role. J. Pierpont Morgan, the financier, was so fond of him that he tried to persuade him to spend a summer holiday as his guest in America. But Mockett could not be induced to cross the Atlantic. 'The ships are too slow. I prefer Margate,' Mockett said.[7]

D'Oyly celebrated with three opening events. His first had been an intimate 'housewarming supper' in late July. This was hosted by his friend Hwfa Williams, one of the seven hotel directors. A man-about-town, Williams was manager of Sandown, the racecourse in Surrey, and a friend of the Prince of Wales. His wife, Florence, was a renowned, well-dressed society hostess. D'Oyly's other directors were Sullivan, his theatre friend Michael Gunn, the former Conservative Party chief whip Earl of Lathom, and two financiers, R. B. Fenwick, and A. G. Weguelin, who liked to turn up in a chinchilla fur coat. Company directors and other investors had put up the money to buy the land, construct the building and start the company. D'Oyly raised £200,000 (£24m) by selling shares, and subscriptions at £10 (£1,200) each had been offered to the public just before it opened.[8]

Hwfa Williams' Housewarming Supper did not start until

midnight, after a performance at the Royal Opera House to which D'Oyly had treated everyone.[9] Carriages brought them from Covent Garden to the flower-filled Savoy courtyard from the Thames Embankment side, allowing guests to admire the prettiness of the gaslights along the waterfront, with the outline of Cleopatra's Needle in the foreground. To enjoy the river from the bedrooms, D'Oyly had his architect cousin Arthur Mackmurdo design long rows of art nouveau balconies along the façade, with striped awnings, a look reminiscent of the cheerful little seaside hotels on the Continent.

Inside, golden ceilings and carved wooden wall panels glinted in the novel electric light of which D'Oyly was so fond. There were acres of William Morris wallpaper and red carpet. He had asked Collinson & Locke, his interior designers for the theatre, to work their magic on the public areas with their gilding and moulding work. Surrounded by all this very Victorian opulence, D'Oyly and Helen welcomed guests as though to their own house. This fitted the hotel's mantra that it had guests, never customers. D'Oyly had forged himself a place in the bustle of his home city, and revelled in finally being able to welcome people in.

As well as his friends and the journalists covering the opening, plenty of aristocrats had accepted the invitation: there was the Duchess of Manchester Consuelo Montagu, Lord Dunraven, Lord and Lady Gosford, Lord and Lady Dudley, Lord and Lady de Grey, Lord Hartington, Lord Hardwick, and the Honorable Algernon Bourke, the owner of White's, who had just lost the best chef in London to D'Oyly's hotel kitchen. Lady Randolph Churchill, born Jennie Jerome in Brooklyn, would become an early visitor, as would her twenty-four-year-old son, Winston. Before moving to England, Lady Churchill had already become friends with Sullivan and Mrs Ronalds, for the unusual reason that Mrs Ronalds had been her father's mistress, and the two had grown close, so they became regulars at the hotel together. Representing the businessmen whom D'Oyly was keen to attract were the English branch of the Rothschilds, and the American Forbes family.

This late-night debut established the convivial atmosphere that D'Oyly wanted. The hotel would offer 24-hour room service, and 'opera suppers', starting at 11 p.m. every night, other than Sunday. Charpentier put together a light midnight feast for the housewarming that would be typical of the opera suppers:

Deutz and Geldermann Gold Lack champagne, 1880

Croustades de Crevettes Dieppois [shrimp croustades in a light wine and cream sauce]

Cailles de Vigne [quail wrapped in grape leaves][10]

The second opening party, described by D'Oyly as a 'private viewing',[11] was to thank the investors and further dazzle the press. His ability to win journalists' attention meant previews in *The Sunday Times*, *Observer*, *The Economist*, *Financial Times*, *News of the World*, *Daily Telegraph* and *Vanity Fair*, alongside fifteen others. He kept their effusive write-ups in an album. One journalist, sent by the *Illustrated London News*, marvelled: 'All the suites of rooms are upholstered and arranged on a scale which can only be equalled in a grand mansion. In all such details as plate, glass, china, and table-linen, great pains have been taken to procure the best. Nothing is wanting to please the educated eye or gratify the taste'.[12] He was bowled over by the 6,000-square-foot riverside courtyard, at the centre of which was a pretty fountain surrounded by an arch of flowers.

The official opening was a week later. This was the general public crunch time: D'Oyly would find out whether anyone would pay to be there. There was one particular guest arriving on whom D'Oyly had been fixated for years. On one of his trips to Monte Carlo with Sullivan in 1887, D'Oyly had been so enamoured by the hotel where they were staying, the Grand, that he had sought out its manager, César Ritz, to compliment him. D'Oyly passed on his frustration about his home city. 'There is not a hotel in London where you can get a decent meal,' he told Ritz, 'much less one where you can dine like a god as one does here.'[13] While his own hotel was being built, D'Oyly began his patient seduction of Ritz, later of The Ritz hotels, telling him that, in London: 'you would make money hand over fist. Hand over fist!'[14] Ritz was unconvinced that the city had much potential at all, and D'Oyly was unable to persuade him otherwise.

A year later, D'Oyly was in the German spa town of Baden-Baden. Both he and Sullivan liked to 'take the cure', which was fashionable among wealthy Victorians looking to soothe a range of ailments using mineral spring waters. One evening he attended a dinner for Prince Radziwiłł of Poland at the Restaurant de la Conversation, newly opened by Ritz. D'Oyly was entranced by the beauty of the evening, and admired the mix of German, French and English high society around him. Picking himself up after the rebuff in Monte Carlo, he homed in on Ritz again after dinner. Sweeping his arm around the room full of ferns and roses, he told Ritz: 'This is the sort of thing I'd like to do at my new hotel in London.'[15] This time he backed it up with a serious job offer and a boast that his Savoy, as the finest hotel in the world, was going to change the city.

Still, Ritz would not budge. D'Oyly toned down his offer. Seeing a chance to work on him over a few weeks, he offered to pay Ritz to come to stay for a fortnight, just for the opening. His knowledge would be invaluable, D'Oyly told him.

For this D'Oyly would pay £350 (£42,000).[16] In the end, successful persuasion came down to offering a lot of money.

Having resolved that London was a lost cause, for purely mercenary reasons Ritz put himself on a train in time for the official opening on 6 August. D'Oyly was waiting to escort him to his suite in person and show him the view from the balcony. To the east, it took in St Paul's Cathedral and the Tower of London, to the west the Houses of Parliament. Across the water lay the open greenery of Lambeth, with the Surrey hills in the distance.[17] As Monet would so romantically depict from his hotel room, the trains from Charing Cross railway bridge left trails of steam and smoke, occasionally hazing up the view of Westminster. He first painted the Thames from the Savoy in 1899, and returned twice, staying each time for two months. He painted *Waterloo Bridge* from room 618. 'London would be quite ugly if it were not for the fog,' he judged.[18] Fortunately, the haze from Charing Cross provided plenty of cover as well. D'Oyly's artist friend, Whistler, stayed for months and worked on lithographs and oil paintings of the view. It was a vista that suited an optimistic, expansionist age: the heart of the largest city in the world, in the largest empire in the world. Taken by his own view as he was, D'Oyly bought many of Whistler's paintings.

Beyond the view from his balcony, there was much for Ritz to explore in two weeks. The hotel itself was a masterpiece, Ritz agreed. There were four hundred guest rooms, fireproof and heavily soundproofed, with electric lighting available twenty-four hours a day. Considering that D'Oyly had started life using a communal pump for water, with no plumbing at home and, of course, no electricity, he was thrilled by it all. He loved to show guests that they could turn the bedroom light on and off using a switch by the bed, so there was no need to get out once they were tucked in.

He had imported six American elevators. Four were for service, which gave a sense of the scale of the operation, and only two were for guests. They were furnished with padded seating, mirrors and lacquered walls, hydraulically powered, and operated by attendants. D'Oyly christened them 'ascending rooms'. They had the benefit of making all of the floors desirable. Traditionally, top floors were servants' quarters. Here the fifth-floor rooms were equally comfortable and D'Oyly charged accordingly. If anything, the top floor was the best, as it had a panoramic view and cleaner air. He promised in an advertisement that the 'ascending rooms' would be 'running all night', making 'top floor rooms equal in every respect to the lowest'.[19]

A double with a bath cost 12 shillings (£60) in the early years.[20] There were two hundred and fifty suites with sitting rooms and multiple bedrooms. Some even had bathrooms with lavatories. Altogether there were sixty-seven bathrooms, a specification that D'Oyly's builder met with incredulity. Would the guests be amphibious? the builder asked.[21] A fairly recent hotel at the time, the Victoria on Northumberland Avenue by Marble Arch, had four between five hundred guests, which was more normal.[22] Most hotel guests of the time expected to bathe in a freestanding vessel, which servants would fill with canisters lugged up to the room.

Instead, D'Oyly's marble bathrooms would be the first in London to proffer constant hot and cold running water and, later, telephones were added. Rather than a quick dip in a portable tub, the experience was elevated to a separate ceremony of ablutions. D'Oyly took bathtime extremely seriously. He hopped fully clothed into tubs in showrooms around Mayfair in search of the most comfortable in which his guests could wallow. It was in America that he had first seen fitted baths. The vast Palace Hotel in San Francisco had impressed him with its remarkable provision of four hundred bathrooms.

In his own, he added two tub-side bells – one to call a female maid and another to call a male valet.

Speaking tubes, little pipes that could carry voices between floors to the kitchen, made room service possible. D'Oyly boasted that food could be served to guests 'in the most perfect manner in their own rooms'.[23] Anything from a cup of tea to a fancy cocktail from the American Bar would appear 'in the twinkling of an Embankment lamp', as he phrased it.[24] Just as he had at the theatre, he eliminated all hidden charges. He did not like being asked for more money for frills wherever he stayed himself. His full-page advertisements in London's newspapers assured that there would be 'no charge for baths, lights or attendance'.[25]

This transparent approach seemed a relief. The *San Francisco Chronicle* reported, a few weeks after the opening, that among a number of Californians, General John T. Cutting, a congressman, was holding forth about his stay:

'I'll tell you, gentlemen [. . .] I maintain that for service there is no hotel in the United States to compare with that Hotel Savoy in London. There is no rush nor excitement when you arrive. You are courteously escorted by an attendant to your apartment, not by an officious bellboy who wants to wear his whisk-broom out on your clothes in the expectation of a tip. You open your trunk and lay out your crumpled clothes and go to your breakfast. You return in the early evening to dress for dinner, and your dress suit is there freshly pressed and ironed for use. In the morning your day suit is similarly fit to wear. You couldn't have your wants better attended to if you were at home. I never had to call for any special service – you don't have to ring for ice water, it's there. That's the way to keep a hotel.'[26]

The ice water that General Cutting so appreciated was another touch to appeal to Americans. Even when Conrad Hilton opened up in London seventy years later, iced water was a remarked-on selling point for Americans away from home, alongside the air conditioning. Many newly wealthy Americans looked to European culture for ideas of style, but they wanted modern comforts added on top. With this in mind, the hotel brought together English country-house interiors, with the American innovations and French fine dining that D'Oyly admired from his travels. It was a winning combination that set the template for the modern luxury hotel. Anyone could come in and be treated like royalty – as long as they could afford it. He could see that, like him, London's wealthy had growing leisure time and disposable income, and he wanted the most illustrious people from around Europe and America there as well.

D'Oyly had successfully sold Americans both Oscar Wilde and the Savoy operas, and he was angling to do the same with his hotel. Part of the skill was to present an appealing version of Victorian Britain. When William Randolph Hearst, owner of a string of American newspapers, started coming to stay in 1892, he bought into the whole British upper-class aesthetic and lifestyle in the way that D'Oyly had hoped. For Hearst, it involved joining in with the 'Season' of annual social events, including horse racing at Ascot, cricket at Lords and the Henley Regatta, and it meant plenty of commissions for D'Oyly's tailor on Savile Row. On just one of many visits, Hearst ordered a tweed short lounge jacket with a waistcoat and plus fours, a blue double-breasted coat with beaver fur on the collar and cuffs, a mackintosh with a cape, a driving cape, and a tweed short lounge jacket and trousers. Hearst was fully ready to buy into the part of an English gentleman.

D'Oyly's Savoy's 1889 prospectus for shareholders made

clear his ambition to appeal internationally. He often repeated this wish in private and had specific guests in mind. He wanted the princely families of Rome, the Rudini family from Sicily, the Crispis, who had the eleventh prime minister of Italy in their family, and the Rospigliosis, who had Pope Clement IX in theirs, to be socialising at the hotel with his theatre and opera friends: Adelina Patti, Polish opera singer siblings the de Reszkes, and French actors Benoît-Constant Coquelin and Sarah Bernhardt. From America he wanted Vanderbilts, Morgans and Rothschilds.[27] He had made a start in his opening week in attracting some of them, but he needed to keep going – and he needed them to pay to be there. This was a show that needed to run and run to break even, let alone make money.

For all D'Oyly's innovative offerings, characteristic dynamism and illustrious early visitors, the hotel suffered a wobbly start. After his three big parties, the fun was over for a while. As he relied on his friends to fill up the bedrooms, the Bar and Restaurant, he could hardly sleep for anxiety, fearing himself to be on the brink of ruin. He offered his friend, American journalist R. D. Blumenfeld, the chance to move from his flat in Mayfair to an empty suite for £2 10s a week (£260).[28] He had created a playground for the rich, famous and talented that he was so keen to bring to London. He had built from scratch a plush, palm-adorned palace for them. Now he could not tell if enough of them would materialise to make it all worthwhile. He only shared the extent of his worries later: 'I extricated the hotel by great work and owing to my relations with the world of finance. I have not spoken much of it, but it was the most difficult and dangerous position in my life.' Even if he could manage to tempt guests in through the door once, it was very possible that the whole idea had been a ruinous folly.

D'Oyly had set the scene and created an initial buzz, but he still needed a stellar manager and chef to keep guests coming back. In the meantime, he had established a loose structure of French chefs, Italian waiters and English management, to which the hotel has always roughly stuck ever since. His first manager, Hardwicke, and head chef, Charpentier, were competent, but he had not given up on the idea of securing Ritz to replace Hardwicke, and, to replace Charpentier, D'Oyly, characteristically, was longing for the best chef not just in London but in the world. This was Auguste Escoffier, known in France as 'the king of chefs, and the chef of kings'. He worked with Ritz in Monte Carlo part of the year, and Lucerne for the rest. The way to Escoffier was Ritz, and so D'Oyly kept working on the latter.

There was already hope. As planned, D'Oyly had convinced Ritz on his fortnight-long stay to see the potential of London. He had impressed the gatekeeper of Continental glamour, and more specifically of Escoffier. Ritz was not on the hook yet, but he was certainly thinking about it. D'Oyly would have to do without him for the next few months, but Ritz was now open to persuasion. He returned home from the Savoy to his new young wife, Marie, as she described it, in a 'fever of excitement'.[29]

An 1891 cartoon of Richard D'Oyly Carte, with architectural plans under his arm.

W.S. Gilbert (*above*) and
Arthur Sullivan (*right*), the
duo behind the famous
Gilbert & Sullivan operas.

A London performance of their opera *Iolanthe*, thought to be the 1915 production featuring Nellie Briercliffe in the lead role.

Billie Carleton, the actress, who was found dead in her room after an apparent cocaine overdose in 1918.

Marguerite Fahmy in 1922, the year before she murdered her husband in a suite at the hotel.

The Art Deco interior of Coleton
Fishacre in Devon, country home of
the D'Oyly Carte family (*above*).

Rupert D'Oyly Carte, 1910. (*left*). Bridget D'Oyly Carte during the 1950s (*right*).

Formula 1 driver Stirling Moss and Katie Molson cut the cake
at their wedding reception, 1957.

Sophia Loren at the hotel, 1965.

Princess Margaret greets fashion designer Valentino, after the unveiling of his winter collection at the hotel, 1968.

Muhammad Ali at a press conference to publicise his autobiography, 1976.

The famous entrance to the hotel today.

SIX

The carpet quarrel

D'Oyly was right to worry for now, though. The hotel had an expensive, fairly quiet winter from 1889 to 1890. In an echo of his disappointment with Gilbert and Sullivan when he ran out of money too early on to commission them at the Opera Comique, it looked as though his hotel might hit the rocks before he could secure his other dream double act, Ritz and Escoffier. He could see exactly what would work, but feared that he might not quite get there. It was taking time to convince Londoners to 'adopt the Continental habit of dining at hotels and restaurants', as D'Oyly's journalist friend Blumenfeld noticed, and so far the hotel was 'given over to people from abroad, and they are not many'.[1]

Meanwhile, at the Opera Company, the New York production of his new opera, *The Gondoliers*, was getting bad reviews, to which he was no longer accustomed. It jolted him into action. He and Helen decamped for three months to iron out its problems. Once *The Gondoliers* in America was fixed, they raced back in March, arriving the day before its royal command performance at Windsor Castle, which Queen Victoria found 'quite charming'.

More existential a threat than *The Gondoliers'* New York reviews, however, was that the fragile peace at the Savoy

Theatre had finally ended. Relations between D'Oyly and Gilbert became so tempestuous that they broke down altogether in 'the carpet quarrel'. On returning from an extended holiday in India, Gilbert combed through D'Oyly's spending for *The Gondoliers*. He perceived unacceptable extravagance: D'Oyly had spent £4,500 (£550,000), including £100 (£12,000) for the dresses of Casilda and for the Duchess. The item that rankled above all was the purchase of a carpet for £140 (£17,000) in the foyer. He was furious that D'Oyly, as the owner of the theatre, was expecting to split the cost with him and Sullivan, rather than paying out of his own pocket.

Gilbert argued that carpet was not an expense 'incidental to the performance' and that their contract referred to collectively paying for repairs, not replacements. He confidently contacted Sullivan, expecting his backing. Sullivan took his friend and patron's side instead. Gout-ridden Gilbert, short-tempered at the best of times, embarked on taking them to court. It became front-page news, as D'Oyly, supported by Sullivan, was sued by Gilbert in acrimonious proceedings from July to September. Sullivan provided an affidavit in support of D'Oyly. This treachery in Gilbert's mind maintained the breach between Gilbert and Sullivan, long after he and D'Oyly reconciled years later.

The legal boiling point came on the day when D'Oyly was due to share out profits from *The Gondoliers* to the other two on 4 July. With the dispute ongoing, D'Oyly held the profits back, on the advice of his solicitor. On the 30th, Gilbert demanded his share, which he estimated at £3,000 (£370,000). D'Oyly sent him £2,000 (£245,000). Gilbert hit back by moving in for receivership of the Opera Company. D'Oyly objected to this 'cruel conduct', but he was ordered to pay the extra £1,000 (£123,000) the next day, and to produce the year's accounts in three weeks. Fans beheld the partnership in tatters as it dissolved with bad grace all round. Gilbert presumably believed more than ever his sour observation that D'Oyly had 'a disposition to kick away the ladder by which he had risen'.[2]

Personally wounded but professionally undaunted, D'Oyly channelled his energy into a new venture, his English Opera House at Cambridge Circus, while the Savoy Theatre would largely tick along on revivals of the hits from now on. He intended his Opera House as a home for serious English opera, which was not a genre that existed as such. As with English light opera, he was more or less starting from scratch at the time. A classical opera house of his own had been a long-standing aspiration, but it was also now needed to placate Sullivan, who was increasingly upset about his career. He was the composer of esteemed hymns and oratorios, had studied music in Leipzig, and was much admired by Queen Victoria, who had knighted him, so he was hurt by critics pointing out that he had been prostituting his gifts at the Savoy. He suspected they were right. That such a paragon had spent his prime writing scores for comic operas was thanks to D'Oyly's persuasion, and ability to generate wealth to fund Sullivan's expensive taste. Convinced that more success awaited him in serious work, Sullivan had told D'Oyly some years ago that he was resolved 'not to write any more Savoy pieces'.[3] Even though he had not stuck to it, yet he had made it clear that he wanted to get away.

Sentimentally, the plot for D'Oyly's Opera House was at the end of Greek Street, where D'Oyly was born. As London theatre was enjoying renewed respectability, with the patronage of royalty and members of affluent society, venues themselves were increasing in number and style. Many former slums in the West End were demolished to make way. The Opera House was at the junction of Greek Street, Shaftesbury Avenue and Charing Cross Road, a new crossroads that was only created between 1877 and 1886. The nearby Shaftesbury and the Lyric Theatres had opened in 1888, but the Opera House would be the most ambitious of them all. By contrast, older theatres were still 'in many cases sandwiched between public houses, their cheaper parts approached from sinister slums'.[4]

Revelling in design details, he furnished his Opera House with his favourite William Morris fabrics, lined its walls with Algerian and Italian marble, and dispensed with a contractor in order to supervise the building personally. The theatre did not have an architect in the regular sense, often being credited to D'Oyly himself. George Holloway, who had built the hotel and D'Oyly's island retreat, provided the initial drawings, while a theatre consultant ensured that sightlines and escape routes worked. It was cleverly built with no pillars to block the view. This was not only for the benefit of the audience, but, as with the ascending rooms at the Savoy Hotel, allowed greater charges for what historically would have been the cheap seats – the ones with obscured views – as for the historically cheap rooms – the ones at the top of too many stairs.

This design by committee could have resulted in a muddle. Instead it created a towering landmark. 'Throughout the length and breadth of England,' judged one theatre magazine, 'there are only two theatrical structures which make any pretence to architectural merit – Mr D'Oyly Carte's English Opera House and the portico of Covent Garden.'[5] D'Oyly added this gushing write-up into his scrapbook, along with his hotel reviews. Long after D'Oyly's time, the poet Sir John Betjeman described it as Britain's 'only theatre architecture that climbs into the region of a work of art'.[6]

On the outside, its red bricks were dressed with terracotta balconettes and friezes. Inside, the audience walked up a marble-and-alabaster staircase, and into the green-and-gold auditorium, lined with cipollino and pavonazzo marbles, inset with panels of Mexican onyx. It was all insulated from the increasing traffic noise by a shallow row of dressing rooms, offices and cloakrooms the length of the Shaftesbury Avenue frontage, and by foyers and staircases facing Cambridge Circus. The relics of its elaborate iron and wood machinery, above and below the stage, are unique survivors in London. Occupying a deep cellar and mezzanine, its moving parts are gone, but a forest of dusty timber with cogs, belts, traps and chariot slots remains.

Altogether, D'Oyly's English Opera House was estimated to have cost at least £150,000 (£18m). It regularly attracted pages and pages of features in titles such as *The Building News and Engineering Journal* and *American Architect*. These cuttings were neatly pasted into his leather-bound scrapbook too. His cuttings give an insight into how fascinated he was by the smallest technical detail of theatre architecture. He kept trade articles about the springs used in seating, about fire safety and cantilever measurements. No detail was too dry, it seemed. Unsurprisingly, he kept an eye on the Continent, as always. The Vienna Court Theatre, new at the time, made several appearances in his scrapbook. It is not hard to imagine him poring over any innovation that he might be able to use himself.

Although unannotated, the scrapbook also gives an insight into his character. It is perhaps the analogue equivalent of his internet search history. The eclectic cuttings have that magpie quality of a person's mind, naturally hopping from one subject to another without any need to order them for anyone else. On the other pages, among clippings about theatre architecture, are descriptions of litigation in which he was involved. It was one quarrel after another: his defeat in court to open another Savoy Hotel in Dublin; the 'Savoy Skyline Case', in which he avoided prosecution by London County Council over the prominence of his hotel sign; and various Gilbert and Sullivan spats. Alongside serious incidents were his passing interests. On one page was an article on the Romans' eating habits, which had caught his attention, on another he was curious about 'hypnotism and murder', and how the American Dental Institute was being sued for uncomfortable dentures.

Now known as the Palace Theatre, D'Oyly's Opera House had been home to *Harry Potter and the Cursed Child* for years at the time of writing. It was not so well-attended in D'Oyly's time. When he finally gave Sullivan the chance to be serious, it was a flop. Few have ever heard of *Ivanhoe,* which Sullivan wrote for the opening season, starting on 31 January 1891. It ran for 160 performances, which exceeded any precedent for any similar work, but it was insufficient to cover D'Oyly's exorbitant costs. More importantly, considering that he had a whole theatre dedicated to English opera, there was a more existential problem. D'Oyly had no other work to replace *Ivanhoe* immediately because they did not exist. He fell back on a French operetta by André Messager, *La Basoche.* In November 1891, D'Oyly pointedly mentioned in interviews that the Opera House's future depended on public support.

He was forced to present a series of plays starring Sarah Bernhardt, opening in May 1892 with Sardou's *Cleopatra,* to fill the bill, and opened negotiations with actor-turned-theatre manager and Savoy Hotel investor Sir Augustus Harris to sell up. Harris was one of D'Oyly's only rivals in his vigour for theatre promotion, although Harris's approach was more hard-nosedly commercial. He was happy to stage unsophisticated crowd-pleasers that D'Oyly would not countenance. Having admitted defeat and sold it on, D'Oyly suffered the indignity of seeing Harris promptly turn his Opera House into a music hall. The English Opera House became Harris's Palace

Theatre of Varieties. Despite Harris's dedication to selling tickets, it did not prosper either. Musical hall manager Charles Morton was called in. He finally made it lucrative with his racy curiosity of *tableaux vivants*.

While D'Oyly and Sullivan had been working together on *Ivanhoe*, Gilbert had been out in the cold. A month before *Ivanhoe* had opened, as a peace offering, D'Oyly had sent him tickets for the first anniversary performance of *The Gondoliers*. Gilbert did not attend.

SEVEN

'Everyone who comes, goes away highly pleased'

D'Oyly's claim for the Savoy Hotel

While D'Oyly's Opera House was proving a laudable but costly mistake, help had at least arrived for his hotel. He had redoubled his efforts in pursuit of Ritz, and managed to get him and Escoffier to London permanently in April 1890, having persevered with telegramming Ritz offers and plenty of flattery. He reminded Ritz of that dinner in Baden-Baden and told him how much he longed to offer that experience in London. Once Ritz was looking likely to come on board, D'Oyly insisted that Escoffier must be part of the deal. Ritz duly turned up in Monte Carlo as D'Oyly's messenger, promising Escoffier the chance to open the best restaurant in the world. Copying D'Oyly's tactic, when Escoffier baulked at London, Ritz told him to try it just for the coming summer. D'Oyly offered carte blanche as terms: Ritz's own team to assemble as he saw fit, no obligation to stay in London over the winter, and joint annual salaries for Escoffier and Ritz and their staff worth a million in today's money. Ritz would have £1,200 (£148,000) and

Escoffier £900 (£111,000) and the other salaries were similarly generous.[1]

Escoffier's arrival at the Savoy was not the slick introduction that Ritz had received. Instead, he walked into his new kitchen to find it trashed. Charpentier, indignant to have been usurped by the most famous chef in the world at short notice, led his men in leaving the fresh food out to rot, or throwing it to the floor, and taking off with the rest. Escoffier's first shift started with clearing up the mess and wondering where he could buy so many replacement ingredients on a Sunday.

Escoffier set an example for British restaurants at the Savoy. He sped up service by instituting a clockwork assembly line, with individual sous chefs responsible for preparing a small stage of each dish, which eventually became standard practice, known as the 'kitchen brigade' system. Each finished arrangement was then inspected by Escoffier before it left the kitchen. He codified haute cuisine as he went with his maxims: '*beurre, beurre et encore du beurre*' ['butter, butter and yet more butter'], '*surtout, faites simple*' ['above all, keep it simple'] and 'fish without wine is like egg without salt', he liked to tell his apprentices. He placed an emphasis on what we now take for granted – that food should arrive hot and quickly. He was stern about hygiene and sobriety. 'We are not drunks,' he told his Savoy cohort, 'we are cooks.'[2] There was to be no more smoking or drinking on the job.

D'Oyly's gamble of spending big on Ritz and Escoffier paid off. The pair brought the Continental level of refinement from Monte Carlo that he had pictured. As German financier Otto Kahn put it, the Savoy now made London 'a place worth living in'.[3] Invaluable to D'Oyly, soon after Ritz arrived, he wrote invitations to his best international customers personally, promising that they would 'find no flaws in food or service at the Savoy but instead perfection'.[4]

The calibre of guest became unparalleled, many of whom were famous enough to be known by their last name alone: Monet, Whistler, Puccini, Vanderbilt, Gilette, Roosevelt. D'Oyly's connections pulled in the thespian crowd that he wanted, including Australian opera singer Nellie Melba; actress and mistress of the Prince of Wales, Lillie Langtry; and playwright George Bernard Shaw, who was still coming to dinner there into the 1930s. A *Pall Mall Gazette* journalist reflected, when explaining the lengths that he had gone to in securing a table one night, he did not want the restaurant manager to fit him into a smaller side room 'as at the Savoy, the view of one's neighbours and their wives is no unimportant part' of the experience.[5]

Novelist Elinor Glyn, who coined 'It' as a contemporary euphemism for sex appeal, which was later used again for 'it girls', kept a journal about her social activities. The hotel was one of her favourite places to people-watch:

'In the evening we dined at the Savoy, the most amusing place in London, everyone smart in town was there [. . .] the gaiety & fun of the Savoy! The beautiful room, the perfect dinner, the lovely music & everyone in their best clothes. [. . .] To dine at the Savoy is the smart thing to do on Sunday night & it is so expensive that that adds to its charm! [. . .] There was an old veteran there (aged 80. I have looked in the Army list!). The gamest old man I have ever come across, he began to make love to me on the second day! He is called Sir Charles Shute. I was in fits of laughter at dinner, if only the rest of the prim party could have heard the things this old reprobate was saying to me! [. . .] Oh, the extraordinary vanity of men! Even at 80 they think any woman is only waiting for them to throw the handkerchief!'

Author Émile Zola came to town from Paris and was 'received like a prince'.[6] He was in London to observe its poor, but at quite some distance. With his wife, Alexandrine, they held court at the hotel, meeting London's literary figures and addressing banquets. He discussed dishes from France with Escoffier, and his favourites at the hotel became the polenta with white truffle and the grilled sardines. This time of luxury and adoration was in contrast to Zola's return to London in 1898. In 'J'accuse', his open letter published in a French newspaper, he had attacked the authorities for their anti-Semitism in the scandal that became the Dreyfus Affair. Found guilty of libel and sentenced to prison, Zola fled with no inkling of when it might be safe to return. When he arrived at Charing Cross the second time, he was a lonely fugitive, carrying his nightshirt wrapped in newspaper, and no longer received like a prince by *le tout Londres*.

In the Restaurant, Ritz introduced the practice of putting 'reserved' cards on the best tables. It allowed him to give prominent placement to glamorous guests, which pleased them, as it made them the centre of attention, and the less glamorous ones could 'star-spot' with ease from the other tables. Ritz took personal sycophancy to a professional level. The Duc D'Orléans, claimant to the French throne, was the first guest for whom the hotel customised a whole crockery service after Ritz arrived, and they extended this service to others later. The hotel obligingly stamped the fleur-de-lis crest on all of the plates and linen that the Duc used whenever he visited.

The Restaurant was open to anyone with money and style, so contemporary social boundaries were, unusually, suspended. Once, money had been entrenched with a small group of aristocrats. Now it was flowing more freely: into the new middle and upper middle classes, and through their spending power into the coupes of champagne at the Savoy.

D'Oyly pitched to a range of wealthy people. Nouveau-riche businessmen, magnates and Jewish bankers, not always warmly accepted in high society at the time, and stars of the theatre and opera, sat alongside aristocracy and royalty from all over Europe. The eventual popularity of the Restaurant confirmed his hunch that Londoners were 'ready to come forward [. . .] when there is really something high class offered'.[7]

Of the British people on his dream guest list, the 'Marlborough House set' were top. Named after his residence on Pall Mall, they were the Prince of Wales' inner circle. His friends included Lord Rosebery, Lord and Lady Elcho, Lord and Lady Gosford, Lord and Lady de Grey, and the Sassoons, a vastly rich family who historically dominated the opium trade between India and China. D'Oyly had made a start before Ritz arrived with Lord and Lady de Grey and the Sassoons, but the Prince himself proved elusive. Nicknamed Tum Tum, the future Edward VII was greedy and enjoyed dining with the Rothschilds in particular, as he was so partial to the truffles and Strasbourg pies that they often served at home. He was a man of taste and one of Ritz's most important clients on the Continent. When it came to the Prince, D'Oyly was yearning for royal patronage and essentially paid for access through Ritz. Sure enough, the Prince soon made the appearance that D'Oyly was angling for. As a gourmand, and such a well-connected one, his seal of approval was a triumph.

Unchaperoned women were admitted – except those of 'doubtful reputation and uncertain revenue'[8] – and were encouraged to smoke alongside the men, which was considered risqué. It had been good business for the theatre to welcome women and D'Oyly was hoping to attract them to eat out too, whether they were joining their husbands or not. An important part of his ventures was to court women who had the money and free time to socialise and entertain. Rich men of the time could go to their clubs, where women were not permitted. They were more than welcome at D'Oyly's Restaurant. The first to give her approval was society hostess Lady de Grey, a close friend of Wilde's, who held a banquet for a group of female friends. D'Oyly hoped that others would follow suit when they read the descriptions in the press. Female-only gatherings started tentatively with a few screens around the table, to make sure that they were not on full view to the Restaurant. As the idea became more accepted, the screens were dispensed with.

The ornate luxury was designed to appeal to women more than the décor of other Victorian establishments. There were bountiful flowers and palm trees, fine china and glass, bespoke crockery and dainty food presentation, which often included sculpted ice and fragile sugar baskets for puddings. The glow of soft lighting on the pink tablecloths was considered more flattering to diners' complexions than the standard white linen. It was all much prettier than Londoners were used to.

The effusive service was another welcome departure. Instead of the haughty detachment of London's private clubs and its few restaurants, smooth restaurant manager Louis Echenard would tell customers 'if it is possible, it shall be done', and Ritz would be careful to massage egos as he moved around the room.[9] The haughty detachment of the diners themselves was livened up with orchestral music, for which Johann Strauss and his orchestra were engaged at great cost. Ritz said that it was needed to 'cover the silence which hangs like a pall over an English dining table'.[10]

Dinner for two cost roughly £3 5s 6d (£370). Having enjoyed his evening with a female friend, one early diner judged the sum 'a moderate one for such an admirable dinner', which included: 'Borsch, sole Savoy, mousse jambon, poulet

Polonaise, salade, foie gras, asperge verts, pêches glacées vanille, one bottle champagne, cafe and liqueurs'.[11]

As well as a social departure, the Restaurant was a culinary epiphany. At a dinner for the Prince of Wales, Escoffier put a dish entitled 'Nymphes à l'Aurore' (Thighs of Nymphs at Dawn) on the menu: Frogs' legs had arrived in London to tempt an unsuspecting public. They were poached in white wine and served with champagne jelly, to resemble water, and tarragon leaves, to resemble grass, set between the legs.[12] It pleased the Prince, but not everyone was impressed by the frills. After scowling at the menu, Prime Minister William Gladstone ordered a hard-boiled egg and toast.[13]

Escoffier created numerous dishes at the hotel and it was canny publicity to name them after celebrities who visited. In honour of Nellie Melba, he invented Peaches Melba and Melba toast. One was for when she was on a diet and one was for when she was not. Escoffier wheeled in his debut Peaches Melba on an ice sculpture to her table. On the back of the swan carved of ice were exotic fresh peaches on vanilla ice-cream, laced with raspberry puree, and crowned with spun sugar between its wings. The ingredients have become hackneyed and cheap to produce, and there is seldom the ice swan presentation, but it was a refined novelty at the time. Other Escoffier creations were bombe Néro (sponge caramel, meringue, truffles and flaming rum), fraises à la Sarah Bernhardt (strawberries with pineapple and Curaçao sorbet), baisers de Vierge (meringue with vanilla cream, crystallised white rose and violet petals) and suprêmes de volailles Jeannette (jellied chicken with foie gras). All were served with *fin de siècle* flair. For extra novelty when serving fruit, guests were presented with tiny peach and cherry trees from which they could cut their own with golden scissors.

To eat out less expensively and without such ceremony at

the hotel, there was the Savoy Grill. Briefly called the Café Parisien, it was created mainly with the performers and audience of the adjoining theatre in mind, where a jacket would suffice and a *prix fixe* menu spared a steep bill.[14]

By September 1890, D'Oyly was able to put on an upbeat show at his first shareholders' meeting. He described how, a year after opening, it had established itself as 'unrivalled for luxury and perfect comfort', with cuisine that was 'second to none in the world'. Crucially, after a bumpy start, 'into the details of which it is perhaps not necessary or desirable to go', he said, it was all now 'in really good working order'.[15]

He went on to make an impassioned case that the shareholders' first dividend should be withheld to invest in champagne and fine wine, arguing that a superb cellar was vital and that the Restaurant was now so popular that the hotel was glugging through its stock fast. The medieval Savoy Palace dungeons under the Thames were now home to magnums of Château Mouton Rothschild 1875, Château d'Yquem 1868, and Pommery & Greno 1874, then a champagne house only a few decades old. D'Oyly's main concern was that, in his opinion, no good champagne had been produced since 1884. He saw it as a matter of urgency to buy up as much as possible of the 1880 vintage, which he thought was decent, before it became scarce and to avoid being stung by the high prices that he foresaw.

This unlikely victory over wine spending was more significant than it might sound. Such tame shareholders gave D'Oyly freedom from chasing short-term profit. This was a large part of what made the place so special. It allowed him to keep on spending to an unconventional, even unbusinesslike, extent. The shareholders might as well not have been there over the coming years, for all the clout that they exercised.

D'Oyly would not skimp on the Opera Company, theatre

or the hotel, or any other venture, for the sake of making money. There was truth in D'Oyly's comment to Sullivan that money was 'not everything' to him. He enjoyed driving a hard bargain, partly, one suspects, because he was good at it and liked a challenge. However, when it came to the experience that guests or audiences would have, that, resoundingly, would not be stinted on. This approach worked incredibly well, not in providing the highest return, but in creating loyalty.

Still, for all the lack of return on their investment, D'Oyly's shareholders were happy in 1890. In fact, they gave several rounds of applause during the meeting.[16] Oily Carte had slipped through a tricky year.

EIGHT

Scandals

'The hotelier who cannot keep his own counsel
had better choose another métier'

César Ritz

By the 1890s, D'Oyly's sons were both teenagers and living
within the rarefied confines of boarding school in Winchester.
Despite being cloistered away, his eldest, Lucas, had already
managed to attain immortality in English literature. He
had the distinction of being the only real person to inspire a
P. G. Wodehouse character. In the introduction to *Something
Fresh*, Wodehouse explained that Psmith, originally named
Rupert, was 'based more or less faithfully on Rupert D'Oyly
Carte, son of the Savoy Theatre man'. Wodehouse heard about
Lucas second-hand from his cousin at Winchester, and seems
to have confused him with Rupert, his younger brother, as
Rupert's daughter Bridget later believed. Wodehouse may have
made a mistake with the first name, but every other detail fits.
Lucas was described to Wodehouse as 'long, slender, always
beautifully dressed and very dignified. His speech was what
is known as orotund, and he wore a monocle. He habitually
addressed his fellow Wykehamists [pupils at Winchester] as

"Comrade". If one of the schoolmasters chanced to inquire as to his health, he would reply "Sir, I grow thinnah and thinnah."[1]

Wodehouse was so attracted to these details that Psmith became the only character of his that, as he put it, was handed to him 'on a plate with watercress round it [. . .] Lord Emsworth, Jeeves and the rest of my dramatis personae had to be built up from their foundations, but Psmith came to me ready made.'[2]

Lucas also piqued the interest of Lord Alfred Douglas, known to his friends as Bosie, who was in the year above him. In Bosie's autobiography, he recalled that he enjoyed friendships at school that were 'neither pure nor innocent'. He started young as a serial seducer and it seems very unlikely that Lucas was not one of his early conquests. When they wrote to each other, Lucas called him 'my dear Bodling'. Bosie wrote a sonnet after leaving Winchester that suggested the depth of his feeling. His 'torch of pleasure' does not sound too platonic:

> To L—
>
> Thou that wast once my loved and loving friend,
> A friend no more, I had forgot thee quite,
> Why hast thou come to trouble my delight
> With memories? Oh ! I had clean made end
> Of all that time, I had made haste to send
> My soul into red places, and to light
> A torch of pleasure to burn up my night.
> What I have woven hast thou come to rend?
> In silent acres of forgetful flowers,
> Crowned as of old with happy daffodils,
> Long time my wounded soul has been a-straying,
> Alas! It has chanced now on sombre hours
> Of hard remembrances and sad delaying,
> Leaving green valleys for the bitter hills[3]

Lucas started at Magdalen College, Oxford, a year after Bosie in 1890. There Lucas pursued him back, writing: 'I love you more now than I ever have before.' Less flatteringly, he goes on to say, 'I never did really love you before, but I do now.'[4] Lucas's growing conviction was perhaps sharpened by competition.

Bosie was introduced by a cousin to Oscar Wilde in 1891, when Bosie would have been twenty, and Wilde thirty-seven. Like Lucas before him, Wilde would find Bosie a painful person to be in love with. He became a fixation for Wilde, and this could not have been much more uncomfortable for Lucas. The only person whom he was ever known to be in love with had moved on to one of his father's star clients, and conducted the relationship at his father's hotel, all while they were at the same Oxford college.

Wilde and Bosie enjoyed an extended sojourn at the Savoy in adjoining rooms in 1893, which ended when Wilde spent his way into financial difficulty. He wrote to Bosie in March from the hotel:

> Dearest of All Boys,
>   Your letter was delightful, red and yellow wine to me; but I am sad and out of sorts. Bosie, you must not make scenes with me. They kill me, they wreck the loveliness of life. I cannot see you, so Greek and gracious, distorted with passion. I cannot listen to your curved lips saying hideous things to me. I would sooner be blackmailed by every renter [slang for male prostitute] in London than to have you bitter, unjust, hating. You are the divine thing I want, the thing of grace and beauty; but I don't know how to do it. Shall I come to Salisbury? My bill here is 49 pounds (£6,000) for a week. I have also got a new sitting-room over the Thames. Why are you not here,

my dear, my wonderful boy? I fear I must leave; no money, no credit, and a heart of lead.

Your own, Oscar[5]

Wilde had not finished paying for that stay. The hotel weathered its first scandal in 1895 as the backdrop to his 'gross indecency' case. In the early 1890s, mainly in room 361, he had entertained 'renters' or rent boys, alongside his relationship with Bosie. They had dined like princes, eating turtle soup and ortolans (tiny songbirds), they had glugged champagne, they had left stains on D'Oyly's high-thread-count sheets, and it was all to become public knowledge, raked over in court.

Wilde's nightmare started in February 1895, when he received a card at his club, the Albemarle, from Bosie's irate father, the Marquess of Queensberry. It accused Wilde of being a 'ponce and somdomite' or of 'posing as somdomite' [sic]. Goaded by Bosie, who was always looking for ways to rile his cruel father, Wilde made a libel claim against the Marquess. It was Wilde's undoing.

He realised that the case was going badly after he had appeared in the witness box, and he attempted to withdraw the claim, on the advice of his barrister. The judge at the Old Bailey disallowed it. Instead, on 5 April, Wilde was arrested for gross indecency based on the evidence from his failed libel action. The next day, he was charged, together with Alfred Taylor, the owner of a brothel at which he had been a customer. The trial ended in jury disagreement. Wilde and Taylor were tried again in May, and found guilty.

Evidence in the libel trial had come from rent boys Charles Parker, Fred Atkins and Alfred Wood, who testified that Wilde had indeed committed 'indecent acts' with them and that they had procured young men for him. Their evidence was supported at the second trial by that of Antonio Migge, the

Savoy's 'professor of massage', who testified that he had seen a young man sleeping in Wilde's bed. Migge used to massage Wilde in his third-floor bedroom in the morning. He told the court that, on one occasion: 'I entered after knocking – I saw someone in bed. At first I thought it was a young lady, as I saw only the head, but afterwards I saw that it was a young man. It was someone about sixteen to eighteen years of age. Mr Wilde was in the same room dressing himself. He told me he felt so much better that morning and that, as he was very busy, he could not stay to have the treatment. I never attended Mr Wilde again.'[6] Jane Cotter, a chambermaid, told the court in some detail about stained sheets. Ritz was mortified to read the coverage – not because of the flouting of any contemporary morals, but at the breach of privacy. A hotelier should, as he said, 'keep his own counsel'.[7] By this measure, the staff had failed their guest. Wilde was sentenced to two years' hard labour. For fear of indictment, Douglas fled for the Continent, leaving Wilde to his fate.

Despite legal and social pressure for Lucas to be discreet about his homosexuality, D'Oyly is likely to have known of his love for Bosie. A few months before that fateful 1893 stay at the Savoy, Lucas's love letters had been stolen from Bosie's collection, which he kept in his 'Morocco box', a gift from Wilde. One of the teenage rent boys, Alfred Wood, whom Bosie had summoned from London to a hotel in Oxford for the night, had a beady eye for an opportunity. The enterprising boy had pocketed the compromising letters, including Lucas's. Wood extorted money from Wilde through Bosie for their return to fund a new life for himself in New York.

Another scandal loomed a few months later that was more damaging for D'Oyly. Ritz was getting greedier than ever, taking on more and more responsibilities. Altogether he was working in Frankfurt, Salsomaggiore, Aix-les-Bains, Palermo, Cannes, Baden-Baden, Lucerne, Biarritz, Wiesbaden, Menton, Cairo and Madrid – all while dining out on an astronomical salary from D'Oyly. Even so, he and Escoffier were happy to steal from him, siphoning eye-watering amounts of food and drink, taking kickbacks from suppliers, and using company funds to entertain potential backers for their new venture, a London hotel.

Suspicion started in earnest in 1895, when, although overall receipts spiked up from the kitchens, the profits fell. In 1897, the kitchen actually showed a loss. By the time of Queen Victoria's Diamond Jubilee that year, the figures were too suspicious to ignore. The board, led by D'Oyly, ordered a secret investigation to establish what they were up to.

The investigation took months of evidence gathering. Escoffier had been diverting food to his own home and to Ritz's, and demanding personal payments from the hotel's suppliers. He admitted to taking 'commission' from them, a regular 5 per cent in the case of Hudson Brothers, grocers on the Strand, amounting to £1.4 million in today's money. Then there was the disappearance of £3,400 (£428,000) of wine and spirits in the first six months of 1897. In the same six months, another £3,000 (£378,000) had been consumed by managers, staff and employees.[8] Had D'Oyly been more circumspect, he should perhaps have worried from the beginning, when Ritz insisted on bringing his own cashier to London, a Mr Agostini, to work as the hotel accountant.

In March 1898, D'Oyly summoned Ritz, Escoffier and Echenard to the drawing room of Adelphi Terrace. When they walked in, D'Oyly was in a wheelchair surrounded by members of the board, with Helen standing beside him, her arms folded. Of late D'Oyly had become physically exhausted. Although only just in his fifties, his body was failing. Depending on his strength, he now moved around in a wheelchair, but could sometimes walk with a stick. He was the most affronted by Ritz and Escoffier's behaviour. He had been such a champion of theirs, given them salaries that were unheard of in the industry, and he had now so clearly been taken advantage of. D'Oyly directed his speech at Ritz, whom he said had used the Savoy simply as 'a place to live in, a *pied-à-terre*, an office, from which to carry on your other schemes'. Ritz, he said, had forgotten that he was a 'servant' and 'assumed the attitude of master and proprietor'.[9] For Ritz, so sensitive about his Swiss peasant background, 'servant' would have rankled.

Sir Charles Russell, the hotel's solicitor, read aloud the conclusion of the investigation. It was then D'Oyly's turn to hand them their notice, written by him. It outlined their 'gross negligence and breaches of duty and mismanagement'. It ended with the request to 'be good enough to leave the Hotel at once'.[10] Ritz, Escoffier and Echenard filed out of his house in silence.

NINE

Fluctuat nec migrator

[Tossed by the waves, but does not sink]

By the time that he sacked Ritz and the others, D'Oyly was frail and increasingly sickly. The day he handed Ritz his notice, his legs were under a blanket, disguising quite how swollen they were. Still, his mind was sharp. Remembering the trashing that his first chef, Charpentier, had given the kitchens on the way out, this time he had called the police in advance. They were stationed by the side entrance, awaiting any sign of trouble.

Guarding against any bad publicity, D'Oyly kept quiet in public about how Ritz had fleeced him. In the end, he managed to recoup today's equivalent of £2.4m. As the hotel's total profit for 1898 was £2.6m, over the course of eight years Ritz and co. had stuffed their pockets with nearly a year's worth of profit, and probably much more before the investigation was able to gather the details. D'Oyly would have surely winced to read the speculation that appeared, despite his discretion. Newspapers offered readers dramatic intrigue: 'The Savoy Hotel Mystery', 'Startling Changes at the Savoy', 'A Kitchen Revolt at the Savoy' ran the headlines. As a struggling *Daily Mail* reporter had to write: 'No one who has an explanation to offer seems to know, and no one who is in a position to know will offer any explanation.'[1] Ritz told the reporter that he had 'no idea' what it was about. As the *Star* judged: 'during the last 24-hours the Savoy Hotel has been the scene of disturbances which in a South American Republic would be dignified by the name of revolution. Three managers have been dismissed and 16 fiery French and Swiss cooks [. . .] have been bundled out by a strong force of the Metropolitan Police.'[2]

Helen, who had always been wary of Ritz, oversaw the packing of his belongings. His wife, Marie, perhaps wanting to detract from her own husband's misdemeanours, found Helen's behaviour 'incredible', she said. She described in her memoir: 'She was in a great hurry to rid our apartment at the Savoy of all our personal belongings. Indeed she practically threw them out into the street, sending precious pieces of Saxe and Sèvres, fragile Venetian glass and Roman pottery to us packed anyhow, helter-skelter, in cardboard boxes.'[3]

However offended they ostensibly were, the Ritzes were soon plotting a comeback, The Ritz in Paris. Ritz echoed D'Oyly in his ambition when he instructed his own architect: 'My hotel must be the last word in modernity. Mine will be the first modern hotel in Paris.'[4] He wanted to do for Paris what D'Oyly had done for London. With a loan from Louis-Alexandre Marnier-Lapostolle, who was grateful to him for serving his new orange liqueur, Grand Marnier, at the Savoy, Ritz purchased a mansion on the Place Vendôme and spent two years having it remodelled and furnished. However, Ritz did not have quite the same feel for building and design as D'Oyly. He left it to others to translate his personal style into architecture, and came in at the end with the finishing touches.

Inevitably, the Savoy share price had taken a hit with the Ritz scandal and ensuing uncertainty. However, D'Oyly had plenty of fresh talent in mind. He bought two restaurants, which gave him a pool of experienced staff to shore up the

Savoy. In London he bought the Savoy's neighbour, Simpsons-in-the-Strand. It had opened in 1828 at 103 Strand as a 'cigar divan', where gentlemen could smoke and drink coffee in hushed surroundings. The later addition of a restaurant offered a table-side carving service so that men could play chess uninterrupted. As in the Savoy, women were actively courted when D'Oyly took over Simpson's. There was an additional dining room decorated in lighter colours for them upstairs, so that they could socialise with or without men, as they wanted.

In Paris, D'Oyly bought the Marivaux, one of his favourite restaurants, near the Opera House. Its manager, Monsieur Joseph, had distinguished himself by inventing crêpes Suzette. D'Oyly brought Joseph over from Paris to replace Ritz in running the Restaurant and to act as the sommelier to replace Echenard. Joseph shared D'Oyly's theatrical approach to hospitality, which made him a good fit. A visiting gourmand, Nathaniel Newnham-Davis, came to interview Joseph at the Savoy and asked about his party trick of flambé-ing and carving dishes at the table-side. Joseph explained that it was his way of adding 'imagination in his art'.[5]

D'Oyly instructed Joseph to bring with him his chef, Henri Thouraud, who had previously cooked for the French President. Joseph liked to imagine new dishes when he was out on afternoon walks and then ask Thouraud if he could rustle them up. Their popular concoctions included homard Randolph Churchill (lobster), poularde Marivaux (fattened chicken) and foie gras Souvaroff (foie gras with truffles). In London, Joseph spent the rest of his free time keeping up his hobbies from Paris: training and flying pigeons, and *la savate*, a French form of kickboxing. All the same extravagance was kept up in the kitchen after the rapid departure of Escoffier, with vegetables and poultry imported from all over France, along with a tonne of Normandy butter a week. Buyers were dispatched to Smithfield market in the early hours of the morning to buy fresh meat every day, and 45,000 rolls were baked in-house every week.[6] Full-time jobs were available for carving ice, and for fashioning baskets and flowers out of sugar. At this time the hotel also invited over celebrated curry chef Ranji Smile from near Karachi, then in British-controlled India, to London. Unfortunately for the Savoy, he was soon poached by the newly opened Cecil Hotel a few doors down.

Newnham-Davis, the gourmand who came to interview Joseph about his flambé-ing, stayed for dinner afterwards and gave an idea of the cost in the Restaurant. He and his date had:

champagne

marmite [casserole]

sole Reichenberg [sole in white wine]

caneton à la presse [pressed duck]

salad

fonds d'artichauts [artichoke hearts]

bombe

coffee

liqueurs

It came to £2 17s (£277). The price did not, however, put Newnham-Davis off declaring that 'the dinner was a perfect work of art'.[7]

As a further lift to morale post-Ritz, D'Oyly's latest venture was ready to open by November 1898. Having pioneered the idea of a luxury hotel in London, he was convinced that there was more demand to go with it, so he had been working on a new hotel for the past five years. D'Oyly had spent his work-ing life in Soho and Covent Garden, but now he broadened his horizon to the west, to Mayfair. He bought an upmarket boarding house called Mivart's on the corner of Brook Street and Davies Street, near Hyde Park. As at the Savoy, he wanted another purpose-built hotel, rather than Mivart's hotchpotch of town houses joined together. He hired the architect of one of his favourite shops, Harrods, to build him a scaled-down sister to the Savoy.

Mivart's had been referred to as a hotel on occasion in the past, but it had few of the features. When neighbours complained that it was a hotel in 1813, its owner at that time explained that it was: 'a Private and distinct Lodging House only, the Apartments of which are always held by the Month, or for certain Periods as may be agreed, and not let by the Night to casual comers, as in Hotels. I beg also to state that there is no accommodation for Business of a Public Description.'[8] This kind of establishment, with such a limited offering, made up most of London's paid accommodation, alongside inns, and some pubs with rooms. Even as late as 1901, *Country Life* complained that what passed for hotels in London were really 'little better than taverns'.[9]

It had been run most recently by a married couple, William and Marianne Claridge, from whom D'Oyly would take their name for his establishment. Another company had pipped D'Oyly to the post in buying it directly from the Claridges but luckily for him, it ran out of money. By 1892 it had ceased to make a profit in the face of 'competing establishments of a more modern nature'.[10] There were only twelve lettable suites of rooms and although these yielded an annual return of £10,000 (£1.2m), it was not enough to meet the running costs and improvements.[11]

D'Oyly, then still working closely with Ritz, had swooped

in with an offer, and he made a similar move in Rome as well. He bought up the Grand Hotel when the company building it was foundering too. On the Via Vittorio Emanuele Orlando, a few minutes from the Borghese Gardens, the palazzo that he completed is now the St Regis. After Ritz's untimely departure, D'Oyly brought all of his new interests together into one company. If you were a lucky shareholder by then, you would have stakes in the Savoy, Marivaux, Claridge's, the Grand Hotel, and Simpson's.

D'Oyly in the 1890s was a Monopoly player in full flow. Making money, buying property, making more money, and buying more. At one point he had started developing the site of an old pub opposite Harrods on Knightsbridge Green, with a view to creating Britain's first serviced apartments. He went a long way in planning a mini Savoy in Dublin as well. In keeping with his taste at the original Savoy, Claridge's and the English Opera House, his Irish Savoy would have been of marble, polished granite and red brick.

He had been back and forth to Ireland since the 1870s with his theatre work, and it had given him the idea. His long-standing friend and Savoy board director Michael Gunn, who had helped him through the scrapes of the Opera Comique, ran a theatre there. D'Oyly had plans drawn up for a hotel not far from Gunn, off Grafton Street, but it never materialised. It was blocked by a local judge over the drinking licence. The *Evening Herald* in Dublin described the 'magnificent hotel and restaurant which he rejected' that would have put 'thousands of pounds' in the pockets of local workers.[12] Landing heavily on the Savoy's side, the newspaper said that as soon as the judge heard the word 'restaurant', 'his liquor monomania seized him and simply hurled the whole scheme from his presence'.

D'Oyly brought up ladies' socialising again to support his Irish hotel idea. According to him, the ladies of Dublin were often lamenting the quality of the cookery and style of existing restaurants. He argued that he could provide them with a ladies' dining room in close proximity to the city's most desirable shops. One Dublin newspaper in favour of an Irish Savoy speculated that many women did indeed simply go home to eat as the wait for food was so long and the service so poor in town.

However, a flurry of letters to newspapers did agree with blocking him. A few readers mainly seemed angry that D'Oyly proposed an 'Anglo-Italian restaurant'. One complained that D'Oyly was the front man of the operation, but that he wanted to install an Italian chef. The reader was suspicious that, no doubt, this would mean a lot of Italian and French waiters too, with their 'greasy ways'. Another pointed out that D'Oyly was a 'gentleman with a foreign name' and that he wanted to bring an Italian manager 'to teach us how to cook and serve food'. The *Daily Express* pointed out that there was a popular petition to uphold Dublin's licensing laws, and scorned the *Evening Herald*'s idea that people would flock to shop nearby 'because a restaurant owned by Mr D'Oyly Carte and some London people had been opened'. D'Oyly's wealth grated for one reader, who grumbled that he already had 'a company wealthy beyond the dreams of avarice'.

So D'Oyly did not have much luck in Dublin. Fortunately, the Duke of Westminster, landowner of the Grosvenor Estate and freeholder of Mivart's, did not share such qualms over drinking, nor over D'Oyly's wealth nor his love of Continental staff. The Duke consented to D'Oyly's architectural plans with the proviso that he did not want 'anything like a repetition of the Savoy Hotel' in a quiet neighbourhood, so Claridge's was half the size.[13] D'Oyly was in time to save Mivart's from 'a vulgar application on the part of its butchers to wind it up', reported *The Caterer and Hotel-Proprietors' Gazette*, but 'happily money has been forthcoming to satisfy Mr. James Ginger's meat-bill and costs'.[14] Ingratiating himself with Lady de Grey, who had done so much to bring her influential female coterie to the Savoy, she was invited to lay the foundation stone for the new Claridge's.

At the opening of the 'luxurious hostelry' in 1898, *The Times* was invited to look around. Its favourite features were the 'magnificent smoking and billiard-rooms which are decorated and furnished in the Old English style with large fireplaces and panels of oak'. Men were intended to congregate in the smoking and billiard rooms, with the lighter reading and drawing rooms decorated to appeal to women, and the coffee room and Restaurant as places for both sexes to mingle. For guests seeking discretion, the first-floor rooms had a private entrance. One particularly lavish suite on that floor was aimed at royalty, with a Georgian-style bedchamber of rose damask. As at the Savoy, D'Oyly reassured that Claridge's 'had all the accessories of that American life which some believe will grow more and more among us'.[15]

As Claridge's was far smaller than the Savoy, it had a naturally cosier atmosphere, starting with an entrance foyer the size of a town house, rather than of a stately home, where the fire was lit on all but the warmest days and surrounded by armchairs. Hidden through a doorway by the fireplace, the small reception was out of sight. It had a lift in the same room, so that guests who might not be looking their freshest after a long journey could hop straight in, having been seen by as few people as possible, before sprucing up in private. Up in the room, a maid would be ready to unpack, draw a bath and press any clothes that needed it. Maids on duty in the evenings there were known as 'dress maids', as they were expected to help female guests to change and to brush their hair.

Typical of D'Oyly's taste in managers, he poached one for

Claridge's from the Grand at Monte Carlo again, this time Henri Menge. He was still stuck for the crucial perfectionist general manager to bring it all together again at the Savoy, though. He needed someone to spot when a jam label was not facing forwards on a breakfast tray, when a cutlery handle was not positioned one inch from the table edge and when the waiters were not keeping two yards apart in the restaurant. D'Oyly did not, as yet, have much local competition to poach from for this lynchpin job. However, he had noticed that a small, faded hotel with only fifty bedrooms on Piccadilly, the Berkeley, was well-run. He looked into its manager, George Reeves-Smith, a man in his thirties who had been trained in France and knew a great deal about wine, earning the accolade of being the most knowledgeable Englishman on claret in particular.[16] Reeves-Smith provided all of the bedrooms with leather-bound books from his own collection, the rest of which he kept at his house in Sussex. D'Oyly took such attention to hospitality to be a good sign. He first courted him with an invitation to the opening of Claridge's. As D'Oyly had won Ritz over with his tour of the Savoy, alongside plenty of compliments and a huge salary, he prepared his set-piece charm offensive again. Hobbling around Claridge's with a walking stick, D'Oyly's tour was not as smooth as it had been at the Savoy a decade ago. He started off by inviting Reeves-Smith on to the Savoy group board. Reeves-Smith demurred, as he had recently led a management buyout of the Berkeley, and did not see that he could do both. D'Oyly saw his point and bought the Berkeley, complete with Reeves-Smith.

It was a relief to have Reeves-Smith overseeing all three London hotels, as he was the precise manager D'Oyly needed, particularly as he grew sicklier himself. As *The Times* reported, Reeves-Smith 'was aware of the slightest derogation from high standards of housekeeping or service [. . .] punctilious and conservative in manner and dress, he had a shrewd business appreciation of practical detail.'[17] To take the strain, D'Oyly appointed him to take over as managing director, while he remained chairman. As part of the reshuffle, D'Oyly elevated his twenty-four-year-old son, Rupert, from the board to become his deputy chairman and assistant managing director to Reeves-Smith. While Lucas chose to go to Oxford, Rupert had come straight from boarding school to become D'Oyly's assistant in 1893, after learning some basic accountancy, aged seventeen, and by the age of twenty-four he was now close to the top of the business.

At the Opera Company, replacing talent proved trickier. While Gilbert and Sullivan were calming down after the carpet quarrel, D'Oyly had commissioned *The Nautch Girl, or, The Rajah of Chutneypore* (1891) for the Savoy Theatre by Teddy Solomon, with a libretto by George Dance. The story of a temple idol coming to life in order to recover his stolen diamond eye kept going for 200 performances. It was the only non-Gilbert and Sullivan work that went well. D'Oyly commissioned *The Vicar of Bray* (1892) and *Haddon Hall* (1892), which opened to lukewarm receptions. He then enlisted his friend, J. M. Barrie, to write the words for *The Good-Conduct Prize* (1893). Of the three, it was the biggest disappointment by far. Barrie could not finish and persuaded his friend, Arthur Conan Doyle, already popular for his Sherlock Holmes novels, to help. Despite frantic revisions during the run by Barrie and Conan Doyle, it was D'Oyly's first flop that never recovered, and it has never been professionally revived since. On the first night, 'towards the end it became more and more apparent that the audience were getting rather bored. The final verdict [. . .] was far from enthusiastic.'[18] Sensing the same, Barrie and Conan Doyle left their box during the second act. The leading lady, who did not have the luxury of leaving early, refused to come out of her dressing room for the curtain call as she was so embarrassed.[19]

Gilbert and Sullivan reunited for two final original productions, *Utopia, Limited* (1893) and *The Grand Duke* (1896), at the theatre, after D'Oyly brokered a peace at Adelphi Terrace. Even then, they quarrelled between the two new operas. The rumour was that the latest clash was over the casting of a revival of *The Mikado*. Gilbert clarified that it was 'purely of a financial nature'. He wrote to the *Sheffield Daily Telegraph* to explain that 'Sir A Sullivan insists, as a condition of his composing music to a new libretto, that I should hand over to Mr D'Oyly Carte unrestricted control of all the London rights of the 14 pieces which Sir Arthur Sullivan and I have written in collaboration and this on terms appear to me to be inadequate and unreasonable.'[20]

In the past when they fell out, it had been worth persevering for the sake of staging another hit. Now there were slowing ticket sales to contend with, on top of the spats. The new audiences, which they had done so much to create, drifted off elsewhere in the 1890s. The popularity of Alfred Cellier's *Dorothy* (1886), Sidney Jones's *A Gaiety Girl* (1893), and *The Geisha* (1896), which D'Oyly dismissed as 'drivel', signalled the arrival of fluffier musical comedy. Gilbert's complex plots assumed sophistication on the part of his audiences, while newcomers' lyrics offered no satire and the emphasis was on romantic entanglement.

The D'Oyly Carte Opera Company made a few nods to this trend in the 1890s with showier staging and more dancing, but D'Oyly was too disappointed to have to change. 'What the public wants now,' he lamented, 'is simply "fun" and very little else.'[21] He tried and failed to find more where Gilbert and Sullivan came from too. He sought out the services of another serious composer, Sir Edward German, to work on the operas *The Emerald Isle* and *Merrie England*. They gave German his greatest triumphs, but, by Savoy standards, they were underwhelming.

The Opera Company continued to tour the guaranteed Gilbert and Sullivan hits around the country, but increasingly it was managed by Helen rather than D'Oyly. Altogether it had 7,000 performers on the books, with the voice, appearance and the ability of each noted down.[22] This talent pool had been brought together by both of them over the past few decades, which gave Helen the grounding to take over. D'Oyly told a journalist with pride: 'She manages these companies [touring companies], arranges all the dates, all the bookings – and every detail of organisation. I have an idea that she does it with some kind of conjuring.'[23] Despite the criticism of *The Gondoliers* in New York in 1891, D'Oyly remained bullish about running all of his touring companies himself: 'I prefer to send my own companies out. If you sell an American manager the rights he is apt to introduce innovations.'[24]

The last original work that Gilbert, Sullivan and D'Oyly would produce together would be *The Grand Duke*. Gilbert, suffering from migraines and gout, had been too ill to work until the summer of 1895, and Sullivan was receiving morphine injections for a kidney complaint, so progress had been slower than usual. It began a run of 123 performances in March 1896. After that, with all of the hotel activity, D'Oyly allowed a lull. Sullivan, the most placid of the three, felt a degree of bitterness over D'Oyly's power towards the end, but they worked together again, without Gilbert, on *The Rose of Persia* (1899). Sullivan was keen to have American soprano Ellen Beach Yaw play the Sultan Zubeydeh, the lead, after he heard her at a private concert at Mrs Ronalds' house. He went to tell Helen at the Savoy Theatre. Sullivan recorded making his case in his diary: 'that Miss Yaw be engaged as must have new blood. She [Helen] promised to think it over and discuss with D'Oyly – let me know early next week, as they were going to Portsmouth next day to look for a yacht.'[25] The sour note came next: 'I fear they won't accept because they didn't find Miss Yaw and they only act on their own initiative.'[26]

Despite Sullivan's cynicism, they did allow Miss Yaw to take the lead but then regretted it, as did Sullivan. He wrote to Helen and D'Oyly that he had made a mistake and that he feared that Miss Yaw 'hasn't got the stuff in her to improve'.[27] He then changed his mind a week later, writing to say that Miss Yaw was 'improving rapidly every night', and that it would in fact be a mistake to let her go.[28] For all of his own indecisiveness, he was still hurt when 'Miss Yaw came and told me that she had been summarily dismissed, and told not to come to the theatre again'.[29] He wrote in his diary, 'The whole thing is quite plain and evident. The Cartes disliked Miss Yaw's engagement from the beginning, as they do everything that isn't of their initiation [. . .] Well, I have now no voice in the management, and claim none.'[30]

After the dust settled on *The Rose of Persia* casting clash, Helen suggested that D'Oyly, Gilbert and Sullivan appear together on stage at a revival of *Patience* in the summer of 1900. Sullivan was not well enough: 'Good luck to you all. Three invalid chairs would have looked very well on stage,' he wrote back, his handwriting looping elegantly, but now shaky in places.[31] Gilbert and D'Oyly went ahead and appeared anyway, just the two of them, leaning heavily on their walking sticks.

The Opera Company triumvirate was permanently dissolved a few weeks later with Sullivan's death. His note regretting his inability to join Gilbert and D'Oyly on stage was his last. He died on 22 November 1900 at home. The death certificate specified 'bronchitis, 21 days, cardiac failure', with no mention of his longstanding inoperable kidney disease.[32] He died in the presence of his valet and his housekeeper, Louis Jaeger and Clotilde Raquet. Both were generously provided for in his will, which included bequests of manuscript scores to the Royal Academy of Music and the Royal College of Music. Mrs Ronalds had rushed over to say goodbye to him, but arrived too late. He left instructions that he should be buried at Brompton Cemetery in the family grave, which had already been opened up when he was given an upgrade to St Paul's Cathedral by his fan, Queen Victoria. D'Oyly had a memorial plaque made for him and placed in Embankment Gardens, and, despite the years of ill-tempered letters and bickering, Gilbert spoke of him generously after his death: 'with Sullivan, I never had to do that fatal thing, explain a joke. I remember all he has done for me, in allowing his genius to shed some of its lustre upon my humble name.'[33] There was nothing humble about Gilbert really, but there was a nice sentiment in there somewhere.

By now D'Oyly needed the care of two full-time nurses and a visiting doctor, and was too ill to attend Sullivan's funeral. He watched, slumped at his bedroom window, as the cortège passed Adelphi Terrace along the Embankment to St Paul's. 'I have just seen the last of my old friend,' he whispered, as he was helped back to bed.[34] Six months later, in April 1901, D'Oyly died at the age of fifty-six from a heart attack, with a longer-term diagnosis of dropsy. His myriad exertions, stresses and indulgences seemed to have taken a fatal toll. The *New York Times* offered the explanation that his weak heart was 'aggravated by the shock he sustained as a result of the death of Sir Arthur Sullivan'.[35] D'Oyly was buried next to his parents, at St Andrew's in Hastings, to where they had retired and a memorial service was held at the Savoy Chapel. Despite the losses of his English Opera House and of Ritz's theft, he left £250,000 (£31m).[36] It was twice Gilbert's eventual legacy, and more than four times Sullivan's.[37]

Exhausted as he was by the time of his death, D'Oyly had much to be proud of. Having not found much success until he had turned thirty-one, he had made sudden, dramatic progress. In twenty years of frenetic activity, he had established a new kind of cosmopolitan glamour in London. His escapist experiences – whether a dinner-dance at the Savoy, cocktails at Claridge's, or a recreation of early modern Japan in *The Mikado* – became magnets for fashionable Londoners and international visitors. He dreamed up places and experiences that barely existed in the imaginations of others when he started. His confections sit alongside Sherlock Holmes, gin and tonic, Wimbledon tennis, grand public spectacles of monarchy and Test Match cricket as rarefied features of Victorian Britain that have proved remarkably enduring.[38] He was so deft in bringing together his mishmash of influences that his theatre and hotel were soon thought of as quintessentially British and timeless, when, in fact, they were cosmopolitan and new. To borrow Gilbert's phrase from *The Pirates of Penzance*, D'Oyly achieved a 'most ingenious paradox'.

Across his various ventures, his overarching talent was to make the fantastical into reality. He possessed the vision, with the hyperactive perfectionism to see it through. This could mean staying up into the early hours watching endless auditions for his operas, commandeering a private train for rehearsals to avoid any plot leaks to the press, or bringing back cookbooks from around the world with novel recipes for the hotel.

It had taken patience and plenty of nerve, but he was right that his brand of light entertainment that *The Times* classified as 'a combination of good taste and good fun' would be loved by others.[39] As *The Observer* reflected, 'Carte took what other people thought were risks but he felt were certainties. His practical judgement was as sure as his sense of artistry.'[40] On closer inspection, there were limits to his practical judgement, but his energy for managing his own reputation ensured that went unnoticed by the public. Starting with that *Observer* obituary, the idea that D'Oyly breezed through life, one inevitable triumph after another, was picked up by an early historian of Gilbert and Sullivan, Hesketh Pearson. This was not borne out by the detail, but Pearson parroted *The Observer*'s description that D'Oyly simply had 'an instinct for success'. Real life had been far more messy than that, but he had taken the things that he loved – the theatre, travel, eating out and London, his hometown – and made them all permanently better.

ACT TWO

RUPERT

TEN

Belle Époque

'If a man can't forge his own will, whose will can he forge?'
W. S. Gilbert, *Ruddigore*

D'Oyly and Sullivan dying months apart meant a lonely few years for those left behind on Adelphi Terrace. Helen had built her whole life around D'Oyly, describing him as 'my one thing to protect and care for'. She replied to one condolence letter: 'I don't know how to write or speak of myself – I am practically dead.' Her other replies shared her ongoing dejection. She wrote back to another: '[he and I were] so close through these years of suffering and weakness that of late he was to me my dearly loved child'.[1]

Not long ago the house had been home to D'Oyly and Helen, Rupert and Lucas. Now it was just Helen: there were to be no more visits from Sullivan, Gilbert lived out in the countryside, more or less retired, Rupert had bought his own house next to Trafalgar Square on Suffolk Street, and Lucas was gravely ill. After Oxford, Lucas had set out on an independent path to the rest of the family by becoming a barrister at the Inner Temple. The *Daily Telegraph* singled him and the son of the Marquis of Dufferin, Governor General of Canada, out as the most notable of the intake of barristers that year, accompanied by the old doggerel verse:

> The Inner for a rich man,
> The Middle for a poor;
> Lincoln's for a parchmenter,
> And Gray's Inn for a bore

Not long into his career, Lucas's most high-profile case had turned out to be a fatal one. In 1899, aged twenty-five, he had acted as private secretary to Lord Chief Justice, Sir Charles Russell, his father's former solicitor, at the Venezuelan Arbitration. The delegation met to resolve the long-running boundary dispute between Venezuela and British Guiana, and awarded Britain 90 per cent of the contested territory. The negotiations took place in Paris, all the highlights of which Lucas knew from childhood holidays. He stayed at the Élysée Palace, the presidential residence no less, for the negotiations, but the opulent surroundings did not spare him from contracting tuberculosis. In November 1900, he had been strong enough to attend Sullivan's funeral. By 1901, he was at the Kelling Sanitorium by the sea in Norfolk – a long way from his favourite haunts, the American Bar at the Savoy and the little bar at Claridge's, where the bartender, Ada Coleman, always had a sympathetic ear for him. He never became well enough to leave.

While Lucas was in his terminal decline in Norfolk, Oscar Wilde's literary executor and former lover, Robbie Ross, published *De Profundis*, Wilde's letter to Bosie from prison. In it Wilde denounced Bosie's selfishness and vanity. He described their hotel stays together as an 'imperfect world of coarse uncompleted passions, of appetite without distinction, desire without limit, and formless greed'. Lucas, confined to bed by the time of *De Profundis*' publication, had hopefully freed himself of his own thoughts of Bosie, having not seen him for years. Bosie himself, rather improbably, had married, and fathered a son in the meantime. There is no record that he came to visit his terminally ill former friend.

Cut off from his work and his family, and with plenty of unhappy thoughts to contemplate, Lucas gave his active mind purpose by writing a treatise on how to provide care for TB patients who could not afford private hospitals. He designed chalets for the grounds of the sanatorium so that he and his fellow sufferers could enjoy fresh air in some warmth. In 1907 he died there at the age of thirty-four. He left Ada Coleman £300 (£35,000) of his £59,000 (£6.8m), which came mainly from his stake in the Savoy.[2] His *Times* obituary remarked that he would be missed by his 'wide circle of friends'.[3]

In another secluded corner of the English countryside, Rupert and Lucas's uncle was confined to a sanatorium for years too. Henry, D'Oyly's only brother, suffered his 'third attack of insanity', as the admission notes phrased it, after D'Oyly's death. He was admitted to Holloway in Virginia Water, five miles from D'Oyly Carte Island, having been committed twice before. The first time he was sent to Jersey in the Channel Islands for a year. The second time he was kept in London, at Bethlem, one of the world's most infamous asylums, from where we take the word Bedlam. The third time he had recently misappropriated funds from Rudall, Carte & Co., which he had taken over after the death of their father ten years earlier. Unlike D'Oyly, Henry had been allowed to complete his degree at University College London before joining the business, and had met his wife there. She had died back in January 1885, which seemed to have triggered the first breakdown.

This time, on New Year's Day, 1902, described as 'a widower of no occupation', Henry was classified as needing urgent attention and certified insane.[4] He had attempted suicide by throwing himself out of a window. His admission notes incorrectly recorded that there was no history of suicide in the family. D'Oyly and Henry's grandfather, Richard Cart, had drowned at a well-known suicide spot in the River Severn near his home in Welshpool in 1846, aged fifty-nine.[5] His legitimate son, Robert, Henry and D'Oyly's half-uncle, had drowned himself in Highgate Ponds. For the Cartes, the ponds were a favoured corner of Hampstead Heath, being near the family home on Dartmouth Park Road, and Robert had regularly come to stay. When he killed himself, Robert had been staying with D'Oyly at Adelphi Terrace, but he had headed out from there to die in a more familiar place. D'Oyly was working on the Savoy Hotel opening in July 1889, hurrying about his last-minute logistics – the scheduling, delivering, staffing and supplies – at the time.

On arriving at Holloway that New Year's Day, Henry was 'confused and trembling', 'incoherent and uncertain', and injured from his fall. His appearance was similar to D'Oyly's. As the doctor recorded, he was 'well-built, his hair is dark brown, as is his moustache'. Where he differed markedly was his 'somewhat vacant' expression. He appeared to be 'very depressed', and had visibly been short of sleep for a long time.

Considered a modern facility, Holloway had opened in the 1890s as an asylum for the middle classes. Rupert paid for his uncle's extended stay. With twenty-two acres of manicured parkland, it was presented as a comfortable residential option and, for the voluntary patients at least, it was a place where professionals who had suffered a breakdown could recuperate before getting back to work. Interred in this Gothic-style red-brick Victorian facility, Henry felt no better: 'he knows that his mental condition is not what it ought to be', but he is 'unable to brace himself up', the doctor wrote. Entry after entry recorded Henry's 'melancholia' with no improvement. On 15 May he managed to elude his attendant on a supervised walk. He threw himself into the lake of Virginia Water by the waterfall. To Henry's dismay, he was saved. After his fractures healed, he was thin but in good health. The doctor judged Henry to be a hypochondriac, because he kept requesting laxatives when he did not need them. A darker reading would surely be that he was trying to starve himself, having failed by falling and drowning.

By December 1907, Henry's notes say simply that he was 'silent, solitary'. The dark leather-bound case book, filled with other patients, is punctuated every so often with a death certificate. This was not the ending for Henry. Despite his reluctance to live, he survived until 1926, when he died aged seventy.

In contrast to the rest of his family, who all endured a run of misery, Rupert came into his inheritance with vigour. He was twenty-five at the time of D'Oyly's death. Not only was he lucky to inherit such a range of thriving enterprises, he had no competition for them. Helen had no children, neither did Gilbert, nor Sullivan, and his own brother had shown little interest before his untimely death. His path was clear. While the country worried that, after Queen Victoria, her louche son Bertie would be no replacement, Rupert was the very model of a good heir. Without the same impulsiveness, he avoided the acrimony and legal tangles that dogged his father's career. In many ways, he was a steadier businessman. However, as any child of high-achieving parents would find, the bar for comparable achievement was daunting. To this Rupert had the extra burden of fame. As *The Times* pointed out, thanks to the globetrotting D'Oyly Carte Opera Company, his surname was known 'wherever the English language is spoken'.[6]

While Lucas had loved attention, playing up to appreciative audiences, Rupert was known for his reserve. He was diffident in unfamiliar company, but managed to be a low key, effective flirt when he wanted to be.

D'Oyly's formula for building up talented staff had been to track down an individual whom he admired, charm them, bring them into the fold, then get them to train a protégé with whom to replace themselves. Most senior management would then die in the job or at least stay until retirement, so turnover was slow. With Rupert, of course, D'Oyly had little choice in the first step, and to begin with he trained both sons. While Lucas did not appear to seize the chance, Rupert certainly did. As young teenagers, both were set the task of critiquing theatrical performances for D'Oyly, comparing cast members and productions in detail, and encouraged to make observations about their stays in the finest hotels of Europe. D'Oyly started with Opera Company work by taking them up to Manchester in 1888 to watch three performances of *Patience* with three different leading ladies, to assess their relative suitability. They were expected to weigh up all of the live entertainment that they saw and use it to improve the Opera Company, just as D'Oyly did.

Having stayed in so many, Rupert had a clear understanding of what a grand hotel should be from a young age, so, as well as joining his father on the board at the age of twenty-one, he was given a fun extra task. D'Oyly invited him on to the 'committee of taste' for the Restaurant, alongside Portuguese diplomat, and friend of the Prince of Wales, Luis de Soveral, who 'made love to all the most beautiful women and all the nicest men were his friends';[7] Austro-Hungarian diplomat Count Albert Mensdorff-Pouilly-Dietrichstein; and Viscount Bertie, who later became British ambassador to Italy.[8] D'Oyly ran all new dishes, drinks and service ideas past them, and they were encouraged to comment on everything, including 'lighting or decoration of the table, ventilation etc'.[9] They were expected to think about how the Restaurant could appeal more to women – although no women were invited to join them, which could have surely eliminated some of the guesswork.

Allowed a two-year ease-in to the job, Rupert took over as chairman in 1903, aged twenty-seven. He had the Savoy Hotel, Claridge's, the Berkeley, Simpson's-in-the-Strand, Marivaux, and the Grand Hotel in Rome to play with, while Helen took care of the theatre interests. Showing all the exuberance that you might expect from a newly powerful twenty-seven-year-old, he started spending, fairly modestly at first. One of his first moves was to secure the services of François Bonnaure from the Élysée Palace as head chef of Claridge's. In haute cuisine, post-Escoffier, this was the pinnacle. The press speculated about how much he must have paid to persuade Bonnaure to make the move to London. Newspapers made the natural comparison between Carte junior and his father's coup in securing Paris's most famous maître d'hôtel, Monsieur Joseph, a few years earlier, and in buying the Berkeley, as legend had it, just because he wanted Reeves-Smith. Rupert took out an advertisement to herald Bonnaure, describing the arrival of 'the renowned Paris chef' at Claridge's, the 'resort of kings and princes'.

He enjoyed a flurry of building that was considerably more costly. By the end of 1904, he had sanctioned £1 million (£116m) of expansions.[10] At the smaller end, this included the steel sculpture of Count Peter of Savoy, owner of the original medieval Savoy palace, which perches on the Strand-side canopy, guarding the entrance. The courtyard over which he keeps an eye was lined with rubber, to muffle the sound of any traffic, as not to upset the atmosphere. The big expenses were the new blocks on the Strand: the very recognisable current entrance and foyer, as well as the modern Savoy Grill and Britain's first serviced apartments, Savoy Court, offering one- and two-bedroom *pieds-à-terre* with all the perks of the hotel. The short drive connecting the new blocks is still the only road in Britain where vehicles, by law, drive on the right; Parliament granted the privilege as the theatre is on the right-hand side when guests are driven in from the Strand. Taxi drivers and chauffeurs can drop guests directly outside under the shelter of the canopy and seamlessly loop past the hotel and out again.

Sarah Bernhardt moved into the Savoy Court apartments straight away with her red setter, Tosco; Lillie Langtry started her mornings there with an 11 a.m. flute of champagne; and Harry Selfridge made it his base when he arrived from Chicago, ready to open a London department store. Sir Thomas Dewar, the Scottish whisky heir, moved in and stayed for forty years. He wondered if he might be the long-est-serving Savoy resident since John of Gaunt.[11] American producer Charles Frohman lived at 81 whenever he was in town for work. It was ideally placed for him, just across the road from Theatreland, and he ate every day at the Grill. As became tradition, on the day a resident's death was announced, their table would be left empty. When Frohman died in the sinking of the Lusitania during the First World War, not only was his table left empty but his friends paid for a plaque beside it.

Rupert had become convinced of the demand for the Savoy Court one Derby Week, when the hotel had turned down a record number of guests, with an estimated 2,500 short of accommodation in town altogether. He realised that, if guests who lived in the hotel more or less permanently could be offered apartments, it would free up plenty of rooms. Such was his confidence that, five years later, he added two new floors to the hotel as well, and had the whole river front removed to make space for the bathrooms that guests now expected, rather than enjoyed as a novelty.

To complement the bigger bedrooms, there was a central new item. Rupert wanted bespoke beds. The design is still used by a company called Savoir Beds, including the distinctive trellis pattern that Helen drew for the mattress. This company had originally been Rupert's Savoy Bedworks. Although Rupert did not want rivals buying them, guests could order in bulk. King Hassan II, who visited Claridge's after a stay at Buckingham Palace, bought thirty to take home to Morocco. They were handmade in the Savoy's little hive of industry on Stukeley Street, next to the D'Oyly Carte Opera Company warehouse behind Drury Lane. This corner of Covent Garden was also home to the Savoy's chocolaterie, coffee roastery, printing press and French-polishing department. Keen on being self-sufficient, Rupert bought his own trawler in Essex that would go out every day of the week, so there was no dip in fresh fish on Sundays. As many of the staff noticed, the Savoy felt like 'a city in itself', such was its range of activity.[12] Thanks to its own electricity supply and its wells, burrowed down to the artesian water table, it could go off-grid too, if it needed to.

As one final splurge, Rupert spent £30,000 (£3.5m) stocking the cellar with champagne from 1898. With all the bravado of youth, he told the shareholders about the spending on the wine, the kitchens and the rooms: 'last year's fashion is dowdy this year. We move forward and introduce something new. That is our policy. It is the basis of our success.'[13]

Rupert was lucky that, as well as having no family competition, his one credible rival to be the most prestigious hotelier in Europe had recently, dramatically fallen out of the running. Rupert was always keen to keep a close and curious eye on what family friend-turned-enemy César Ritz was up to. Ritz would have been a nightmare competitor. If there was one hotelier who could cultivate a discerning fan base and retain them, it was Ritz. He had come back to London to open the Carlton near Trafalgar Square in 1898, within months of D'Oyly opening Claridge's. Then, in 1906, came The Ritz on Piccadilly, directly opposite the Berkeley. The location could hardly have been more provocative if Ritz had pitched up on the Strand. There was plenty of ongoing rivalry over the years: whenever an important appointment was about to be made at the Savoy, a counter offer could be expected from The Ritz, and vice versa.

Rupert wanted to modernise Claridge's after 1906, to keep ahead of The Ritz. He had not yet bought the freehold, so improvements had to be approved by his aristocratic landlord, the Duke of Westminster. There were complaints from local residents about disturbances from Claridge's already. Rupert, for his part, felt dampened in his improvement attempts. He pleaded with the Duke of Westminster's Grosvenor Estate that, since The Ritz opened, Claridge's had suffered a good deal 'by reason of the inadequate accommodation for balls, large private dinners, wedding receptions etc.'[14] After some resistance, the estate relented. So Claridge's gained a beautiful ballroom, decorated by Parisian artisans in Louis XV style, with reliefs by Marcel Boulanger, also employed to decorate The Ritz, and chandeliers imported from Paris's most venerable glassmakers, Bagues.

Over at The Ritz itself, although it bore his name, César was not actually in charge. It was Marie who oversaw the proliferation of Ritzes in Madrid, Budapest and London. César had next to nothing to do with them. He took part in planning the outpost in London, but he was never able to return to managing anywhere. He spent the last years of his life at a private hospital in his native Switzerland, unable to muster interest in a career that had been his obsession.

The doctor who first saw Ritz when he had passed out at work judged it a 'complete nervous breakdown'.[15] On the day of the intended coronation of King Edward VII in 1902, Ritz had collapsed when addressing staff at his new Carlton hotel. He had worked himself into a frenzy for the day, intending to beat his rivals in offering a spectacular gala dinner. Crowds were lining the streets from Buckingham Palace to Westminster Abbey, and the build-up around the hotel was hectic. After the scandal with D'Oyly, it was Ritz's big return to London. He was in the foyer when he was handed a telegram that broke the news of the king's coronation ceremony being postponed, due to ill-health.[16]

Pale and dejected, Ritz walked into the restaurant where lunch was being served to announce that the gala dinner was cancelled. A few hours later, without warning, he passed out, and woke up delirious and incoherent – it was to be his last day at work. His breakdown left London a fairly open field for Rupert and Ritz's replacement, Reeves-Smith. However, there were other smart hotels to keep an eye on – in addition to The Ritz, as run by Marie, there was the Coburg, soon to be renamed the Connaught, and the Cecil, which was virtually next door to the Savoy. The Cecil made an open pitch to the same customers, promising that 'American requirements are understood and catered for'.[17] Fortunately, the Savoy was already set up to offer feasts for those with money to burn – American or otherwise – and had its fan base. Even so, Rupert took it up a gear. As Claridge's now had its high French-style ballroom, the Savoy would soon have its Lancaster Ballroom, given pride of place by the river, with its own entrance that offered privacy from the rest of the hotel. Decorated in a style that mingled Louis XIV with that of his great-grandson,

Louis XV, it was edged with dainty columns, mirrors, arches and gilded moulding. As Rupert no doubt hoped, its parquet oak floor would be worn thin by thousands of parties, wedding receptions and balls.

One particularly good customer was New York champagne importer George A. Kessler. Fancy dress was fashionable in Edwardian London and Kessler's party highlight of 1905 was a *Gondoliers*-themed birthday dinner. Before Rupert transformed his father's courtyard into the Lancaster Ballroom, for Kessler's birthday the hotel obligingly flooded the courtyard to a depth of four feet to conjure the Grand Canal of Venice by the Thames. The banqueting department painted frescoes in front of its walls, strung up fairy lights to illuminate the night sky, and dressed the waiters as gondoliers. Dinner was served on a gilded, silk-lined floating gondola, covered in carnations, in the middle of the 'canal'. Real swans were swimming in the water, or at least they were at the beginning. They fell ill from the chemicals that tinted it blue and were scooped out. Once the ailing swans were out of the way, Savoy regular, the Neapolitan tenor Enrico Caruso, serenaded the guests under a paper moon while a hundred white doves were released to flutter above. As a final flourish, a baby elephant borrowed from London Zoo pulled a five-foot-high birthday cake up the little bridge to the gondola. As accompaniment, Caruso warbled 'O Sole Mio'. There was no such thing as overkill at the Edwardian Savoy.

The banqueting department was kept busy by Kessler and other magnates with imaginative requests. For Christmas, Kessler asked them to recreate the North Pole with all the trimmings. Crossing a floor of artificial snow in the Restaurant, his guests, in their winter finery, walked past icebergs of silver tissue to tables decorated as snow drifts, where waiters in Eskimo dress served dinner, and handed out the presents: gold Cartier cigarette cases for the men and diamond brooches for the women. In the spring, the hotel made the fountain in the courtyard gush with unending champagne for steel tycoon Gustav Krupp, who had a near monopoly on German arms manufacturing.[18]

In 1906, they managed to fly a plane briefly during the New Year's Eve party. On the stroke of midnight, an 'aero-mobile' (a hybrid motor-car and aeroplane) set off on rails fitted to the roof of the foyer, becoming airborne for a few moments before landing and running between the diners, as two women on board showered the party with gifts. At one 'Midnight Ball' raffle, winners took home diamond pendants, an oil painting by Irish landscape painter John Lavery, and the new Daimler limousines, the Royal Family's car of choice until the 1950s. For Fourth of July celebrations, the Banqueting Department thought to start cooling the ballroom with a chilled mist to spray over perspiring dancers. If the guests were creative big spenders, so was the Savoy.

For more casual celebrations, there was the American Bar. It was presided over by Ada Coleman, one of the few women to work in a cocktail bar anywhere in the world at the time. Rupert had met her at his golf club and wanted to help when she explained that her father, who also worked at the club, had recently died. He invited her to work in the floristry department at Claridge's. When she started, she learned on the side from the wine waiter how to make cocktails, starting with a Manhattan, and became Claridge's first female head-bartender. This snowballed into a long, trailblazing career as the 'world's most famous barmaid'.[19] Promoted to head-bartender at the Savoy's American Bar in 1903, she leapfrogged over the existing one, Ruth Burgess, known as Miss B. In twenty years, the two women never worked at the same time. Coleman declined to share her recipes with Burgess, and it caused plenty of animosity, so they worked different shifts. Both Coleman and Burgess would be entirely surrounded by men at work, as no female customers were allowed in. Having female bartenders at all was controversial. Campaigns were underway to bar women from the profession. A 1905 parliamentary committee 'on the Employment of Barmaids' met to consider whether it was morally proper to allow such a thing.

Part of Coleman's draw was that, alongside technical skill, she grasped that hospitality should be genuine and warm. In much of Edwardian London it was still starchy. The affection between her and the guests was such that, when she had private parties, many of her own guests were American Bar patrons. These invitations were not extended to her colleague, Miss B.

One of Coleman's inventions was the Hanky Panky for actor-turned-manager Charles Hawtrey. Bearing a resemblance to the Negroni, it was an entirely alcoholic blend of gin, Fernet Branca and vermouth, with an orange twist garnish. It seemed that all was forgiven between the hotel and Hawtrey, after they had taken him to court to settle his bar bill one year. He had possibly hit another one of his financial rough patches in his career as the manager of the Comedy Theatre, and said that he would not pay until he was 'compelled to'. True to his word, he waited until he was ordered by a judge. Hawtrey was not a total anomaly, in that many regular visitors were allowed to run up bills before being chased for payment, but few took advantage to the extent that court action was then involved. The hotel was always keen to keep relations cordial in bill disputes. When Churchill's private secretary wrote to quibble a bar bill, the Savoy took the chance to be ingratiating. 'Mr Churchill is surprised at the amount of this bill, which works out at almost £3 a head,' wrote the secretary. The hotel reply came and stated that it concerned a half-drunk bottle of port, 'being kept at the bar for Mr Churchill's use next time we are honoured with his patronage.'[20]

Ada Coleman and Miss B aside, while there was no flurry of promoting women from Rupert, there was a hint of sympathy for women's rights. Both the theatre and the hotel hosted suffrage events. This happened several times, even though the press coverage was not entirely favourable. Christabel Pankhurst, co-founder of the Women's Suffrage Political Union, took over the theatre for a rally in November 1906. She addressed the recent wave of window-smashing in London by telling her receptive audience that men had won the vote by riot and rebellion, and defended attacks on private and public property to loud cheers. In the trial of her mother, Emmeline Pankhurst, for damage to property, the Theatre came up often as a suffragette meeting place that had been infiltrated by the police. A month later, the hotel allowed campaigner Millicent Fawcett to hold a banquet for 250 guests to celebrate the freedom of the first ten suffragette prisoners from Holloway Prison. Fawcett, as toastmaster, referred to in the menu as 'Madam the chairman', wore a necklace of rubies and diamonds and a bunch of lily of the valley on her dress in suffragist colours.[21] She toasted the Royal Family and 'success to the Women's suffrage cause'.[22] When Emmeline Pankhurst herself ended up in prison along with her mother, James Murray, a Liberal MP, had several courses, wine and three waiters sent over to her cell from the hotel, which said that it was all on the house.

While Rupert channelled his energy into the hotels, Helen ran the Opera Company, fitfully. Laid low by grief herself, other managers leased the theatre between 1903 and 1906. Following D'Oyly's death, the Opera Company's number of repertory companies touring Britain dwindled down from its peak of eight to one. After the remaining company visited South Africa in 1905, more than half a year elapsed with no productions at all. It did not seem as though the Opera Company was destined to flourish post-D'Oyly. In the early decades of the new century, the popularity of Franz Lehar's *The Merry Widow* (first seen in London in 1907), Frederic Norton's *Chu Chin Chow* (1916) and Harold Fraser Simpson's *The Maid of the Mountains* (1917) threatened to overshadow the Savoy operas. Gilbert apparently expected no better: 'Posterity,' he once remarked, 'will know as little of me as I shall know of posterity.' And so it seemed, for a few years.

Such pessimism was not necessary. By the mid twentieth century, as *The Times* lauded them, the operas would 'become a national institution'.[23] Part of that longevity undoubtedly lies in the zeal with which Rupert would exploit his inherited exclusive rights of performance when he took sole control. It meant that, during the twentieth century, the Company gave at least 40,000 performances. For now it was just the beginning of the resurgence. Helen's first major revival took place in London between 1906 and 1908, with the productions supervised by Gilbert. She renegotiated the performing rights from him, to add to Sullivan's, giving her and Rupert the ability to continue their monopoly.

It took the greatest tact for her to handle Gilbert in his role as director of the production of *The Yeomen of the Guard* in 1906. He had difficulty in accepting that he was no longer an equal partner, as he had been (financially at least) in productions with D'Oyly, and he was angry that he had not been consulted regarding casting. However, the season, and the following one, were triumphs. At the opening night of the 1906 revival, Helen, dressed in white, carrying white flowers, peeped out shyly from the side of the stage. She trembled visibly at the 'hurricane' of applause when she stepped out to take three curtain calls with Gilbert, now seventy-one. This was one of his last public appearances. He retired to his estate, Grim's

Dyke in Harrow, where he spent the rest of his life. He died there in 1911, attempting to help a local girl, Ruby Preece, who was in difficulties while swimming in his boating lake. The girl was fine, but Gilbert's lifeless body was recovered from the lake after he suffered a heart attack while hauling himself through the water to save her.

Although only in his twenties in the early 1900s, Rupert had few close relatives left. With his mother, brother and father gone, of his immediate family he had only Helen. She had sold Adelphi Terrace and moved into the Savoy Court with her second husband, Stanley Carr Boulter, a barrister friend of D'Oyly's who was on the Savoy board. Aged thirty-one, Rupert decided to marry too. He swiftly proposed to eighteen-year-old Lady Dorothy Gathorne-Hardy, the Earl of Cranbrook's daughter, in the April just before her debutante season. The marriage created a stir, as it was unorthodox for an Earl's daughter to marry into an upper-middle-class family, however wealthy.

Dorothy's grandfather, the first Earl of Cranbrook, Gathorne Gathorne-Hardy, had been included in the cabinet in every Conservative government from 1858 to 1892. Gathorne-Hardy had to wait until the 1890s for a title, but he had a fitting property ready from the start of his career. In 1858 he had bought Hemsted Park in Kent, and begun an immediate overhaul, flattening the original Elizabethan house and commissioning a replacement Victorian mansion, lodge and cottages, alongside acres of formal gardens and a pinetum. In 1891, when the census was taken and Dorothy was staying as a baby, sixteen servants were in attendance.

Known as Dolly to her family as a child, one of her earliest memories was contracting double pneumonia at home in Chelsea and having four doctors evaluating her chances at the foot of her bed. In those days, if someone was gravely ill, straw was scattered on the road outside to muffle the sound of horses' hooves so that the invalid could rest in as much peace as possible. The housemaid laid straw outside Dorothy's family home at Cadogan Square day after day until her recovery. Taught at home by governesses, Dorothy lamented having few children her own age to play with, as her brothers went away to school. She described one governess, who would beat her with a ruler when she played the wrong notes on the piano, as 'quite hideous'. Another one, she complained, was 'old and prissy', and a third she managed to escape by behaving so badly that she left straight away. Dorothy writhed on the floor, scratching the carpet as though possessed, causing the governess to tell Dorothy's mother that her daughter was going mad and that she would like to leave.

Newly elevated to the peerage as the Gathorne-Hardys were, it was quite a leap up the Edwardian social ladder for Rupert. His father had been born to parents who had eloped, one of whom was illegitimate, in a flat surrounded by brothels and theatres. It had not been an auspicious start. A generation on and the picture was radically different, but from the Gathorne-Hardys' point of view, there was plenty to be dubious about. As well as illegitimacy and a lack of breeding, in their prospective son-in-law's family there was homosexuality – then a religious and legal offence – and suicide – also a religious and legal offence. Theatres and hotels were also not considered an upmarket or intelligent way to make money. As one of the Savoy's privately educated hotel managers recalled, his parents found his career choice 'odd for a well-educated boy'. Other than wealth, the son of Oily Carte did not tick many aristocratic marital boxes.

Rupert and Dorothy's wedding went ahead in June 1907 at St George's, Hanover Square, having moved from the Gathorne-Hardy's Kent estate to Mayfair at the last minute.

St George's was perhaps an unwitting choice for Rupert. His paternal great-grandfather, whom he had never met, Richard Cart, had married his wife – rather than Rupert's own great-grandmother – there in December 1820. Rupert and Dorothy's short-notice reception was held at her uncle's house at 30 Grosvenor Square, a few streets away.

With pale skin and dark hair, Dorothy had a fashionable beauty. She was a considerable catch by the standards of the day, or at least that is how she appeared. A prodigious drinker, smoker and gambler, Rupert's teenage wife would turn out to have a streak of unpredictability. After their honeymoon in Cornwall, they settled into his house on Suffolk Street, between the National Gallery on Trafalgar Square and Ritz's Carlton hotel. It was an astute location for Rupert. Suffolk Street adjoined Cockspur Street and Haymarket – it was between his three London hotels, in the heart of Theatreland, and next to the agencies of the ocean liner Cunard, and of Pacific & Orient cruises, and the map and travel bookshop Stanford's. This meant that Cockspur Street was lined with exotic window displays, travel brochures, and dinky model ships. At number one was Oceanic House, the London office of the Oceanic Steam Navigation Company, which most notoriously operated the *Titanic*, and 14–16 was home to the Hamburg America Line. All of their customers were potential customers for Rupert. Keeping an eye on them on the way to work was invaluable.

Rupert and Dorothy's first child, Bridget, was born at Suffolk Street in March 1908. They lived in London during the week, but Bridget remembers many a weekend in the summer swimming in the river around D'Oyly Carte Island. Three years later her younger brother, Michael, was born on the island. While Rupert settled into a new family life, Helen, like D'Oyly before her, was burning out by her mid-fifties, increasingly prone to illness. She had been the foremost businesswoman of her time, but she was in decline. By 1910, she was too ill to sit for a portrait, which other London theatre managers wanted to commission to honour her work. Instead she asked for the cost of the portrait to be donated to the Actors' Benevolent Fund and to Great Ormond Street Hospital, a children's hospital. She died a week short of her sixty-first birthday in May 1913 at Savoy Court of a brain haemorrhage complicated by bronchitis. Her will suggested plenty of close relationships with the staff. She left large amounts to everyone from the messenger to the chief wardrobe mistress of the Opera Company to the hotel pianist. Her ownership of the Opera Company, the theatre and her shares in the hotels passed to Rupert. At her wish, her funeral at Golders Green crematorium was private.

ELEVEN

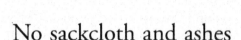

No sackcloth and ashes

The First World War interrupted the start of Rupert's control of the entire D'Oyly Carte fiefdom. His office dominated the 'directors' corridor' at the Savoy, along which the senior management had a room each. To keep an eye on Claridge's and the Berkeley, liveried clerks came from both at the end of each working day to present the takings to him by hand, as if in a pageant. Reeves-Smith, who lived at Claridge's, briefed him every morning.

At his desk Rupert had a direct line to the stage, so that he could check up on the theatre at any time. He wondered what to do with the Opera Company, concerned by how dusty that particular heirloom was. Picking up his father's habit of turning up unannounced to performances, in 1913 he sat in a 'dreary' theatre on the outskirts of London, sizing up his Opera Company during a production of *Iolanthe*. He found the sets 'unattractive and without character' and, when he went to talk to the wardrobe mistress about how 'dowdy' the dresses were, she did not see what he meant, which made him worry even more.[1] When she told him that the 'chorus ladies' were still being issued with flannel knickers, he decided that there needed to be a twentieth-century revamp.[2]

Rupert did not get the chance to make improvements, however, before he volunteered for the Royal Navy. He had the honour of being chosen as a King's Messenger, which involved the undercover movement of diplomatic documents across occupied Europe. Before the intelligence services became more professional, they recruited businessmen and journalists, who used their own credentials as cover. Rupert's extensive travel at the time was hoped to be above suspicion, given his line of work, so he conducted official naval work throughout the war, with the occasional clandestine King's Messenger mission.

In the meantime, Reeves-Smith was more than capable of keeping everything ticking along. He started working days by riding in Hyde Park, before returning home to Claridge's to spruce up for his first meeting of the morning with the general manager there. He then walked over to the Berkeley to take the same meeting, and on to the Savoy, arriving for 10.05 a.m. He would summon in the reception manager to his office to discuss important arrivals and departures, and special events, and then he read the night manager's report. This was the routine into the 1940s.

For all the anxiety and upheaval of war, the hotels thrived. Many aristocrats were forced to sell their London mansions, as upkeep became prohibitively expensive. A suite at Claridge's or the Savoy for the Season was considerably cheaper. With these long, repeat stays in mind, Claridge's set aside permanent stores for their regulars. Housekeeping would lay out return guests' belongings in their room for next time, to save any lugging or unpacking. Each floor was tended to by six waiters, six maids and two valets over the course of each day and night, and guests were matched to their previous floor when possible, so that they were met by familiar faces.

Carrying on the hotels' tradition as a backdrop for illicit relationships, Princess Alice, or to give her full title, Her Serene

Highness The Princess of Monaco, spent most of the war in Claridge's with her lover, at a safe distance from her irate, humiliated husband, Prince Albert. Her affair with the British composer Isidore de Lara, whom she had met through her patronage of opera, had resulted in Prince Albert slapping her in full view of an audience at the Salle Garnier, home of the Opéra de Monte-Carlo. They separated days later. When de Lara moved back home to London, Princess Alice moved into Claridge's and stayed for years. When marriages broke down, Claridge's often acted as upmarket temporary accommodation while more permanent arrangements were made. Margaret, first wife of the newspaper proprietor Viscount Rothermere, following their separation, arrived with her five-year-old son. She and the infant third Viscount Rothermere shared a suite for years. Later the boy would be ferried back and forth by a governess between her house in Dorset and his father's house in Mayfair until he reached adulthood.

Rupert enjoyed a much more profitable few years than The Ritz, which ran a reduced, loss-making service, but Ritz himself was too ill and vacant to register the rocky patch. He died after a long period of unconsciousness in the private hospital in Switzerland where he was resident. The Carte approach, in some vaguely Keynesian spirit, was, as usual, to keep on spending in a time of crisis. As Reeves-Smith said, appropriating the Bible in the service of luxury hospitality, no wars had been won with 'sackcloth and ashes'. Therefore, they should carry on as normal. In 1915, P. G. Wodehouse wrote about Simpson's, Rupert's restaurant adjoining the theatre, that there were no wartime corners cut:

> 'Here, if he wishes, the Briton may, for the small sum
> of half a dollar, stupefy himself with food. The God of
> Fatted Plenty has the place under his protection. It is a

pleasant, soothing, hearty place – a restful temple of food. No strident orchestra forces the diner to bolt beef in ragtime. There he sits, alone with his food, while white-robed priests, wheeling their smoking trucks, move to and fro, ever ready with fresh supplies'.[3]

Further into the war, however, supplies were rationed by the government. By 1917, restaurants were obliged to have a meat-free menu one day a week. Rather than directly deny guests anything, if possible, the management served polite notices when times became desperate. One at Claridge's from 1917 read: 'In view of Lord Devonport's [Minister of Food Control] warning and the increased shipping losses, many visitors may wish to abstain from bread at luncheon or dinner', along with the suggestion: 'to meet the wishes of such visitors, polenta and rice cake, both of which are efficient substitutes, will be served'.[4]

When he returned from naval duty, Rupert had a flurry of peacetime activity in mind. He started with the Opera Company. It had not appeared in the West End since 1909, while the theatre had been leased out to other managers. Instead a touring company had continued on its circuit of Britain's towns and cities. Rupert wanted a London comeback with aplomb, while keeping up international tours and provincial ones. He scouted for designers and conductors to present the first fresh productions since taking charge.

While most works that had once been popular in Victorian Britain disappeared without trace, Rupert's enthusiastic running of the D'Oyly Carte Company ensured that Gilbert and Sullivan reached more people than ever. He reassured fans that the operas would be produced 'precisely in their original form, without any alteration in their words, or any attempt to bring them up to date'.[5] The fan flicks for dramatic and comic effect and the semi-circular chorus formations were non-negotiables, but he made adjustments where he could. When he gave permission to amateur societies to perform them, it was on the same exacting conditions, and they had to supply him with the programme of their production in advance for his approval. For smaller societies, however, he often waived the royalties that they owed.

For his first London theatrical season, while sticking to his pledge to keep to the 'original form', he had strongly held opinions on the smallest details of stagecraft. This extended to fabric for individual costumes, discussed at length with the costumiers. For the rarely performed *Trial by Jury*, he commissioned a new wardrobe for all of the cast, and for *Iolanthe*, he combed through fashion history books and samples of crêpe-de-chine and taffeta, along with boxes of sample headdresses, looking for the right new clothes. At work, he tended to be referred to as RDC, and this can be seen on queries that needed checking. They were 'RDC approved' – or not.

Although Rupert liked to invest in big creative showpieces, he had his father's beady eye for niggling charges. In correspondence regarding the *Iolanthe* chorus, he wrote to say that he expected the cost of the stiff petticoats and pantelets to be included in the quoted prices. As he was a valued customer, the costumiers hurriedly, obsequiously agreed. Their replies were peppered with grovelling comments and apologies for small matters. In Rupert's business correspondence, once he had flexed his muscles and made a few demands – whether he was dealing with builders, designers or amateur operatic groups – he would often then make a sudden, unexpected kind gesture or compliment. The surprise seemed to make the recipient even more thrilled.

This firm of obsequious costumiers were one of only a small group in the theatre industry who had a clue what

Rupert was like. His enterprises were *sui generis* and set apart, and Rupert himself was largely the same. He was rarely seen at the usual thespian haunts, The Ivy or the Savage Club on Drury Lane. He was a member of the Garrick Club, as was customary in theatre management, but hardly spent any time there. His name was everywhere on programmes and posters, as he sent out his Opera Company touring companies around the world year after year, but fellow thespians had few insights into his life – and that was deliberate. One of his most long-standing employees was a J. J. Jennings, who handled any public relations matters. He must have had a pretty quiet job. 'RDC never gave but one interview in his life,' Jennings recalled.[6] Jennings was at least kept busy publicising the Opera Company, if not the owner. The importance of American fans was again suggested by that one RDC interview being in New York, when he changed the habit of a lifetime, aged seventy.

As a quiet, intense and 'at times distinctly taciturn' man, he was a hard person to get to know – even his daughter was not convinced that she had properly.[7] One of few photographs that the press were given was of him at his desk, with a Bakelite telephone receiver pressed between his face and his shoulder, and his eyes looking down to his work. It was hard to see much of him.

His reserve may have stemmed from his fear that stressful situations could bring on a seizure. He did a good job of keeping the hemiplegia he suffered from a secret and, although the attacks were infrequent, it meant that he lived in fear of temporarily losing control of half of his body without warning. Hardly anyone knew of his neurological affliction, but it caused him a great deal of pain by middle age. It seems unlikely that he was born with it, as he was a keen swimmer and footballer at school and both activities would have been dangerous if he had already been having seizures, which leaves the possibility of an accident in adulthood, in which he sustained permanent brain damage.

When asked what Rupert was like to work for, Alfred Nightingale, one of his Opera Company managers, simply said that he was a 'true English gentleman'.[8] This was echoed by his stage director, who chose 'true gentleman' too, adding 'he was loved by everyone, at all times working hard but never looking for credit or publicity for his efforts'.[9] If his reserve was noted frequently, he was also noted for being fastidiously polite, and he enjoyed public and private socialising, on his own terms. He held parties for the departures and returns of every tour and a popular annual staff boat trip on the Thames. This boat party had started as early as the days of the Comedy Opera Company. D'Oyly was an early adopter of the staff 'away day' and his first was sailing to Cliveden, a stately home in Berkshire, for a picnic lunch. D'Oyly himself could not make the inaugural one, as he was snowed under with work. It was a shame that he could not go for the food alone: a lunch of lobster salad, pigeon pies, lamb with mint sauce, tarts, cakes, cheeses and jellies.

In his own discreet way, Rupert was thoughtful. Dorothy did not display much maternal feeling, either towards her own children or anyone else's, whereas family friends remember Rupert gamely hunching up under the stairs for a game of teddy bears' picnic, and taking their children to the theatre at Christmas. From his correspondence, he took a patrician approach to his staff. In an age before elaborate pension schemes, he received many plaintive letters from former workers at the hotels and the theatre, and their widowed wives, some from far, far back in his father's career, describing the straitened times in which they now found themselves. Having not earned a great deal in the first place, many were short of money towards the end of their days. Rupert was not keen to advertise the fact, either out of modesty or for fear of encouraging more requests, but an appeal to him was seldom in vain. One employee told a *Daily Mail* reporter, 'The old man never let anyone know how much he gave away – but it was plenty.'[10]

On a smaller, personal scale, if anyone expressed the most passing of interests in his belongings, he was apt to give them away, to such an extent that it often caught the recipient by surprise. A compliment could result in being sent home carrying a hefty item of furniture. To his assistant, Stanley Parker, who joined him straight from school, over the years he gave his dinner jacket, tails, dressing gown, a table from his country house, an original cartoon by the caricaturist Fernando Autori, and his father's monogrammed pocket watch.

Importantly for his line of work, Rupert had an eye for a nascent trend. Already in 1918 he was keen to make use of the new gramophone. Starting with *The Mikado*, he supervised complete recordings of the operas with His Master's Voice (HMV). This brought the operas to a far larger audience than ever before, and was financially appealing compared to labour-intensive performances – from one set of recordings came a hassle-free flow of money. They sat alongside his other hassle-free flow of money: souvenirs. He sold merchandise from badges to tea towels to dolls, which were no trouble to produce compared to the operas themselves.

With the new-fangled records a hit, the Opera Company began to broadcast live from the stage as well in the 1920s. The 1926 BBC opening night broadcast of *The Mikado* was heard by eight million people. The *Evening Standard* suspected this was 'the largest audience that has ever heard anything at one time in the history of the world'. Rupert also experimented with early colour film to promote *The Mikado* too, showing his friend and set designer Charles Ricketts at work in his studio, using his dirty paint water as an ashtray.

One of the few criticisms of the Opera Company under him was that productions stuck so closely to the originals, but he ruffled fans' sensibilities at his peril. Even critically acclaimed new costumes or orchestral novelties drew harrumphs from purists. Rupert asked the esteemed conductor Sir Malcolm Sargent to interpret the original score of *The Mikado* for the 1926 production. There were complaints before Sargent even started, to the extent that Rupert felt compelled to promise in *The Times* that Sullivan's score would be followed to the last note. *The Times* then reviewed the performance itself: '*The Mikado*, refurbished in some of its details, made a brilliant opening to the eagerly awaited season last night. Refurbishing of any sort is regarded with some slight suspicion by the faithful [. . .] *The Mikado* dressed like that may or may not be more Japanese than the old setting; it is certainly less English. Again, the faithful may complain that it is less "Gilbertian," that Yum-Yum and her companions should remain pretty girls according to thoroughly Western notions.'[11] In his defence of making minor changes, Rupert said: 'Artists must have scope for their individuality, and new singers cannot be tied down to imitate slavishly those who made successes in the old days'.[12] His balancing act of keeping fans happy while avoiding the rigidity of 'the old days' was a regular conundrum.

At the hotels, Rupert had made ambitious post-war plans too, but to begin with there was unwanted publicity for a peace-time celebration gone awry. It would be the Savoy's first public brush with scandal since Wilde's 'gross indecency' of the 1890s. This time it was the untimely death of theatrical soubrette and Savoy Court resident, twenty-two-year-old actress Billie Carleton. It overshadowed the most respectable of events, the teetotal Victory Ball in November 1918 at the Royal Albert Hall. Carleton had first dined at the Grill with Fay Compton, an actress friend who had performed many times at the Savoy Theatre, and they left together for the Albert Hall, where they met their friend Lionel Belcher, another actor. He had a gold box full of cocaine waiting for Carleton. It came courtesy of an exchange in the lavatory with costume designer Reginald de Veulle, who often procured drugs for himself and for friends from Ada and Lau Ping, a Scottish-Chinese couple who lived on Limehouse Causeway, London's original Chinatown.

In the early hours, Carleton and her friends returned from the Albert Hall to the Savoy Court for breakfast together. By the time that the maid came in to clean at 11.30 a.m., Carleton was on her own, snoring in her kimono. At around 3.30 p.m. the snoring stopped. The maid tried to rouse Carleton, and called for the hotel doctor. Artificial respiration and an injection of brandy and strychnine were administered to no avail. The inquest into her death, held through December 1918 and into January 1919, featured heavily in the newspapers. De Veulle was found guilty of manslaughter.

Carleton's death was Britain's first big drug scandal of the twentieth century, and it prompted soul-searching in the press. *The Times* pursued an anti-drugs campaign in its wake and published many features exposing the trade around the docks of the East End, where the Pings lived. In the theatre, the death of a pretty young actress who lived at the Savoy sparked the imagination. Within a year, there were three plays with drug themes running in the West End. Noël Coward, who had known Carleton personally, acknowledged her death as inspiration for his *succès de scandale*, *The Vortex*, about a cocaine-snorting young composer. In the cinema, the silent film *Broken Blossoms* featured American actress Lillian Gish as a vulnerable girl in a frightening Limehouse opium den full of nefarious characters. By 1920, Britain's first law explicitly banning cocaine possession for anyone without a prescription was passed: the Dangerous Drugs Act.

After such a public brush with the world of cocaine, the Savoy was back to its own agenda. Rupert's own wholesome peace-time celebrations included late-night candlelit performances by the Ballets Russes, and Fred and Adele Astaire. For the hotel's all-important accompanying publicity photography, the Astaires were pictured giddily twirling on the roof, the Thames and the London skyline spreading out behind them. Dining became even more elaborate and intellectual thanks to a new head chef with a love of history. Rupert had hired François Latry, who had grown up near Lake Geneva learning about cooking from his hotel-keeper mother.[13] In 1919, 'stoutish and very merry', Latry took charge at the Savoy, and stayed in the post into the Second World War.

He was encouraged to think big and, over the twenty-year stretch, he became the 'chef to sovereigns', as the *New York Times* crowned him. He whipped up novel, exotic dishes. For banker Lionel de Rothschild, he served plump quails from Egypt stuffed with truffles on solid silver platters. For a German industrialist's Easter treat, he made a chocolate egg that, with tiny catches and pulleys, 'hatched' diamonds. For authors Arthur Conan Doyle and Hilaire Belloc, he braised turbot in vintage burgundy.[14] For a lunch in honour of his hero, nineteenth-century French gastronome Jean Anthelme Brillat-Savarin, he prepared crayfish with foie gras imported from Brillat-Savarin's native village of Belley.[15] Latry prided himself on being the first London chef every year to offer grouse at the start of the season on 12 August.[16] He had the birds flown down on the day and cooked in time for dinner. In 1921 he managed to procure a fresh consignment, by aeroplane, of the first Russian caviar in London since the war.

With the big budget available to him, Latry pushed the boat out for Christmas lunches in particular. 'No meal in the world has such a history,' he enthused. His menu was a Continental extravaganza: 'Le Pot Henry IV; Les Filets de Sole Richelieu; Le Dindonneau a l'Anglaise a la Reine Elizabeth, Torta Fiorentina de Catherine de Medici; Le Mousse au Cliquot, and Les Gourmandises du Père Noël'.[17] His 'Henry IV soup' was in honour of the Battle of Arnay le Duc, in which the soldiers sustained themselves on rice and tomatoes with capon, a forgotten delicacy of a castrated male chicken fed a rich diet of milk or porridge. The Cardinal Richelieu sole, after being buttered and braised in white wine, was served on green Marennes oysters. For the turkey with sausage-meat-and-breadcrumbs stuffing, Latry tracked down a 1573 recipe. Interwar dining at the Savoy was nothing if not extensively researched. Extolling the underrated virtues of herrings, he explained: 'It is, I believe, only the herring's abundance (its name is derived from an Anglo Saxon word meaning "army") and consequent inexpensiveness that prevents it from ranking with salmon and trout as a supreme delicacy.'[18]

One of the few mentions of children as hotel guests was in the menu that Latry designed for them. Rather than having a 'children's menu' as such, he made skilled imitations of their parents' food. His 'lobster' for children was a blend of potatoes, white sauce and milk, served in the natural shell, with coloured semolina as an imitation caviar garnish.[19]

In the spirit of the Savoy's modernity and self-sufficiency, Rupert's other interwar pet project was his workers' paradise, the Savoy Laundry. While politicians pondered how to make a 'home fit for heroes', after the war Rupert's own patrician initiative was well underway on two acres of wasteland by

Stockwell underground station. His new 300-strong laundry workforce had free visiting doctors and dentists, self-improvement classes in singing or needlework, a subsidised canteen, two baths a week, and affordable housing on site.

He launched the Laundry in 1919 with typical D'Oyly Carte largesse, shipping in newly invented electric washing machines from America and building his own water-softening plant. The Laundry sprang into action briskly, cleansing the fine silks, cottons and linens of the Savoy, Berkeley, Claridge's and Simpson's, and the Opera Company's costumes, seven days a week. Rival London hotels began to dispatch their linen there and private individuals, most frequently Noël Coward, sent their shirts for the whitest cuffs and the stiffest collars. If a prospective customer wanted to get in touch, they telegrammed 'Unblemish, London' with their request. Theirs would be among 150,000 items cleaned and pressed every week.

Of all Rupert's considerations for the staff at the Laundry, the courtyard garden was the most unusual. It was an English country garden behind a nondescript London street. Workers walked in through the wrought-iron gates and smart outer white-and-black tiled laundry walls and were transported to a quadrangle of trees, shrubs and delicate flowers. The garden could accommodate up to 100 people at a time, with the fountains and flowers intended to offer respite from the washing and drying. As Rupert was surely gratified to hear, many turned up early for their shift to enjoy it.

Heat from the laundry machines and hot water allowed rare plants and trees to flourish in what was effectively an urban walled garden. In the sheltered environment a Napoleon cherry tree that grew by the canteen survived from 1920 until the laundry closed in 1999. As did the fig tree that spread its broad leaves across the northern corner, helped through the winter by a steam pipe running along behind from the dry-cleaning department. The plants strategically screened off any unsightly pipes or vents.

Oswald Milne was likely to have designed the garden and laundry, as Rupert commissioned him for his country house in Devon soon after, and immediately again for Claridge's, and they all have common features. Milne had a large canvas to play with for the laundry, and made as his focal point an elegant tapering chimney that became a local landmark. Collcutt & Hamp, responsible for the river-front foyer of the Savoy in 1910, and D'Oyly's English Opera House, did the building work itself. The only remnant of that quadrangle now is the honey-coloured brick gatehouse, hidden these days behind a modern office block.

As word of the walled garden spread, guests began to request visits from the hotel to have a look. Rupert proudly took the occasional visitor on a tour himself. All of this care meant that the staff tended to stay for an eternity. Decades of service were not uncommon. When the last general manager of the Laundry took up his post in 1971, he met one female worker who had been there since 1920.

Bridget was a child of twelve when Rupert first took her there on a guided tour. In later life, she often arranged a car from the Savoy to take her over to relax among the shrubbery. Because many employees found Rupert quiet to the point of mysterious, they began to believe that there was plenty to hide. A rumour started that the Laundry was in fact where he kept any papers that he did not want to risk anyone in the office seeing. The reason that Rupert, and then Bridget, went often was not for the scenery but to squirrel away documents, so the rumour went. It was dismissed as nonsense by a later managing director. Nevertheless, there was a recurring sense from staff outside the inner circle that the family were strangely defensive.

TWELVE

Rupert's roaring twenties

'I want very little in this world. All I want is the best
of everything and there is so little of that.'

Michael Arlen, Savoy regular and actor

As the roaring twenties gathered momentum, the hotel
flourished as a second home to thespians and bohemians,
royalty and aristocracy, to nouveau-riche businessmen and to
the women who pursued them. It was so full of Americans,
who had started travelling again after the war, that it acquired
the nickname 'the 49th State'. Vanderbilts, Stuyvesants and
Guggenheims slept on its handmade beds, which would have
thrilled D'Oyly. Rupert had a ticker-tape machine installed
to keep tycoons in touch with Wall Street, while the American Bar, famous for its martinis, catered for a steady stream
of drinkers enjoying the frisson of escaping Prohibition. The
strictures in America made cocktails in London even more of
a treat.

Unfortunately for Harry Selfridge, founder of Selfridge's,
vaudeville stars the Dolly Sisters arrived in town on tour
and seduced him out of millions. Having earned a great deal
themselves in silent films and on Broadway, Rosie and Jenny

stayed and entertained at the Savoy when they performed in the West End. Already infamous at the racetracks and casinos of Continental Europe, they persuaded Selfridge to fund their nightlife in London. They reportedly gambled away $4 million of his money. For all that, he still offered Jenny $10 million to marry him. In a calamitous attempt to have her cake and eat it, she went for one last hurrah with a French pilot before giving Selfridge an answer. On the drive back from the Riviera to Paris, they had a car crash that left her disfigured. Selfridge donated funds towards her surgery but they never married and she killed herself eight years later, having been depressed ever since her accident. Selfridge did not fare well either. He came into the Savoy for a commiseration lunch in 1941 when he was forced off his own board, before ending his days in relative poverty in a flat in Putney, laid low by back taxes and debt.

Heading up the Californian contingent were ballerina Isadora Duncan, silent film actresses Lillian and Dorothy Gish, the Barrymore family of actors, and the studio moguls of Warner Brothers and of Goldwyn Mayer. There were so many Hollywood parties at the hotel that when British actress Lady Diana Cooper went to Los Angeles, she was disappointed by the socialising. In her diary she wrote about the first night of her play, *The Miracle*, which was 'packed with screen celebrities', that 'to my surprise no one did anything in honour of [. . .] any of us – no party, no flowers, no telegrams, no visits to congratulate. It would be impossible for, say, the Fairbanks or Guitrys or Stanislavsky to have a first night in London and not be feted by the profession at the Savoy.'[1]

All of this popularity with Americans was not entirely organic. Rupert actively courted both them and other overseas customers. Reeves-Smith told a shareholders' meeting in blunt terms: 'we are endeavouring by intensive propaganda work to get more customers; this work is going on in the USA, in

Canada, in the Argentine and in Europe'.[2] Rupert did not see the main competition as other London hotels. He believed it was Paris, which was attracting a lot of American visitors after the war. With this in mind, the Savoy became the first British hotel to actively promote itself in America by sending over a representative to canvas travel agents. Rupert believed that this was more subtle than paying for advertising. As it seemed to be working, Reeves-Smith was dispatched to set up an office at the new Waldorf Astoria in New York on Park Avenue and he invited other hotels to club together to improve their collective clout. They initially called it, in 1928, 'The Luxury Hotels of Europe and Egypt', and it is now the Leading Hotels of the World group.

Rupert also felt the benefit from some unplanned literary promotion. It was during this decade that the hotel was first immortalised by authors. F. Scott Fitzgerald came to toast the 4th of July with his wife, Zelda, and decided to set a short story, *Two Wrongs*, at the Grill. Inspired by the Cartes once again, P. G. Wodehouse had Bertie Wooster flitting between the Grill, Wooster's fictional gentleman's club The Drones, and Goodwood races. Arnold Bennett set a whole novel, *Imperial Palace* (1930), among the staff, and dedicated it to Reeves-Smith. He stayed for three months for the research, then another three to write. Armed with his notepad, Bennett diligently recorded the minutiae of every department, back and front of house. He was charmed by the place's hint of raffishness and intuitive service, and explored them both in detail. The chefs perfected his eponymous fluffy omelette of smoked haddock, hollandaise sauce and parmesan while he was staying. He was so delighted that he insisted on it when he travelled, spreading the omelette's fame, and his own.

Bennett was in residence when a starstruck young novelist, Graham Greene, was nervous to meet him at 'a great banquet' in 1929. Greene confided in his diary: 'I found myself a junior guest, very much "a stranger and afraid" [. . .] having the dinner at long tables, set at right angles, seemed a kind of frozen geometry [. . .] I found myself with my coffee seated beside Arnold Bennett, who, when a waiter gave me a glass of "something" remarked sternly, "A serious writer does not drink liqueurs".' Greene took Bennett's rebuke to heart and steered clear thereafter.[3]

The theme of being intimidated by the Savoy's company and surroundings appeared in A. A. Milne's novel *The Birthday Party* as well. Milne made the meta point that the Savoy was often appearing in novels. The main character finds the idea of going to the Grill for the first time a daunting one; he tells himself: 'what was there frightening in that? Nothing. He had the money in his pocket, he was ready for anything, afraid of nobody'. The girl in his party that evening, Charmian Flyte, when asked whether she is enjoying herself, nods and shows off:

> 'I always say there's nothing like the dear old Savoy. It's sort of different, if you know what I mean.'
>
> 'Another glass of Pommery?' asks her male companion.
>
> 'Just what Mother ordered,' laughed Miss Flyte, as he picked up the bottle.'[4]

These days London hotels are not so popular among Londoners themselves, but plenty of locals back then used the Savoy habitually. Many were angling to bump into people they knew. As old members of staff reminisce, it was more of a club than a hotel. The sociable founder of a venerable accountancy firm, William McLintock, knew how to network, as we would now call it. Accordingly, he 'loved the limelight' and 'held court' at the Savoy, hovering about on the lookout for clients or potential employees. McLintock and other business-men brokering deals over lunch, earned the Grill Room the nickname of the 'bosses' canteen'.[5] One shareholders' meeting ventured that the nickname should be 'the brain exchange', for all of the ideas, agreements and enterprises being discussed.[6]

Other patrons were far less productive but just as regu-lar. Twenty-two-year-old Richard Beaumont, whose family were the hereditary rulers of the tiny Channel Island of Sark, explained his routine in the 1930s: 'You get up at twelve, breakfast on a champagne cocktail. There's a cocktail party at six, then dinner, a theatre, supper and a night club. You go to bed about three.' Beaumont added that his friends 'live on credit. They are always borrowing, always in debt'.[7] The idle rich were good for the hotel – as long as their cheques did not bounce, as Beaumont's often did.

Wealthy actor-director Sir Gerald du Maurier and his wife, actress Muriel Beaumont (no relation of Richard Beaumont), treated it as a change of scene from their mansion in Hamp-stead. They brought their daughters, Angela, Jeanne and future novelist Daphne, to eat out with their thespian friends. At the Savoy and Claridge's, Daphne and her sisters enjoyed dances, first night parties, lunches and dinners, interspersed with their holidays abroad. However, Sir Gerald's back taxes caught up with him and by 1929 the Inland Revenue were in hot pursuit. Although he did not smoke them himself, as he preferred his unfiltered, to pay his monster tax bill, he lent his distinctive surname to Du Maurier cigarettes. The company partly chose him for his name but also for his on-stage smoking.

According to Daphne, if an actor approached a scene ener-getically, her father would immediately direct him to tone it down. He would ask, 'Must you kiss her as though you were having steak and onions for lunch? It may be what you feel but it's damned unattractive from the front row of the stalls.

Can't you just say, "I love you", and yawn, and light a cigarette and walk away?' This nonchalance was how Du Maurier approached all of his plays. His languid signature cigarette at moments of high emotional tension made him an ideal brand ambassador.

For every Evelyn Waugh, H. G. Wells, Alfred Hitchcock or Presidents Wilson or Eisenhower, there were hundreds of hangers-on angling to be in their aura. In the Restaurant, clientele were unkindly described by one magazine as 'a few truly smart people and a crowd of well-dressed non-entities'.[8] As well as non-entities there were also hacks. The Savoy was a handy source of stories, particularly as it was so close to Fleet Street, then the heart of Britain's print press. Editor Aylmer Vallance of the *News Chronicle* prided himself on being so decisive in handling the prickliest of editorial or printing staff that he could put a daily paper to bed in plenty of time to dine well at the Grill afterwards. John Gordon, editor-in-chief of the *Daily Express*, stayed over every Saturday night, so that he was well-rested and ready for the Sunday edition.[9] The owners of the *Daily Telegraph* from the 1920s to the 1980s, the Viscounts Camrose, held the paper's election-night parties there, with big results boards set up for its 2,000 guests to check between dancing and drinking champagne.

Dandyish columnist Hannen Swaffer was one of the main fixtures in the Bar and Grill for decades.[10] He wore his hair long over a silk cravat and high-winged collar. As he never used an ashtray, he was flecked in ash, allowing it to fall on to his waistcoat from the cigarette balanced between his lips. His boss at the *Daily Graphic* referred to him as Swaffer the Poet, thanks to his bohemian appearance, but officially he went by 'Mr. London' on his gossip page. He became the drama critic for the *Daily Express*, and was so scathing that he boasted of being banned from twelve West End theatres. He also campaigned against what he considered the Americanisation of the stage. As a result, he was smacked in the face 'on behalf of America' by an actress who recognised him in the hotel foyer. He celebrated his forty years in Fleet Street there with a dinner. In his sociable career he had made friends in film, journalism and politics, including the minister of war, Leslie Hore-Belisha; American actor and producer, Douglas Fairbanks Junior; producer of Cole Porter musicals, Charles B. Cochran; the proprietor of his newspaper, Lord Beaverbrook; and two Labour MPs, Nye Bevan and Tom Driberg. They all turned out for his big honorary party.

To impress all of these discerning guests, for service Rupert encouraged new levels of attentiveness. Rules included no running under any circumstances in front of house, and absolute silence in moving crockery, glassware or cutlery. Among the niche jobs on offer were a waiter to spend hours in the subterranean ice cavern at -17°C in a fur coat, chipping away at the walls to supply the American Bar; a 'plongeur' to scrub pans in the kitchen using their bare hands, sand and vinegar; a maid to sweep up the beads from the flapper dresses in between dances; a pageboy to tactfully put out footstools for tired ladies to rest their feet; and a detective to subtly identify confidence tricksters and thieves without alarming the guests.

Every morning the hotel was supposed to be returned to perfection. With this in mind a carpet spotter patrolled the halls with eyes cast down, looking for loose threads and stains, one of whom scoured the floors for thirty-three years. Similarly there was a painter whose job it was to go around every day with a tray of twenty little pots and fine brushes, looking for nicks and scratches on the doors, chairs and skirting boards and make them disappear.

Detailed index cards listing guests' age, interests, travelling companions and career highlights acted as crib sheets for making them feel at home. The staff recorded everything from guests' preferred porridge temperatures and mattress firmness[11] to diagrams of how they liked their toiletries laid out in the bathroom, which started with Noel Coward, who had a precise way of ordering things. The notes grew so extensive that they occupied their own room, presided over by the reception manager. For the actor Lionel Barrymore, one of the Barrymore acting dynasty, housekeeping provided a fire retardant eiderdown every time he stayed. There had been an incident with singeing the bedding because he liked to smoke while reading in bed, the notes recorded. Marlene Dietrich's card described the twelve pink roses and bottle of Dom Pérignon that she liked to have in her room on arrival, and less glamorously that she was partial to the suet pudding. After some testing, the hotel came up with enough strategically placed soundproofed padding to allow Louis Armstrong to practise his trumpet in bed and the layout was drawn for future reference.

Displays of devotion towards the guests were useful not only because they flattered the guests themselves, they also provided great publicity. A Savoy pageboy was made available to take an all-expenses-paid trip to India at the behest of the Maharajah of Patalia, to personally deliver a small parcel, and it made a novel photograph. When the Maharajah took over a floor in 1930 with fifty attendants, the hotel installed a silver bathtub especially for him. Again the newspapers loved it.

Rupert's flair for live entertainment meant that he secured British dance premieres of the Lindy Hop, Charleston Blues and the Rumba. He believed that his in-house Savoy Orpheans and Savoy Havana Band, whom his head of entertainment had talent spotted and brought over from New

York, were 'the best-known bands in Europe'. Their names were synonymous with the dancing of the twenties, and daily appearances on BBC radio in the earliest days of broadcasting, starting in 1923, brought them to the masses. After he had closed down the BBC studio around the corner on Savoy Hill at 10.30 p.m., presenter Stuart Hibberd would walk up to the hotel to announce their songs from backstage. Microphones suspended from the ceiling of the Ballroom, high above the band, would pick up the music and the swishing of dancing, giving far-flung listeners a vicarious evening out.[12] The general public knew the Savoy in particular of all hotels in the 1920s because of this publicity from the BBC broadcasts, and from the records of the bands released by Columbia. It meant they could hear the Savoy in their living rooms, and no other hotel had that reach. What listeners at home did miss, however, was the sight of the gowns and huge bouquets of flowers reflected in the Ballroom's mirrored alcoves, and the scent of perfume and whisky and smoke in the air.

The *Evening Standard* saluted the Savoy Orpheans' debut under the headline 'London's brighter evenings'. The correspondent wrote: 'They play beautifully with a swing and rhythm that set the feet stepping and tapping'. The hotel's publicity machine was in gear, making it known that the band contained a number of top American musicians and had a '£900 (£50,000) piano with its double keyboard, which is making some interesting experiments with the fox-trot rhythm'.[13]

Having hosted broadcasting from its earliest days, it was in the Lancaster Ballroom that Italian inventor Guglielmo Marconi made the first wireless broadcast to the United States in 1923. A simple exchange of messages was transmitted in the middle of a programme by the Orpheans, which went out at least weekly to British audiences between 1923 and 1927.

Marconi's suite at the hotel had been padded with screens and layers of felt while he conducted experiments ahead of the broadcast. Part of the fun of staying, for Marconi, as with Hearst and many others from abroad, was buying into the whole aesthetic. Marconi's wife, Maria Cristina, recalled in her memoir that her husband 'looked even more English than usual' when they were doing the Season, and at the dinner parties he threw at the Savoy and The Ritz.

The first full-scale wireless overseas transmission in the world took place two years later, when the Orpheans played two hours of dance music live to the East Coast of America from the Ballroom in 1926. A fan of securing debuts, in the same year, Rupert had a tip-off from his pianist with the Savoy Havana Band, Billy Mayerl, that it would be a coup to have the British premier of George Gershwin's 'Rhapsody in Blue'. Gershwin himself played at the piano, and the performance was broadcast simultaneously by BBC radio.[14] Mayerl himself became so famous, having worked at the Savoy, that he set up a long-running spin-off correspondence course, 'How to play like Billy Mayerl'.

Gershwin was invited back to perform at the new regular cabaret when it started in 1929. The stage stood where the counter area of the modern Beaufort Bar is now. A hydraulically raised dance floor allowed diners to watch the can-can and ballroom dancing between eating and dancing themselves.[15] After the Orpheans moved on, the management went on the hunt for replacement crowd-pleasers. They found Gerald Bright, whose first professional engagement was as a pianist accompanying silent films at a cinema on the Old Kent Road. More exotically, Bright then spent time in Argentina and Brazil studying Latin-American rhythms and returned to form his Gaucho Tango orchestra, which started at the hotel in August 1930. The 'tango teas' remained a fixture for ten years and the orchestra gave more than 2,000 broadcasts. In keeping with his Latin-inspired offering, he took the stage name Geraldo.

Alongside the tango teas and cabarets, the hotel was a hub of events that are almost extinct now, including the dinner-dance, of which it had been a pioneer. More sedately than with the tango and can-can, the stage hosted Johann Strauss III, who was brought over from Austria and played waltzes for romantic dinners, in an echo of the earliest days of César Ritz, when his uncle had provided the soundtrack to the Restaurant. Following the hotel's tradition of theatre-set standard decoration, the Savoy threw The Strauss Ball, with Strauss himself as the centrepiece. Tickets were three guineas (£180), and included supper, champagne and a late-night buffet. The ladies' gowns harked back to the days of Old Vienna. As *The Times* reported the next day, 'there was, directly the orchestra under the inspiration of Herr Strauss struck up the opening bars of The Blue Danube, the sensation that time had ceased'. The journalist was relieved to have a break from jazz, it seemed: 'Herr Strauss must have been proud of his name, as he saw for one night, a London ballroom rescued from the paradoxes of Harlem and dedicated to the sense and sensibility of melody'.[16]

THIRTEEN

Curzon Street Baroque

Away from the constant bustle of the hotel, Rupert had sold D'Oyly Carte Island and was searching for somewhere even more secluded for the weekends. On one of his many Devon sailing holidays, he was rounding the coast between Brixham and Dartmouth when he spotted a secluded natural harbour, Pudcombe Cove. He wanted this secret Enid Blyton-esque corner and its surrounding combe as a retreat for his family, which by now included sixteen-year-old Bridget and fourteen-year-old Michael.

It was a wild, elemental setting for a house, but the family had a gift for making something sublime out of nothing. Rupert made an energetic start on the twenty-five acres of scrubby bumpy farmland that sloped up from Pudcombe Cove. The first step was quarrying the land for the stone to build the house. Rupert kept a photo album of his designs as they came together, starting with the construction of a temporary railway to haul shale up from the cliff to the head of the combe. There he had the house built into the curve of the hillside, cradled by a grassy bank, out of the worst of the weather. With all of the houses's windows facing out to sea, there were no signs of other people or the modern world – only rock, water and earth. Its view was framed by the valley that led down to Pudcombe Cove, from where the salty scent of the English Channel drifted up towards the house. Access was via a winding single track, which in itself started from a narrow, unmarked gap in the foliage of a country lane. It was a place of splendid isolation that was almost impossible to find if you did not know where to look.

While the house was coming together, out of the acres of sloping farmland, Rupert and Dorothy created a sub-tropical wonderland of plants, lawns, ponds and glades. With its cliffs softened by pines and its warm microclimate, it had an almost Mediterranean atmosphere. For the spring they planted camellias, snowdrops and daffodils in the glades, these were followed later in the year by bluebells and wild garlic in the woods. Close to the house, the gardens were formal, with neat lawns, a bowling green and an ornamental stream. The stream fed into a waterfall and series of lily-lined ponds, ending at the sea. Further from the house, the garden was wilder. At the end of a narrow path, it opened up out of the woods on the cliff edge, with the quarry and the sea below.

The head of the combe was crowned with their eleven-bedroom Arts and Crafts-style house, Coleton Fishacre. The exterior would have fitted D'Oyly's taste perfectly, but Rupert had fresh plans for the interior. He experimented with a combination that he replicated at Claridge's – Victorian on the outside with an Art Deco surprise inside. It was rare to build a country house in this period at all, let alone one with an Art Deco interior. The Exposition Internationale des Arts Décoratifs et Industriels Modernes, which gave Art Deco its name, had only been held in Paris a year earlier in 1925.

Coleton Fishacre's style was a rare example of 'Curzon Street Baroque': modernism with an element of Baroque, named in honour of the town houses of Mayfair. At Coleton this meant Italian details of white marble carving, Venetian mirrors, scagliola table tops and a painting of St Mark's Venice as the focus of the staircase. In keeping with Art Deco principles, the colour scheme was mainly monochrome: pale walls and dark floors, white marble fireplace surrounds with black marble shelving, and black tiles on the windowsills. Outside was a stone sundial with Ancient Egyptian symbols, a popular Art Deco theme thanks to the recent discovery of Tutankhamun's tomb.

When Rupert and Dorothy were still close enough to be sharing a bedroom, they chose the best one for themselves at Coleton Fishacre. Its view was over the landscaped gardens and magnolia-lined paths, to the sea in the distance. Their windows were covered with bat screens to keep a breeze flowing without any nocturnal disturbance from the resident pipistrelles.

Downstairs was a stage set for entertaining. It started with an entrance that borrowed an idea from the Savoy. Coleton Fishacre's drive ended in a curve by the front door to allow chauffeured cars to sweep around and out again fluidly, just as they did on the Savoy Court, the private road that joins the theatre, the hotel and the apartments. The drive provided the first view of the sea, glinting behind the trees at the end of the combe. If arrivals had brought their own car, it was then parked up by the chauffeur, Ned, who drove it to the 'motor house' or garage, back down the lane. Rupert, and Dorothy in particular, were unusual in being able to drive in the 1920s. Ned looked after all of the cars, the main one of which was Rupert's Bentley. They were kept at the motor house, which had its own petrol pump and forecourt, with Ned's flat on the floor above.

Once a guest had been ushered in through the front door, they could hand over their gift of a bouquet to a housekeeper in the flower room, which was dedicated to fresh arrangements and flower pressing, to their left. To their right, they were suddenly on parade to anyone in the saloon. Framed by an arch, entering the room involved walking down a flight of shallow semi-circular steps, and on to the narrow rug that acted like a red carpet, ending in seats that were facing each other in a circle. The long central aisle allowed a good view of arrivals. Learning plenty of tricks from work, Rupert had the same flattering lighting. They were a mixture of the honeycombed hexagonal glass ceiling lights, and glowing alabaster wall lights as at the theatre, all set at a low voltage. As he knew, the trick for being as flattering as possible was to avoid any bare bulbs. Here he tried out the Lalique cut-glass lights that he would later use at Claridge's, the same armchairs and turquoise-glass bathroom tiles as at the Savoy, and the modernist geometric Marion Dorn rugs of all his hotels. Dorn's rugs were limited-edition works of art, for which she became known as 'the architect of floors'. It was well worth Dorn landing the Savoy account: the carpet in the foyer and restaurant alone covered half an acre.

Rupert's architect was Oswald Milne. As a protégé of Sir Edwin Lutyens, a pioneer of the Arts-and-Crafts movement, Milne was the ideal bridge between D'Oyly's tastes and Rupert's. Milne trained with Lutyens at his office on Bloomsbury Square. By the time Milne arrived for his apprenticeship, Lutyens was already famous for his Edwardian country houses, which fitted harmoniously into the British countryside. Thrilled with the house, Rupert invited Milne to stay several times to advise on interior design, and then asked him to make a start on the masterpiece of Milne's career, the new Art Deco Claridge's ballroom.

The family moved in properly for April 1926, just before Bridget turned eighteen. In went the dressing tables, the cocktail cabinets, the Royal Doulton baths, the cantilevered cigarette boxes, chaises longues, and the rosewood grand piano. Dorothy made it her home while Rupert spent the working week back in London. On Friday afternoons, he would catch the train to Devon with friends whom he met through work, including his costume designer, Charles Ricketts; conductor, Sir Malcolm Sargent; and the first woman to sit in Parliament, Viscountess Astor, to spend the weekend sailing and drinking cocktails – often at the same time.

On Saturday mornings, Rupert and Dorothy would wander the combe with his Dalmatians and her Cairn terriers, discussing what to plant where. They were known to ask their most esteemed guests to pitch in with the weeding. They took the gardening so seriously that Dorothy was often in correspondence with the head gardener on the nearby Isles of Scilly to compare notes. Less arduous weekend activities included bridge parties, tennis, fishing and swimming in the sea. It became a hidden-away party house.

Cutting-edge technology was brought up from London for the drinks. In the dining room, there was a forerunner of the modern wine cooler, covered in scagliola to match the rest of the furniture. This mahogany cabinet housed a cumbersome contraption with lead lining, an air vent and a drain, to keep cold water flowing around the bottles inside. Clunkier still were the ice makers and the soda siphon 'back of house', in the servants' quarters. As a mini version of the American Bar's soda siphon, the Coleton Fishacre one was an 'early apparatus for aerating liquids'. A fizzy pre-prandial cocktail was an impressive novelty in the 1920s. Service came at the touch of a dainty lapis lazuli hand-held bell with a jade button, connected to the dashboard of bells in the servants' quarters.

When Rupert and Dorothy entertained on a large scale, they borrowed staff and linen from the Savoy, collected from the station by Ned the chauffeur. The rest of the year, alongside Ned, there was a butler, housekeeper, housemaid, cook and five gardeners as permanent staff. Jack, the head gardener, lived on site, and shared Ned's flat.

For days spent down by the water, guests would wait for the butler to set the changes on the tidal clock in the hall. In the library a wind detector attached to the chimney indicated whether or not it was sailing weather. At the end of the day, a ship's bell on the loggia would summon swimmers, sailors and sunbathers back from Pudcombe Cove to start changing, ready for more cocktails, cigarettes and a few gramophone records before dinner.

In the same summer as Coleton sprang to life in 1926, Savoy regular F. Scott Fitzgerald wrote to his friend Ernest Hemingway from the French Riviera: 'It's one of those strange, precious and all too transitory moments when everything in one's life seems to be going well'.[1] Rupert, from his sunny corner of the English Riviera, would come to know exactly what he meant.[2]

FOURTEEN

A scrum in Mayfair

Thursday, 7 October 1926, was eighteen-year-old Bridget's wedding day. For the past five weeks, Reeves-Smith had been preparing. Having awoken especially early on the day, he set off from his top-floor suite at Claridge's with his pocket watch, as ever, close at hand. After a minute or two in the lift, he was down in the foyer, ready for work.

Holding the morning meeting, he reminded staff that the next few hours ahead required their most dedicated service. Not only were they to keep the usual service of Claridge's running smoothly, but they were also to host three hundred wedding guests for the proprietor's daughter. He went on patrol as staff scurried to their tasks. By lunchtime the linen was starched, the calla lily centrepieces tweaked, the cut-glass crystal buffed. The soft lighting and autumn sun reflected in Claridge's polished panelled mirrors. Little escaped Reeves-Smith's eye as he made his rounds. A frayed tablecloth or drooping flower would result in an immediate summons for the person responsible and he had a particular intolerance for any uneven bow-ties.

Reeves-Smith, who had known Bridget since she was born, was determined to give her the most sparkling send-off that

Claridge's could offer. Too conscientious to attend the ceremony, he stayed to oversee final preparations while his wife, Maud, headed down Brook Street to the church on Hanover Square.

A few streets away, Rupert and Bridget were at home, preparing to be driven to St George's in a black Chrysler saloon, his wedding gift to her. Inside their Mayfair town house on Derby Street, presents overflowed the surfaces downstairs. They were everywhere – table glasses, clocks, vases, bespoke cufflinks for the groom, lamps made from antique Chinese tea caddies, 'innumerable lunch-baskets' and ivory dressing-table accessories.[1] Among the bounty of silver and glassware, villagers and staff from the bride and groom's respective country houses had clubbed together to send carved oak chairs and silver salvers. Of the more pedestrian offerings, Dorothy had bought a selection of cookbooks to encourage Bridget to cater for her new husband. They would never be put to much use.

Looking at Bridget's other sartorial choices, it seems that her bridal outfit was put together under Dorothy's direction. She wore a cream chiffon-velvet gown with a pearl-embroidered sash, a top that gathered over her hips, and a skirt that opened to reveal an ethereal silver silk underdress. It was expensive, fashionable, and a little coquettish. This was Dorothy's style and not Bridget's. A stately train of old Brussels lace, a gift from Bridget's future mother-in-law, was fashioned into a flapper-style cap over her dark hair for a contemporary flourish. Behind Bridget's ears were sweetly scented orange blossoms, to symbolise eternal love and fruitfulness. In her pale hands she held a bouquet of flame-coloured lilies surrounded by autumnal foliage, and around her neck a diamond necklace was 'something borrowed' from her groom's grandmother. Her engagement ring was a square sapphire set with diamonds, with a matching brooch of sapphires and diamonds. Crowning the display was a tiara of diamond wreaths, from her future mother-in-law. There was barely an inch of Bridget not contrived to glint or glisten.

After leaving the tranquillity of Derby Street, when Rupert and Bridget's Chrysler pulled up at Hanover Square they battled to get out. At the porticoed entrance to St George's, onlookers were crammed five-deep along the pavement, spreading up the church steps and across the road. Police came to the aid of the ushers and the elderly verger in holding back the wedding enthusiasts as they crushed together, encircling the car for a good look. In eighteen years of society weddings, the vicar had never seen a crowd like it.

In the bluster of the warm, thundery afternoon, Bridget struggled to keep her dress and veil in place as she was helped out on to the pavement. Reporters, dispatched by several national newspapers, noted that she looked startled and afraid. She followed this with a rather un-bridal dart up St George's stone steps, where married life awaited.

Around the church, the crowd, mainly of young women, became chaotic as she and Rupert waited outside under a striped silk canopy draped between the Corinthian columns. In the melee, the silk canopy was torn, policemen lost their helmets and reporters their notepads. The church doors had to be forcibly closed as onlookers pushed in behind the wedding party into an already-full church.

It seemed that Dorothy may have been partly responsible for the circus outside. She provided the press with the dress details in advance, which piqued readers' curiosity. She also seems to have furnished a story that presented the groom as a daring adventurer, which whetted their appetite for romance. Several newspapers referred to the incident in which he had been rescued from a North Sea gale while sailing to Holland, saved by a trawler minutes before the yacht sank. He was presented as a buccaneering interwar ideal of a man – army-trained, aristocratic, tall, dashing, confident, and a pillar of the empire and the establishment.

Details of the day were fawned over by the press: *The Times* shared everything from highlights of the extensive guest list to Bridget's 'going away outfit' of a beige-and-blue sports suit. It was a day of tasteful display, and the newspapers were not disappointed. A couple also marrying that same day at St George's were dispatched with one sentence lower down the page.

When the church doors were finally shut, the onlookers' din was overtaken by organ music, and Bridget could see her hundreds of guests – the actors and actresses, businessmen and debutantes who filled the pews and the surrounding gallery – for the first time. On the red carpet, she faced them demurely through her veil before starting off down the nave. She had a lifelong tick of twisting fabric through her hands when nervous, so she must have been relieved to have her father's sleeve for such an occasion. Five sombre flower girls and a maid of honour processed along, wearing green taffeta dresses gathered around the hips in the contemporary fashion, bandeaux of green-and-gold tulle in their hair, and delicate posies in their hands. Dull gold threads sewn into their hems picked up the bronze of their shoes and the chrysanthemums that lined the aisle. The two youngest carried Bridget's extensive lace train.

For a high-profile wedding, St George's was a classic choice. Previous brides included George Eliot, Margot Asquith, Nelson's mistress Lady Emma Hamilton, Harriet Shelley, and Edith Roosevelt, for her marriage to Theodore Roosevelt. Dorothy, as an eighteen-year-old herself, had married Rupert here, with Bridget's groom as her page boy. Sitting in pride of place in the front pew today, Dorothy was resplendent in a black velvet fox-fur-trimmed coat, and a black velvet hat with scarlet feathers, alongside her mother, Cicely, in a black lace dress with silver trim. Rupert went to sit beside Michael, his fifteen-year-old son and heir.

Under the white-and-gold vaulted ceiling, Bridget took her place next to her groom, a man whom she had known all her life, twenty-six-year-old old-Etonian explorer, Lieutenant John (known as Jock) Gathorne-Hardy, the fourth Earl of Cranbrook. After the noise of the crowd, the bells and the organ, the church was finally hushed. Jock and Bridget were joined in holy matrimony in the chequered marble chancel, beneath two great chandeliers and a brooding eighteenth-century painting of The Last Supper.

When the new couple emerged from St George's, Bridget could be forgiven for being even quieter than usual. For this was not really her day. Under duress from her mother, she had married her first cousin. From the outset it was an idea that Bridget had resisted. Now it was too late. Facing the spectators and photographers, she managed a tentative smile on the steps, arm-in-arm with Jock, the ravaged silk canopy now cleared away to perfect the scene. The wedding party, with an awkward, muted couple at its heart, headed down Brook Street to Claridge's on an unseasonably warm October afternoon, surrounded by cheery female well-wishers.

Within Claridge's, the little marble foyer rapidly filled up wall-to-wall, as hundreds of guests arrived en masse. Just inside the door, every available member of staff was lined up to greet the bride and groom. Jock and Bridget were then shepherded in front of a flower-covered trellis for the receiving line, before being photographed alongside the sizable cake. Bridget posed with a sword poised to cut it, Jock standing stiffly some distance behind her. In other pictures she stood by the cake, apologetically dwarfed by both it and her bouquet, Jock with his hands clasped behind his back, in others with his fists clenched – surely never a good sign in a wedding photograph. Even taking into account the formality of the age, the photographs look uncomfortable. Meanwhile guests filed from the foyer along into the Drawing Room, its floor-to-ceiling windows letting in the last of the afternoon sun, and into the mahogany-lined 'French Salon' next door, furnished with Louis XV antiques, for dancing later.

As Rupert and Dorothy headed back to Derby Street at the end of the night without Bridget, they might well have been pleased that their only daughter was married off into the aristocracy. However, this stylish day full of family resonance would create misery for all involved. After 1926's Indian summer, on Bridget and Jock's Scottish honeymoon, the weather finally broke.

Following their frosty honeymoon, Bridget and Jock set up home, as planned, at the Gathorne-Hardy family's current seat, Great Glemham House near the Suffolk coast. The nineteenth-century landscape designer Humphry Repton had contrived its main avenue so that the dainty Georgian mansion emerged with sudden panache out of the trees. Acres of parkland, woods and fields spread out across the horizon behind it, giving a sense of grand remoteness. It was a view that Bridget knew well from childhood holidays.

By the time that Bridget arrived in late October, her mother-in-law had moved out with her staff and two youngest children to Snape Priory, a smaller Victorian house nearby, so that Bridget, the new Countess of Cranbrook, could enjoy the semblance of an independent married life. While she unpacked trunks and trunks full of clothes and wedding gifts, her new husband left for India, back on duty with the Royal Field Artillery. She settled into Great Glemham's echoing corridors largely on her own.

For Jock, marrying his wealthy teenage cousin had been

a tremendous practical relief, if nothing else. His father had died of tuberculosis back in 1915, making him an earl unexpectedly early. This had exerted pressure on him from the age of sixteen, imbuing him with a stern sense of duty and bossiness that he would carry through life. At the time of his marriage, as a premature paterfamilias, he had plenty of financial headaches to contend with. He had a younger brother and sister to put through private education, and in London his brothers Eddie and Bob were carousing with the Bright Young Things as a near full-time diversion from their rare books careers, for which Jock was expected to pick up the bill. Although he strove to keep his siblings in the lifestyle that they expected, a year earlier he had enforced a round of downsizing by selling off the family villa near Hyères on the Riviera. Further back in time, they had already scaled down considerably during the First World War from their sprawling seat in Kent, where Dorothy had spent her childhood holidays. The red-brick Victorian mansion built by the first Earl of Cranbrook had been sold to newspaper baron Lord Rothermere after Jock's father had died suddenly. Eventually it became its current incarnation, the girls' boarding school, Benenden.

Jock lamented on more than one occasion that he was the only sane one of his siblings. By many people's standards, he would hardly qualify himself. While his brothers hosted raucous parties around Bloomsbury and Mayfair, Jock's extra-curricular activity took a very different form. When on leave from the army, his Gussie Finknottle-esque passion for nature involved hours of rooting around in the Suffolk countryside making notes, breeding rats in his bathroom for experiments, and pondering the possibility of getting bats to nest in the pelmets of the drawing-room curtains. He once asked a family friend if he could sit bats on top of her red hair to see how they reacted to the colour. Bats were to Jock what newts were to Gussie, and he became renowned in both Suffolk and Borneo for his specialist knowledge.[2] When not foraging or observing, he was keen on hunting as Master of the Easton Harriers, which rode across his estate. He may have inherited this intense love for nature from his mother, as he had grown up at Great Glemham with constant canine companions, always in the double figures, and a plethora of colourful birds, who were encouraged to swoop in and out of the house at will. Bridget complained that Jock had more interest in the animal kingdom than in her, which could well have been the case.

It did not take long to realise that Jock and Bridget were a mismatch – however unpalatable this was to their families. Not only did Bridget fail to appreciate Jock's gung-ho virility and rebuffed his occasional advances with weary disdain, she could not enjoy his companionship either. Jock's nephew remembered him as having an 'often bullying personality' and 'no small talk'.

Surprisingly for an interwar teenager who was often out at nightclubs, Bridget had not been a smoker when she started married life. It seems that her formidable habit took hold in the lonely hours at Great Glemham. In the time she spent there, she was often home alone while Jock was abroad with the Army, in London sitting in the House of Lords, or outside documenting Suffolk's flora and fauna.

At the time of her marriage, she had been named 'pick of the Season' as a debutante by a few society magazines. One remarked how quickly she had made friends as an 'exceptionally witty' girl. Now, less than a year later, she was involuntarily living in a hamlet with only a pub and a church for entertainment. From her bedroom window, the Suffolk countryside spread out to the horizon, flat and nearly featureless beyond the estate walls. Bridget was, literally and figuratively, stranded.

Although the pressure to keep up appearances was great, she would not carry on. As divorce legislation was not relaxed until 1937, it would take a painfully long time to extricate herself. For the first three years no petition could be made, except under exceptional circumstances that had to be agreed by a judge. After those three years, grounds available were adultery, desertion without cause, cruelty and incurable insanity. She regretted having consummated the marriage as she could have annulled it immediately otherwise.

Instead, divorce on the grounds of infidelity was chosen as the most expedient escape. They needed proof, so Jock arranged to be 'discovered' in bed with a woman in a Brighton hotel by a private detective whom he had also hired. This widely used ruse of the time was known as the 'Brighton quickie'. These staged trysts were used to obtain evidence for divorces, and often took place in the cheap seaside hotels near London, where a maid would agree to catch a husband supposedly in flagrante for a fee. A few weeks before the Christmas of 1929, Bridget accordingly presented Jock with the petition for divorce. As the three-year threshold had only just passed, Rupert became suspicious. When he discovered that it had been staged, he felt compelled to inform the court. Proceedings were halted.

This was followed by an impassioned intercession by Jock's mother. When the Dowager Countess heard what Rupert had done, she drove through the perilous December weather to Coleton Fishacre to challenge him. After half an hour of her fury that Rupert was prolonging the misery, he was in tears and conceded not to interfere again. She climbed into her car with the Parthian shot, 'And you call yourself a Christian!', before storming off.

Bridget and Jock's arranged marriage was finally dissolved in January 1931, just down the road from the Savoy, at the Royal Courts of Justice. They went through the whole staged adultery rigamarole again. This time it was alleged that Jock had had an affair with a Miss Joan Ebridge in June at the Bath Hotel in the seaside town of Lynmouth, and again in November, just to be sure, at the Bull Inn Hotel in Suffolk. 'Decree nisi against an earl' ran *The Times* headline. Perhaps not knowing the messy details of the first attempt, *The Times* delicately mentioned that Bridget had previously tried in 1929, but that 'owing to attempts of the family to secure a reconciliation it was not proceeded with'. Bearing in mind the extent to which Rupert avoided personal publicity, and how rare it was in 1932 to divorce, however unhappy the circumstances, he must have found the coverage mortifying.

Jock returned to live alone at Great Glemham, where he threw himself into his nature and local history work, and into finding another wife. In both pursuits he was successful. A year after his divorce was concluded, he married another heiress. This time it was twenty-year-old Fidelity Seebohm, daughter of Quaker financier Hugh Exton Seebohm, who owned one of the founding banks of what became Barclays. Fidelity provided the much-needed fortune and fresh blood. They married in July 1932, and initially moved into the servants' wing while the rest of the house was spring cleaned and redecorated for Jock's second Countess of Cranbrook. Unlike Bridget, Fidelity was relaxed about his eccentricities and cashflow problems. With her blonde curls and rounded figure, she was strikingly different in appearance too.

This time round, Jock made a match of attraction and practicality. He had kept a diary in which he mourned the passing of his first marriage, but as soon as he found Fidelity, the diary stopped. Together they channelled their love for the surrounding area into founding the Aldeburgh Music Festival, with performances initially at Great Glemham itself. The music started in their drawing room, spilling out on to the terraces on sunny afternoons, and singers, musicians and composers were looked after by Fidelity 'backstage' in the kitchen. She and Jock brought up their five children in pastoral bliss, where the children were lucky enough to have their parents' friend, Benjamin Britten, compose *Let's Make an Opera* for them.[3]

For Jock, ready money continued to be a headache, however – visitors remember him borrowing the 'odd fiver' from the butler before speeding off to the House of Lords, but he was undeniably happier.[4] His home became the jumble of children, friends and dogs that had always been envisaged for him.

Bridget did not fare so well. After her false start at adulthood, she had returned to her parents in Devon, aged twenty-three. While her brother prepared to join Rupert in the family business, she found herself a spare part in her own family. After such a lack of chemistry with Jock, she worried that there was something wrong with her. She paid a handsome acquaintance to sleep with her – and was pleasantly surprised to have enjoyed it. If it sounds an odd thing for her to have done, her cousin put it down to her being 'practical, wealthy and secretive'.

After Dorothy's plans proved such a painful failure, back in Devon Bridget was allowed to take a few decisions of her own. One of the first was signing up for adult education at nearby Dartington Hall, where she took courses in modern dance, art and design. Here she gained a small circle of close friends, including the future Opera Company set designer Peter Goffin. Having been educated by a governess on Sloane Street in Chelsea through her teenage years, it was one of only a few chances that Bridget had after her debutante season to make friends her own age.

Relations, chilly for a long time, were even more strained between Bridget and Dorothy after the divorce. When a family friend overheard the coldness with which Dorothy spoke to Bridget, it 'went right through her'.[5] With characteristic understatement, Bridget simply said of her mother, 'I don't think she likes me very much.' In the summer of 1932, Bridget returned to the name of D'Oyly Carte by deed poll. She expunged Cicely, the middle name that Dorothy gave her from the Gathorne-Hardy side of the family, while she was at it.

FIFTEEN

An heir and a spare

While Bridget, divorced and out of favour with her parents, was at a loose end in Devon, her brother and father were actively preparing for the future together in London. Phase one of the succession was the Opera Company. When Michael was seventeen, Rupert took him along on its 1927–8 tour of North America and Canada. It was a field trip to show his son first-hand what an undertaking it was to take the operas on the road.

As Rupert liked to say, his ambition was to 'always be up-to-date – and a little ahead if possible'.[1] Within the confines of the national treasure status of his inheritance, he wanted everything modern and freshened up, and ready for his son to join him. This resulted in a flurry of Art Deco makeovers for the Savoy Theatre and Hotel, and for Claridge's. He started with Claridge's, and the hotel was thereafter made up of two buildings: D'Oyly's original Victorian design of 1896 and Rupert's 1929 Ballroom Wing. The cleverness of the design was how the disparate Art Deco and Victorian styles fitted together, and retained the original scaled-up town house feel, despite the new size. Milne's mirrored foyer was a very un-Victorian palette of silver-grey and glossy black, and the external entrance made guests' arrivals much more uplifting. He did away with the

Victorian drive that allowed horse-drawn carriages to pull up and replaced it with a highly polished canopy inlaid with glinting chrome panels and chevrons.

Inside, designer Basil Ionides put together navy-silk furnishings, etched mirrors, chrome fittings, and cut-glass Lalique screens. In the restaurant he replaced the heavy wooden panelling with engraved glass and lights in the shape of elephants, some of which have been retained in Claridge's most recent incarnation. The billiard room was converted into a lighter grill room, and eighty bedrooms were added. Each suite had a foyer that connected with the one next door, so that a private interior corridor could be created for guests with an entourage. Since at least 1914, Rupert had wanted to expand on such a scale. Finally buying the freehold for £113,500 (£3.5m) from the Grosvenor Estate gave him the freedom to pursue his plans.

Meanwhile, having been commissioned in May 1929, his revamped theatre reopened just 135 days later. As at Claridge's, the interior design was by Ionides and, like Milne, Ionides' most famous commissions came from Rupert. The theatre was his pièce de résistance of mirror and glass, and had Rupert's taste written all over it. The seats were variously of vermilion, amber, honey, fawn and crimson velvet, to replicate his favourite beds of flowers in Hyde Park and gentle recessed lighting gave the velvet an intended hazy autumnal glow.[2] The Victorian auditorium walls were entirely covered in brushed silver and gold leaf. For the Grand Opening Season of 1929, Rupert permitted one of the operas to be broadcast on Christmas Day.

When not occupied by operas, Rupert leased the theatre out for the premiere of R. C. Sheriff's *Journey's End* in 1929, set entirely in a claustrophobic First World War trench and starring a twenty-one-year-old Laurence Olivier. The hotel would take on an extra resonance for Olivier, as he met his future wife Vivien Leigh at the Grill. She was at a nearby table while he was having dinner with his first wife after the show. But they would not start an affair until seven years later, when they starred as on-screen lovers. They divorced their spouses in 1940, and married each other straight away.

Around this time, the theatre often offered a place for plays that were having trouble securing other West End slots. 'Every management in London had turned the play down,' R. C. Sheriff recalled. 'They said people didn't want war plays [. . .] How can I put on a play with no leading lady?' one had asked complainingly. Then, in 1930, there was *Othello*. Its lead, Paul Robeson, son of a slave turned preacher, was one of few black actors who had ever played the role at that time. He had dined many times at the hotel, but when he had been in a West End musical, *Showboat*, the year before and come in for dinner, he had been asked to leave the Restaurant. It was apparently due to complaints from American diners, rather than due to the management – or at least that was Robeson's belief.

When he came back to the Savoy Theatre to play Othello, his previously-held belief that race was less of an issue in Britain than in America surprisingly remained unshaken. At a meeting of the League of Coloured Peoples in London, 'Mr Paul Robeson, the famous actor startled many of those who heard him by denying that there was any discrimination against coloured persons in Britain. Any prejudice, he said, that may exist is due to the presence of Americans in this country [. . .]' He took the role of Othello all over the world from the Savoy Theatre and never lost pleasure in it. For him, it was more than a role: it was, as he said, 'killing two birds with one stone. I'm

acting and I'm talking for the negroes in the way only Shakespeare can.'

The American Bar enjoyed renewed energy in the interwar
period as the capital's whole nightlife scene became more
vibrant. Ada Coleman retired in 1926, having particularly
enjoyed meeting Mark Twain, Charlie Chaplin and 'Diamond'
Jim Brady, the railroad magnate known for his love of jewels
and feasting, in the course of her cocktail shaking for tens of
thousands of guests. Rupert kept a soft spot for Coleman,
having employed her in the first place, and remembering how
caring she had been towards Lucas. He wrote to thank her,
saying, 'my brother was always grateful for your sympathy'.

After Coleman, Harry Craddock, one of the most influential barmen of all time, took charge behind the sweeping
mahogany counter in his white overalls, white shirt and black
tie. Having identified the magnetism of the Bar, in 1930
Rupert capitalised with *The Savoy Cocktail Book*. The Savoy
was the first hotel to publish its own book of cocktails and,
never out of print since, it is the best-selling drinks book in
history. As with the music records and live broadcasts, the
cocktail book spread the Savoy name. Containing 750 recipes
and Art Deco-influenced illustrations, it was a treat to look at,
even if the reader had no intention of making a single drink.

Craddock wrote characterful recipe introductions. He
insisted that drinking in the morning was an excellent way
to rouse oneself, and recommended that his 'anti-fogmatic'
cocktails, as he called them, be drunk 'before 11 a.m., or whenever steam and energy are needed'. One was the unappetisingly
named Corpse Reviver No. 2. With a dash of absinthe on top
of gin, Cointreau and Kina Lillet, Craddock did, at least, offer
the health warning: 'Four of these taken in swift succession will
unrevive the corpse again.' He was well aware of the potency

of his own concoctions. He advised for the Bunny Hug, a mix of whisky, gin and absinthe: 'This cocktail should immediately be poured down the sink before it is too late.' Laurel and Hardy would bring their own copy along to the Bar with them as a way of ordering, often going for a White Lady or a Side Car, but nothing stronger.

It was unfortunate that, having recently spent so much on Art Deco finery, the hotels were then hit by the Great Crash of October 1929. This meant that 1932 was the first time since 1910, when Rupert had gone on the last spree, that the hotel had been unable to pay its shareholders a dividend of at least 10 per cent. Although in attendance, Rupert was not speaking at so many meetings, possibly as he feared a seizure in public. As Reeves-Smith explained in his place, all of Europe's grand hotels had been built 'to provide visitors from America with the accommodation they desire' and the Savoy was suffering from 50 per cent fewer American bookings in 1932 than just before the Crash.

Spending on customers remained sacrosanct, however. Rupert insisted in his shorter speech at the same meeting that even in this 'very bad year' it was 'not a business in which it is possible to make drastic economies [. . .] its very essence being to supply only the finest provisions, liquors and materials that can be bought'. Still, cuts had to be made somewhere. Staff 'from the directors downwards' had 'loyally accepted' wage reductions, other than the 'lowest grades of employees', he announced, who would be spared. Another tricky shareholders' meeting ended with applause.

When Michael turned twenty-one in 1932, Rupert stepped up his induction. Instead of going to university, Michael had a tailored introduction to the art of hotels. Full of enthusiasm, he set off around Europe on a tour of his father's friends' establishments. On the itinerary that summer were the major wine-growing regions and the fine hotels of France, Switzerland and Germany.

A diarist for the *Evening News* sat next to Michael at a dinner at the Berkeley, when he was back briefly to visit his family. He found the 'pink cheeked, dark-haired, slight and athletic' twenty-one-year-old was 'tremendously energetic and keen to learn all he could about the business'. His French was already fluent and he was tackling German. Michael had, by this time, already served several apprenticeships as a waiter.

Back on the road after seeing his family, he was joined for a few weeks by his friend Richard Snagge, who was training to become a doctor. Like Rupert, Michael loved sports cars and he was driving around the Continent in a British sports model. Together the boys drove from Germany to start the Swiss leg of the tour in Lausanne. On 23 October they stopped off in Zurich for the weekend, to see Rupert's friends, the Manz family, who ran the St Gotthard Hotel, and indeed still do. From there Michael needed to make his way to Monte Carlo to start a job in a hotel kitchen.

That Sunday afternoon, Michael was driving them from Zurich along a mountain pass when two motorcyclists who were travelling in the opposite direction tried to pass on the wrong side. To avoid the first motorcycle, he slammed on the brakes. The force of braking swung his car around and the motorcycle, driven by a local workman, crashed into the back. This hurled Michael out of the car and on to the road, where he died immediately. The second motorcyclist and his passenger crashed into the wreckage, and died later. With the fatalities, casualties, broken motorbikes and smashed car, Reuters' Berne correspondent wrote that the scene resembled 'a battlefield'. The local police told the *Daily Telegraph* correspondent that Michael had been 'an innocent victim of the folly of others'.

Rupert flew over to arrange Michael's burial in Switzerland, along with Richard's father, Sir Harold Snagge, director of Barclays, the Savoy's bank. There was no mention of Dorothy joining them. Although Richard had also been thrown out of the car, he had escaped with minor injuries, so his father was able to bring him home immediately.

Rupert and Dorothy did not face their son's death together and family life unravelled slowly. Rupert moved to the far side of Coleton Fishacre, to the small East Bedroom that faced the sea he found so comforting. The rift became visible in the garden, as he grew his favourite bright colours at the sea end of the house and Dorothy stuck to her pastels at the other. One of Rupert's Opera Company colleagues recalled: 'the heart fell right out of him'.[3] Martyn Green, a principal actor for the Opera Company, noticed that 'his interest in both the operas and the hotel seemed to fade away'.[4]

Michael's death altered Bridget's life radically as well. She had lost the one person in her family to whom she felt close. From having no involvement in the businesses, with one fatal accident, she was the 'opera and hotel boss' in waiting, as one tabloid heralded her. She became Rupert's assistant the following year and was given a box-room office at the Savoy Hotel to make a start: she would have to work her way up to a place on the directors' corridor. As she shared Rupert and D'Oyly's talent for design, she took responsibility for the Opera Company's theatre sets and for the interiors of the Savoy, Claridge's and the Berkeley.

From now on, she would choose every mirror, marquetry screen and chandelier for all of the hotels – a job that, fortunately, she loved. The hotels all had their own exclusive upholstery from the workshop in Covent Garden, so all of the cushions, quilts and curtains needed to be commissioned, and all came with an identical set for speedy swaps in the event of spillages. Each room was designed by her too,[5] with one floor closed once a year for redecoration.[6] Her first duties were to design a pared-down 'six guinea suite' (£65) for thriftier guests of the Savoy, and to oversee the floristry department at Claridge's, which employed twenty girls and ran a small shop for guests, and she built up from there. With typical D'Oyly Carte attention to detail, she thought of having small brass fixtures on the arms of restaurant chairs to stop handbags slipping off the end and on to the floor. She had to change her attitude to Gilbert and Sullivan quickly. She remembered that, as a child: 'At home, we weren't allowed to *hum* Gilbert and Sullivan; in fact we were fined for it, because it annoyed my father. We were allowed to sing it properly, but my brother and I couldn't – in my family the fact that I wasn't Mozart at about three years old was thought of as rather disappointing. So I went through a phase when I was very anti-Gilbert and Sullivan; I became rather a highbrow, and my father thought I was a bit of a snake-in-the-grass because of it.'

In a bid to smooth things over with Dorothy, Rupert took her on a cruise in 1933 to the West Indies. She had read an article in *The Field* magazine about the beauty of Speyside, a village in Tobago, and mentioned that she wanted to go. After that winter, according to shipping records, she appears to have returned every year for the next four, but without Rupert or Bridget. The repeat trips may have been to see her next husband. It was in Tobago that she met French Creole count St Yves de Verteuil. His family described him as 'a perfect gentleman', a man who seasoned his conversation with Shakespeare, and never did a full day's work in his life.[7] By 1936, Dorothy, now in her late forties, separated from Rupert, and left to join de Verteuil on a forty-two-acre farm, now known as the Adventure Estate, by the Great Courland River.

Back at the Savoy, it was just Rupert and Bridget. He sold the family home in Mayfair and moved into the hotel. Rather than living at one of the hotels as well, Bridget became a lodger with family friends in Maida Vale. On the weekends, Rupert and Bridget would catch the train to their secluded cove in Devon. When it became clear that Dorothy was not coming back, he divorced her on grounds of adultery, shortly before Christmas in 1941. She married again the following July, which gave her the new title of Lady Dorothy, Countess de Verteuil. Her new husband was fourteen years her senior, as was Rupert, and they spent much of their time on the island horse racing and gambling.

SIXTEEN

Essence de civilisation

In 1939, Rupert, now aged sixty-three, his wife absconded and his intended heir dead, resolved to steer his little empire through another World War. On Sunday, 3 September, two days after the outbreak, the government ordered the indefinite closure of all theatres. So Rupert's first job on the Monday morning was to shut his own, and to disband his touring companies, which were ready to set off around Britain for their autumn tour. Less than a week later, the government changed its mind and theatres were permitted to reopen. Having already sent the cast home and cancelled venues, Rupert decided to concentrate on keeping the hotels afloat, with only a scaled-down tour to start on Christmas Day in Edinburgh. After this initial glitch, the Opera Company kept touring throughout the war. A bomb that hit the warehouse on Drury Lane during the Blitz destroyed the galley decking of HMS *Pinafore*, but singed sets aside, it all ran close to normal.

The war stirred Rupert out of his years of heavy-heartedness and detachment. Bridget even coaxed him into investing in a new production of the rarely performed *The Yeomen of the Guard* in January 1940. He seemed reinvigorated by planning the set and costumes. His old perfectionism was back. While the Opera Company ticked along, the hotels were more complicated. The Savoy itself endured bomb damage, rationing, air raids, staff shortages and an initial plunge in foreign visitors. In wartime, its prime location was not a selling point. During the seventy-six consecutive nights of the Blitz, bombs fell in the Strand and along the Embankment, and the hotel was damaged three times. The force of one blast in Embankment Gardens threw bandleader Carroll Gibbons off the stage at dinner. While Gibbons regained his composure, Noël Coward, who had moved into the hotel, came up from his table to the piano to belt out hits. Coward quipped that he was just pleased to have a captive audience. He recorded the evening in his diary: 'Had a few drinks. Pretty bad blitz, but not as bad as Wednesday. A couple of bombs fell very near during dinner. Wall bulged a bit and door blew in. Orchestra went on playing, no one stopped eating or talking. Blitz continued. Carroll Gibbons played the piano, I sang, so did Judy Campbell and a couple of drunken Scots Canadians. On the whole a strange and very amusing evening. People's behaviour absolutely magnificent. Much better than gallant. Wish the whole of America could really see and understand it. Thankful to God that I came back. Would not have missed this experience for anything.'[1]

The Savoy was necessarily inventive in maintaining a sense of luxury. For the air raids, Rupert put together London's most comfortable shelter, with velvet curtains around the beds, sound-proofed sections for snorers, and 24-hour maid service.[2] Greta Hofflin, the wife of the assistant manager, ran a Red Cross unit in one corner, and in another, room was kept free for dancing. Set apart, in so far as that was possible, was a miniature royal suite. It was occupied, on occasion, by the Duke and Duchess of Kent, and by Prince George and his wife, Princess Marina of Greece.[3] Prince George was safe in the shelter but did not last much longer. He died, aged thirty-nine, on an RAF flight when his plane crashed into a Scottish hillside two years later.

In order to be braced for the air raids, staff were hurriedly trained as wardens, and provided with racks of gas-proof clothing and improvised changing rooms by August 1940. Up on the roof, staff from all departments took it in turns to keep watch in a makeshift concrete observation post with a telephone line, pictures of enemy aircraft, and a stock of tin hats. The Ballroom was filled with scaffolding in the hope of preventing collapse in the event of a direct hit. Blocking the view of the river, of which D'Oyly was so proud, was now a forbidding brick blast wall running the length of the Embankment entrance. One of the most vulnerable corners of the hotel was the private dining room, Pinafore, thanks to its vast, expansive windows facing the river. Churchill had been dining there fortnightly when parliament was sitting since 1911, with the society that he founded, the Other Club, for plenty of port-drinking, and hours spent re-enacting battles with the salt and pepper shakers. He, and nearly every other prime minister of the twentieth century, was a member: Anthony Eden declined however, as he did not like dining clubs.

Although all of the private dining rooms had been re-inforced with iron girders, Hugh Wontner, Reeves-Smith's assistant, gently told the Other Club secretary, when Churchill became prime minister, that dinners should surely move to a safer place. Churchill summoned Wontner to his bunker under Whitehall, where the concern was not well-received. There Wontner found him, mid morning, in bed reading the *Daily Mirror*. Churchill looked up after a long pause without greeting him and dismissively told him that the Other Club would meet in Pinafore, just as before. After trudging over to make his case, Wontner thought better of arguing and said nothing, deferentially leaving the prime minister to his newspaper, and reassuring himself that he had warned him. For rare emergency meetings of his cabinet at least, Churchill did use the more secure basement of the hotel.

The Blitz was the only time when D'Oyly's idea that the top-floor rooms should be as desirable as the lower ones stopped working. The wartime rates at London hotels declined the higher the room. Bargains were available, if you were willing to take the risk. One of those intrepid bargain-hunters was Viscountess Lymington, who took up residence on the top floor of Claridge's in a glass-roofed penthouse when few others fancied a clear view of the Luftwaffe. A standard room there in wartime cost only thirty-five shillings (£100) a night.

Margot Asquith, widow of the former Liberal prime minister, took a similarly defiant approach. By now, in debt and having lost her London home, she moved into the Savoy. A statuesque woman, she caught the eyes of fellow diners, as she dressed for the Restaurant in a long white evening dress with a train, paired with leather boots. She stood out even more when it was time for everyone to head to the air-raid shelter. Having long suffered insomnia, she would sit late into the night in the Thames Foyer instead, playing cards with anyone foolhardy enough to join her.

For rationing, the hotel took the lead in negotiating with the government how much hoteliers and restaurateurs could offer. They came up with a cost of five shillings (£16) and three courses per person per sitting as a limit. As one diner recorded in his diary, it did not have to mean too much hardship, in this instance: 'Pimms, consomé frappé, salmon in white-wine sauce with new potatoes and asparagus tips, praline ices and coffee'.[4] Wine and cigarettes became scarce of their own accord and many fruit and vegetables were no longer being imported. Most fruit, except home-grown apples, disappeared from the markets. As did any British shopper of the time, Latry, the head chef, encountered extreme difficulty in obtaining any onions, and became acquainted with a narrow selection of homegrown vegetables in a way that he never had been before. 'I make up 50 dishes from potatoes alone,' he was proud to tell a journalist. The most famous of Latry's wartime inventions was the Woolton Pie, a dish with enough herbs and pastry to make the root vegetables exciting, named after minister for food, Lord Woolton. Short of dairy products, he also learned to make 'ice cream' without cream or milk, and reported that customers swore they could not tell the difference.[5]

Under cover of darkness, black marketeers would draw up outside the hotel meat department on Savoy Hill to offer carcasses. Although the hotel did not accept such meat, it did get into trouble for buying chickens at more than the price controlled by the Ministry of Food. To get around the shortage, the hotel then set up its own poultry farm in Berkshire to provide a steady, legitimate source of chicken and eggs. The farm continued to supply the hotel until 1979.

During the Blitz, the BBC and the Columbia Broadcasting System (CBS) began a series of programmes which took listeners on a 'sound-seeing tour', called London After Dark. The series was intended to give American audiences an insight into what Londoners were going through. An announcer set the scene at the Savoy on 24 August 1940: 'And so, just after the air raid warning is announced, the dancing goes on [. . .] Upstairs are suites named after the Gilbert and Sullivan Savoy Operas. Below stairs are the kitchens and cellars, and even in wartime London, few spots are busier on a Saturday night, air raid warning or not, than the Savoy kitchen. Bob Bowman of the CBC [Canadian Broadcasting Corporation] is stationed there now, with the Savoy chef Monsieur Latry. Take over, will ya, Bob.'

We hear Bob walk along: 'we are switching you now from the upper dance room down to the kitchen here and what you're hearing is not excitement because of an air raid, but just the busy orders.' He explained to listeners back home: 'A lot of you will know it is presided over by no less a person than François Latry, who certainly is one of the most famous chefs in the world. Well tonight he's presiding over this white-tile kitchen with its red floors. His battery of flying black-coated waiters are serving those people who are staying on right now, staying on and still dancing upstairs. It's wartime and we have rationing, nevertheless, I don't think you'd notice any difference at all. The menu tonight includes eight hors d'oeuvres including caviar, eight different kinds of meat and game.' With a last-minute note of self-awareness, Bob adds: 'I don't want you to think that we're living luxuriously. Keeping with the war effort, printed in red letters on the menu is this sentence: "By agreement with the Ministry of Food, only one dish of meat or fish or poultry may be served at a meal."'

Upbeat as ever, over the din of the kitchen, Latry tells Bob and the listeners: 'I'm very happy to say hallo to my friends across the Atlantic, and to tell them we are well, and food is plentiful. The war has not affected my cooking.'[6] Other American journalists picked up on this hook for wartime stories and a syndicated interview with Latry introduced him with the headline 'New Rations Challenge London's Best Chef'. He was described to readers as 'rotund' and the 'czar of the kitchens at the swank Savoy Hotel'. As on the radio, he insisted that he was enjoying solving the problems. 'It will test my ingenuity,' he said, chuckling. 'I remember things now taught me when I was a kid in France. My mother used to teach me to use every last bit of everything. I am doing just that now.'

Alongside his Woolton Pie, Latry offered other improvised treats, such as his 'chausson de fruits de mer' – a baked potato skin stuffed with herring, mussels, scallops and other shellfish. 'And we do not waste the inside of the potato,' he pointed out. 'We serve that with the chicken course.' He was also proud of solicitously making soup out of fish heads. In preparing meat, before the hotel had always just ordered the cuts that it wanted; now Latry was puzzling over how to make use of the whole carcass. 'Even when serving chicken, we are popularising parts which seldom satisfied our customers before the war. They used to like only the breast and wings. Now I have prepared tournados made from the leg and people seem to like them.'

While the 'business as usual' message in the press was no doubt intended to be jolly and morale-boosting, the apparent bounty was just the thing to cause anger in some quarters. It undermined the wartime narrative that everyone was 'in it together'. In September 1940, the hotel's air-raid shelter was occupied by protesters, who pointed out that while the East End burned, 'the Savoy Hotel parasites' slept soundly in a reinforced basement with its own dancefloor. During the protest, an air raid started. Rupert had recently appointed Willy Hofflin as an assistant manager. As with so many others, Hofflin had practised his craft at another one of the hotels, the Berkeley, before being promoted to greater heights at the mothership. Hofflin invited the protesters to stay in the shelter and they accepted, which took a little heat out of the situation. A few months later, other protesters, angered by the hotel's continued ability to supply guests with good food, disguised themselves as ladies who lunch and ripped off their fur coats to reveal banners that read 'Ration the Rich!' at the Grill.[7]

Latry had been resilient for years, but the strain began to show by 1942. Although he became too ill to work, he was reluctant to leave. As the *Evening Standard* reported, 'M. François Latry has not been well for some time. He took a six months' rest on his farm in Maidenhead and then returned to his kitchen. But after a few days M. Latry has found the work during this boom period too heavy for him and he has decided to retire.' In private, Latry was also sick with worry, because his son, who was in the French Resistance, had been imprisoned at Belsen and was believed to be dead. It was only at the end of the war that Latry discovered he was still alive. Father and son moved to Montelimar in the south of France, where they ran an auberge together. Latry was replaced by two French chefs in quick succession before the hotel settled down to the failsafe August Laplanche, who remained in charge until 1965.

As well as Latry, Rupert lost Reeves-Smith, his managing director of forty years. He died from pneumonia at the end of the Blitz in May 1941 in his suite at Claridge's, still in the job at the age of seventy-seven. Thankfully for Rupert, Reeves-Smith had been preparing his thirty-three-year-old deputy, who was the same age as Bridget, Hugh Wontner, to take over. Like the D'Oyly Cartes, Hugh Wontner's name was more exciting than it should have been. He was born Hugh Smith, but his parents changed their surname and, when he was eventually knighted, he ended up as the altogether more distinctive Sir Hugh Wontner.

As *The Times*' obituary for Reeves-Smith noted, when Wontner took over, he brought with him 'a discerning palate for wines, a taste for travel, and a consuming passion for the theatre' – in short, as *The Times* pointed out, he was 'ideal Savoy material'. Guests found him faultlessly polite. Many members of staff found him haughty, steely and controlling. Susie Willis, briefly his personal assistant, recalled that he made her cry every day. As Reeves-Smith had enjoyed before him, one of his perks was a permanent Claridge's penthouse. He moved in straight away, while his young family stayed out of London for the duration of the war.

Business picked up from the time America joined the Allies in December 1941, by which time the Blitz had finished and Wontner was smoothly in place. Spies, prisoners of war, journalists, diplomats, financiers and exiled royalty found themselves living next door to each other along the Savoy's thickly carpeted corridors. As the East End protestors had identified, the Savoy, fairly or unfairly, provided a soothing refuge for those who could afford it.

Among statesmen, the Savoy became home to two recent Viceroys of India – General Wavell and Lord Mountbatten, as well as Czechoslovakian foreign minister Jan Masaryk, and members of the Free French movement. Their leader, Charles de Gaulle, carried on toasting Bastille Day late into the night at the American Bar after hosting a reception in the Ballroom for his fellow expats. The hotel had also made a windowless speakeasy-style bar, where guests could carry on drinking into the early hours during blackouts, and the network of large private dining rooms made it suitable for serious business too. Waiters remained in the corridor outside and were summoned by a bell, when needed, to ensure privacy.[8] The emerald green carpet and orchids of the Grill provided the backdrop for the first gathering of the Benelux ministers, when exiled representatives of Belgium, the Netherlands and Luxembourg discussed a potential customs union in 1943. They went to Patience to sign monetary agreements, with others to follow.

Once-expensive suites became temporary newsrooms from where war correspondents could file reports. Often, if there was work to be done by a guest, and they could afford it, they would hire two suites: one for themselves and one to act as a private office. When President Truman came to stay, he had this set-up on an even larger scale. He and his wife took a suite on the fifth floor while two on the fourth were filled with industrious secretaries handling his correspondence and schedule.

Churchill was back and forth from Westminster all the time. Not only was he attending the Other Club fortnightly in Pinafore while parliament was in session, he often commandeered a room with a river view to nap in after taking his cabinet out for lunch. He had happened to be dining at the hotel when, in 1940, he had received the phone call summoning him to form a new government. As a regular, he had his favoured entrance by the kitchens – and his own whisky too. As Joe Gilmour, who worked behind the bar, remembered: 'due to the war, whisky couldn't be made, so we only had three stock whiskies. Churchill came in with a good bottle of Black and White and said, "Joe, that's for me."'

With America now part of the war, a mix of transatlantic celebrities, some of them reporting for military service, pitched up in the Savoy foyer. John Wayne, Clark Gable, in his US Army service uniform, Danny Kaye and Groucho Marx all booked in. When asked how long he intended to stay, Marx drawled: 'until it stops raining'. Spotting international stars Gina Lollobrigida, Sophia Loren, and Frank Sinatra, who played the piano in the cabaret, helped to keep staff's spirits up.

Charles Bennett, an actor and screenwriter for Alfred Hitchcock, was one of many who found himself 'all alone in this city' and at a loss for a place to hunker down. He had been working in Hollywood in the 1930s but he was back visiting his soon-to-be ex-wife. He was shocked to see that 'hundreds of hotels, apartment houses and homes had been wiped out' by the Blitz. So he headed to an old favourite. Although its windows had twice been bombed out and replaced, on entering the Grill he was relieved that it looked the same as it did seven years ago when he had last visited. He described how the 'always graceful' maître d'hôtel, Benito Manetta, 'ushered me to my favourite old table – his memory equal to his charm'. For someone alone in a bombed-out city, such a welcome was just what Bennett wanted. As with many other memoirs that include a trip to the Savoy, Bennett bumped into a coterie of creative friends. John Gielgud had soon come over to re-introduce himself, after they had first met appearing in *Othello* back in 1927. Over the course of dinner Bennett chatted to actors Ivor Novello and Gladys Cooper, and he was lucky to bump into film producer Jimmy Woolf, whose father, C. M. Woolf, was an early pioneer of British cinema. Bennett did not miss the chance to pounce on Woolf for a business chat. Four years later, back in the Grill again, he convinced Woolf to lend him his aunt's flat on Baker Street for free.

Looking for sanctuary in worse circumstances was Sir Michael Turner, a banker with the Hong Kong and Shanghai Bank, now HSBC. He had been sent to Singapore to oversee the opening of a new branch in 1942. He was almost immediately detained after the Fall of Singapore in February at Changi Prison. When released, Turner was skeletal. The bank gave him a rehabilitation fund of £2,000 (£112,000). He decided that he wanted to spend a month reunited with his wife, who had escaped to her native South Africa, at his favourite hotel. The Turners eventually left for Hong Kong, where he became instrumental in the bank's post-war expansion.

Joseph Kennedy, brother of the future President Kennedy, came to stay on leave from pilot duties, as a guest of William Randolph Hearst. In October 1943, he came to see Hearst, and his beloved sister Kathleen, who was working for the Red Cross. The weather proved too bad for Kennedy to fly back to his base, so he stayed overnight with Hearst at the Savoy. The following day, the weather had not improved and so he stayed again. He dined in the hotel with Kathleen, Hearst and, this time, a few other friends. One of those friends was Patricia Wilson.

She was married to a major in the British army who was out fighting in Libya. Wilson was Anglican, already once-divorced, and had three young children. She would never be 'meet the parents' material for Kennedy's devoutly Catholic mother, Rose, and his ambitious father, Joseph Senior, the former American ambassador to Britain. However, over dinner, it came up in conversation that Kennedy Junior's airbase was on the same train line as her house, Crastock Farm in Surrey. He was welcome to stop by any time, she told him.

Joe took her up on it regularly and brought Kathleen along. The fact that Joe was with his sister made the visits slightly more respectable, but, by the early summer of 1944, Joe and Patricia were spending a great deal of time together and speaking on the telephone every day. In August, he volunteered to test a new kind of drone bomber loaded with explosives, which had been designed to destroy a rocket launching site in Normandy. Instead it exploded over the Suffolk coast near Blythburgh and he died. When Joe had told his father that he was leaving law school to volunteer in the war, he had reassured him: 'It seems that Jack is perfectly capable to do everything, if by chance anything happened to me.' So it proved, as Jack became their father's presidential hopeful after his death. As for Patricia Wilson, she lost her lover and her husband within the same week. Two days later, she was informed that her husband had been killed in Italy.

As could be expected with the *Casablanca*-esque cross-section of wartime guests, there were often spies about the Savoy, but all of the known ones were friendly.[9] Dusko Popov, a Serbian agent codenamed Tricycle, became a full-time resident. Partly thanks to his powers of seduction, he was one of the inspirations for Ian Fleming's James Bond. Even Bond's code number was based on the detail that, when Popov needed advice, he would call his uncle in Belgrade and the number he needed to remember was 26-007. Fleming thought it had a ring to it. Popov was welcomed to Britain by an MI5 chauffeur, who took him from an airfield straight to the Savoy. He was met in the foyer by Major Thomas Robertson, who specialised in double agents. In his tartan trousers, Robertson looked, Popov thought, 'like Hollywood's concept of a dashing British military type'. 'Let's get acquainted,' Robertson greeted him, steering Popov towards the American Bar. They did indeed get acquainted and not only did Robertson find him a promising spy, the two bonded over their loucheness. They spent a particularly enjoyable Christmas Day together. The two men headed out for lunch at Quaglino's first, then to the Lansdowne Club in Berkeley Square for billiards, before heading back to the Savoy for more dining. Robertson recalled: 'I think he (Tricycle) enjoyed himself thoroughly once he took part in the Christmas bonhomous rioting, well lubricated by champagne. We were picked up by a couple by the name of Keswick who took us to the Suivi nightclub [on Stratton Street in Mayfair] where we danced. Early in the morning, we returned to the Savoy, both viewing things through rose-tinted spectacles.'[10] It was quite a Christmas.

Popov was from a wealthy Dubrovnik family and refused payment from the British secret service, saying that he was happy to work for a country for which he had 'whole-hearted admiration' and that his payment from the Germans was enough. As he had chosen to live at the Savoy, however, MI5 did on occasion have to bail him out. As one record puts it: 'I met a somewhat tired Tricycle for luncheon at the Savoy when he told me he had discovered that he had not enough money to pay his bill. From this, it would seem that his previous evening must have been a somewhat expensive one.'[11]

Claude Dansey, assistant chief of the British Secret Intelligence Service, was an altogether more sober spook. He often
took his lunch at the Grill before finding somewhere more
secluded to interview potential recruits. One, James Langley,
was told to 'go to the front hall of the Savoy and make himself
known to a man with a folded copy of *The Times* under his arm
and a red carnation in his lapel' and this was Dansey.[12] Dansey
had been a patron since the 1890s. Like Lucas D'Oyly Carte,
he had narrowly escaped being publicly shamed for sexual
encounters with Bosie and, in Dansey's case, also with Wilde,
and Wilde's literary executor, Robbie Ross. While still a teenage
schoolboy, Dansey had been befriended by Ross, and taken to
a house that Wilde rented for the summer in Berkshire. When
Dansey arrived back at boarding school late, he was questioned
by his headmaster, and Dansey told him what had happened.
He had started off in a sexual relationship with Ross while
staying with him in London, whereupon Bosie had become
jealous and taken Dansey to Wilde in Berkshire. 'On Saturday
the boy slept with Douglas, on Sunday he slept with Oscar.
On Monday he slept with a woman at Douglas' expense,'[13]
the headmaster's brother-in-law later recalled. Dansey's father
stopped short of taking the three men to court for fear of the
publicity.

In the 1930s, having spent his career in the army, Dansey
had been assigned as chief of station for MI6 in Rome, in
Mussolini's Italy. He was convinced that the shambles he
witnessed in the organisation there was a disaster waiting to
happen. He set up a parallel MI6 structure, a shadow network
called Operation Z, that could take over when Britain was
short of information at the outbreak of another war, as he
predicted. He was at the peak of his power during the war,
and in hiring agents for the Eastern Front in particular.

Alongside the actual spies lurking among the guests, the

febrile atmosphere in the country meant that foreign-born staff came under suspicion. D'Oyly had gone out of his way to attract talent from all over Europe, as had Rupert. Now those star employees were suspected as potential enemies within. Even such a suave, well-connected Anglophile as Loreto Santarelli, known as the 'most popular restaurant manager in Europe', was not above governmental suspicion. As the hotel's publicity manager remembered, 'with the same deferential charm he would congratulate an actress on her new play or a debutante on her spring ensemble. He made every woman feel that she was the best-looking and most elegantly dressed of any one in the room'. In the twenty-two years that he worked at the Savoy, it was his pleasure to pull out all the stops. When he received a wire from the Maharajah of Rajpipla to book a table for a party of seventy at short notice, he procured an Indian elephant from London Zoo, which he dressed up in purple-and-cream garlands to welcome him, and Santarelli cherished the diamond-studded cigarette case that he received in return at the end of the Maharajah's stay.

What the most popular restaurant manager in Europe did not know was that he had been under surveillance for years. Although a British subject, he was born in Rome and MI5 had had him under observation since 1935. An informer had tipped them off that he was supposedly the head of a Fascist cell, 'who would form a good nucleus for anything the Duce might require' in London.[14] For wartime, the Home Office had a policy ready to distinguish between citizens of enemy countries who were a danger and those who were not. However, Churchill had his own, less subtle, policy: 'collar the lot'. Accordingly Santarelli and the rest of his Italian colleagues, including the head waiter, the head of banqueting and the assistant head of banqueting, were detained. Regulation 18B, under which Britons of Italian background were classified as being 'of hostile origin', moved them from the world of seating plans and flower arrangements to the grounds of an old circus ground in Berkshire, refitted as an internment camp with guns and barbed wire. Wontner was shocked when Santarelli, whom he regarded as 'a prince of the trade', came to his office to tell him: 'they're waiting upstairs to take me away'. Wontner was incredulous, as he believed that all of the Italian staff were 'absolutely innocuous'.[15]

Both the Savoy and its influential diners lobbied for Santarelli's release. Sir Guy Hambling, whose father was knighted for his work at the Ministry of Munitions in the First World War, told the Home Office: 'he discussed with me the advisability of purchasing from me one or two pedigree Tamworth pigs, as I happen to breed them. I only give this as a small example of how British his outlook was.' Santarelli also had George Balfour, the MP for Hampstead, and Sir William Fraser, director of the Anglo-Iranian Oil Company, speaking on his behalf. For all of his friends' efforts, Santarelli was released in the end because he became so ill.[16] 'With regard to his mental condition the change is very great,' read his medical report. 'If he remains in confinement at the Camp [. . .] he will become a complete nervous and physical wreck and likely to be certifiable.'

The Savoy's three high-profile Italian prisoners, including Santarelli, all died within a few years. Santarelli's freedom was no triumph: back at work, his hands trembled as he poured the coffee, and Wontner could see that he had become 'distorted' and 'dejected'.[17] A Mr Webber in the accounts department, who was still suspicious, had campaigned to prevent his re-employment. Webber did not have to wait long to see the back of him. Having collapsed at the Restaurant, Santarelli died of a heart attack in October 1944.

The other two prisoners, banqueting manager Ettore

Zavattoni and his deputy, Fortunato Picchi, were both killed by the Axis powers.[18] Of the three, Zavattoni was the only real admirer of Mussolini, although even he was unlikely to pose much practical danger.[19] Still, he was one of 500 Italians put on a boat, the *Arandora Star*, headed from Britain for longer internment in Canada. Also on board were Italo Zangiacomi, manager of the Piccadilly Hotel, and Cesare Maggi, restaurant manager at The Ritz. When it was torpedoed by the Germans in the Atlantic, 805 people died, including Zavattoni.

Fortunato Picchi, Zavattoni's assistant, had returned to the hotel after a briefer internment, but a few months later he volunteered to join an experimental airborne mission, Operation Colossus, in 1941. The idea was eventually to create a parachute regiment. Operation Colossus was an initial run at destroying an aqueduct in Calabria to disrupt supplies to southern Italian ports. There was a great deal of planning regarding landing the troops in the dark, but little attention paid to how they would be extracted afterwards. Thirty-eight soldiers took part, with Picchi there to speak Italian. They detonated the explosives as planned, before starting on their way to the coast, where they were to be collected by a waiting submarine. After the bombs went off, the men split into three groups to get walking. They were all captured within hours. Even if they had made it, no one was waiting for them. It was feared the rendezvous point had been leaked, so the submarine was not dispatched. While everyone else was sent to a prisoner of war camp, Picchi was taken to Rome by Mussolini's Blackshirts. His cover as Private Pierre Dupont had not proved convincing.

Picchi was executed and not given any known resting place. Both sides of the war seized on his death. In Italy, it was announced that a traitor had been successfully apprehended and shot. In Britain, a hero had been murdered by fascist thugs. Florence Lantieri, Picchi's elderly landlady in Sussex Gardens near Paddington Station, heard what had happened on the BBC Home Service. She was crying when she turned up at the Savoy, smartly dressed, with her hair starchily permed, to collect his belongings. She called the BBC to confirm his identity and sent a notice to *The Times*: 'On Palm Sunday 1941 Fortunato Picchi sacrificed his life for the cause of freedom. A brave man of high ideals.' The *Daily Express* ran a larger tribute, giving him the front page: 'Savoy's Picchi dies for us'. He was the first Italian to die helping the Allies.

Fear of fifth columnist Italians loomed large at Claridge's as well. A covert witch hunt ensued after a Savoy board member, a solicitor friend of Rupert's called Miles Thornewill, had lunch with an old friend, Guy Liddell, at the Restaurant. Liddell was MI5's director of counter-espionage, and he had heard some unwelcome news. A former American diplomat had been on a holiday with a former Italian diplomat, Count Carlo Sforza, who claimed that the Italians had bugged Claridge's. Liddell wanted Thornewill to procure the master key so that his men could search the bedrooms for microphones. Thornewill agreed and Claridge's fine plasterwork was duly picked away. Nothing untoward was found. However, a diplomat at the hotel, Norman Davis, complained that his papers had been rifled through on at least one occasion. The entire American Foreign Service contingent moved out to the Dorchester nearby, just in case. Both angry about the loss of valuable American custom, and genuinely believing that Claridge's' Italian general manager, Ferruccio Cochis, must be a fascist, Thornewill wanted him sacked. The Americans, led by their envoy Herschel Johnson, came back to entertain. Nevertheless, Thornewill told Liddell that, personally, he would rather lose the whole Claridge's staff and start again than sacrifice any more American custom.[20] Thornewill's campaign worked swiftly. Cochis was given a month's notice and asked to vacate his staff residence. He went from living on one of the prettiest streets in Mayfair to an internment camp on the Isle of Man. Few staff protested on his behalf because of the fits of pique that they had endured from him over the years. Thornewill ran a Belgian, Henry Van Thuyne, past Liddell as a suitable replacement. Judged not to be a risk, he took up the job and stayed until 1968.

The American panic over, reports of Claridge's being a supposed den of Italian espionage did not seem to reach Europe's royal families. Presumably with their taxpayers footing some or all of the bill, the Kings and Queens of Greece, Norway, Holland, and Yugoslavia stayed there for years, and the Duke of Windsor, formerly Edward VIII, came and went regularly during and after the War. Exiled royalty were joined intermittently by the President of Poland, the President of Czechoslovakia, and Gandhi.

Being away from home posed a unique problem for the Yugoslavian royal family in particular that required a unique solution. At the request of Churchill, suite 212 was temporarily declared Yugoslavian territory for the benefit of Queen Alexandra, so that her son could be born on home soil. Some Yugoslav earth was placed under her hospital bed, which had been borrowed from the nearby London Clinic, to help the conceit along. On 17 July 1945, Crown Prince Alexander took his first breath on Yugoslav soil. As an adult, the Prince has explained that he never received a British birth certificate because he was not technically born in London.[21] He was baptised by Patriarch Gavrilo of Serbia at Westminster Abbey, with a teenage Princess Elizabeth as his godmother. As history turned out, with the rise of Communism in Eastern Europe, suite 212 of Claridge's would be as close as his parents came to Yugoslavia again. When Alexander was finally presented with citizenship, to what is now Serbia, the ceremony in 2001 was held in the suite.

ACT THREE

BRIDGET

SEVENTEEN

Reluctant heiress

'The meeting of two personalities is like the contact of
two chemical substances: if there is any reaction,
both are transformed'

Carl Jung, one of Bridget's favourite writers

For the duration of the war, Bridget had been cosseted away
at Coleton Fishacre. The nearest other house on the headland
was a mansion called Nethway, requisitioned to house evacuees from nearby Plymouth. Bridget, now in her mid-thirties,
busied herself with looking after them. Working with and raising money for vulnerable children would be a lifelong interest
for her. After the war, back in London, she carried on working in the childcare office in Bermondsey. As one of her few
extravagances, she paid for a taxi to and from work every day.

While evacuees occupied Nethway, its owners, the
Llewellyns, and their butler and their housemaid, moved in
with Bridget. Kitty Llewellyn and Brigadier General Evan
Llewellyn for years used to go on month-long holidays to the
Isle of Lewis in Scotland with Rupert and Dorothy, and their
London house was on Curzon Street in Mayfair, which made
them near neighbours twice over. The Llewellyns now occu-

pied Rupert and Dorothy's old marital bedroom at Coleton Fishacre. On the weekends, Rupert came to join them all. This close proximity apparently prompted Rupert and Kitty to embark on an affair. On leave from the army, the Llewellyns' son George would stay in one of the guest rooms, the Turret bedroom. He did not seem overly horrified by his mother's indiscretions and jokingly wondered if his father might be Rupert. Other than anecdotal evidence and a large sum left to Kitty's children in Rupert's will, there is little to go on to back-date the affair. The Brigadier did not seem to have cottoned on at least, as he and Kitty carried on living at Coleton Fishacre even after the war. Nethway became dilapidated and required too much spending for them to put right. They never moved back into their old mansion, and never divorced.

Back in the thick of it in London, when peace was declared in 1945, the Savoy's sandbags and girders were heaved away and the blast wall dismantled to reveal the Thames once again. Although he was so fond of the Savoy, it would be to Claridge's that Churchill retreated following his election defeat that year. Lady Churchill rang Wontner in some distress to say that they had nowhere to go when they had to leave Downing Street. He went to pick her up in his car, and, to his surprise, she chose Claridge's over the Savoy. All of their boxes started to arrive and there they remained. Half the size and with fewer press events, it was a calmer place to recover as her husband mulled over his defeat in one of the penthouses, often inviting his former cabinet members over to dinner to commiserate.

Claridge's relative distance from Fleet Street compared to the Savoy made it more suitable for dignitaries who were not at the peak of their health or fortunes. Churchill came back to recuperate from illness in later life, as did fellow Conservative prime minister Harold Macmillan, and the Duke of Windsor. It was a short drive to the private hospitals of Harley Street in Mayfair, which made it convenient for recovering from an operation before heading home, as they all did.

Churchill was still at Claridge's in September when victory in the Pacific was announced. He was having dinner with his former ministers when his private secretary brought a note from Attlee to tell him of the surrender of Japan. The dinner party sat listening to the radio for the announcement. One of the guests remembered that 'on a borrowed wireless set in a hired room in Claridge's, Winston heard the end of the war, and I think that there wasn't a single one of his former colleagues who wasn't near to tears at the irony of the situation'. Churchill ended the evening by going out for a walk in the rain on his own.[1]

Having been surplus to requirements in wartime, the Savoy's banqueting department was re-established, hastily preparing for victory dinners, debutante dances, and charity galas. As so many members of old banqueting staff had gone, a young Italian, Paolo Contarini, was brought in to start again.

Contarini had fled Mussolini's Italy with his wife, and had hoped to carry on working in hotels in Britain. Instead, he found work as a translator for prisoners of war on a farm in Suffolk, and delivered its produce. On the farm he read an article about the Savoy and told his wife how much he wanted to work there. She encouraged him to write to Wontner, who replied, but had no budget for more staff at the time. In 1945, Wontner remembered Contarini and his enthusiasm – and Contarini would need it. Wontner often had him working sixteen-to-seventeen-hour days, with one assistant and two clerks, to get the department up and running.

Victory parties were thrown straight away for Field-Marshalls Montgomery, Alexander and Wavell. The Russian Embassy in London was not yet ready, so the Soviet foreign minister, Vyacheslav Molotov, held his caviar and vodka receptions at the Savoy in the meantime. Debutante social-ising had been an integral, lucrative fixture of the calendar before the war, so it was a relief to have them back in earnest. Over the course of a Season, there could be 400 events around the city. With an average guestlist of 200, the minimum cost of a ball at the Savoy was £1,000 (£34,000), so it was vital to get that custom back.

One of many eligible young women to be coaxed out to socialise in public after the war was a twenty-year-old Princess Elizabeth. In 1946, she was first spotted with her husband-to-be, Prince Philip, at a Savoy wedding recep-tion. She was acting as a bridesmaid for her cousin, Captain Andrew Elphinstone, and his wedding was the first time that the entire Royal Family had gathered in public since the war ended.[2] Other than Edward VII, eating out had been unusual for the Royal Family so far during the twentieth century, but they were becoming increasingly relaxed about it.

Throughout the war, journalists had never really left the hotel, where their main haunts were the press office and the American Bar. Propping up the bar from nearby Fleet Street were, editor of the *Daily Express* Arthur Christiansen, *Daily Mail* foreign correspondents Noel Barber and Noel Monks, editor of *The Transatlantic Daily Mail* (an abridged version of the paper for Americans) Don Iddon, and Bertie Gunn, editor of the *Evening Standard*. They were there in some combination every weekday in the 1940s. Women were still not allowed in the Bar as patrons, so the few female journalists that there were had to socialise elsewhere. This was fortunate for Inez Robb, as it turned out, for she happened to be in the foyer when Prince Philip walked in while her male counterparts were in the bar. Few American readers were familiar with the Prince, so, ready with her snippet of what he looked like up close, Robb hurried to her room to type up the details for her nationally syndicated column. Appropriately enough, she called her memoir 'Don't Just Stand There!'

Press attention was, however, a balancing act. If publicity was unwanted, the hotel went to great lengths to maintain privacy. Inside there was a strict 'no photography' policy, unless agreed in advance by the guest, and the dingy side entrance on Savoy Hill that Churchill and other famous people favoured was hard for photographers to use for good pictures, so that was often suggested as an alternative. The press office sent out a stern reminder after Princess Elizabeth's picture was taken outside that, among other things, no details of guests' habits or orders should be made public.

When Princess Elizabeth and Prince Philip married in 1947, the hotel had three kings, four queens and a 'crush of princes, princesses and grand dukes' staying. Just when it was brimming with demanding dignitaries, there was a strike. Five hundred of the catering staff joined in for a fortnight over the sacking of a waiter, Frank Piazza. It was apparently a dispute over whose job it was to carry dirty plates away from the Grill to be washed. However, the Labour government of the time feared 'reds under the beds' were attempting to sabotage the royal wedding. Clement Attlee's Cabinet met three days before to discuss intelligence that Piazza was an Italian Communist and wartime internee who had been planted by the British Revolutionary Communist Party. That the police were criticised for being too brutal in quelling the strike makes sense when, behind the scenes, there was so much panic and political pressure to end it quickly. Nye Bevan, the health minister, warned that Communists might attempt to control London's best hotels using managers who could be open to blackmail about their influential guests.

Communist conspiracy or not, in the end, the future Queen and the soon-to-be Duke of Edinburgh married without a hitch, and their first public engagement together was back at the Savoy for The Pilgrims of Great Britain, an Anglo-American club. Immediate members of the Royal Family were customarily invited, as were American secretaries of state and ambassadors. The club tended to throw parties at the Savoy, and they held a 900-guest dinner for the unveiling of President Franklin Roosevelt's statue in Grosvenor Square. That night it was the first time that the club's all-male dinner had been attended by female guests, with former First Lady Eleanor Roosevelt as guest of honour and the young Queen becoming their patron.

With the hotels doing well, aged seventy, Rupert was feeling energetic enough to join an acclaimed Opera Company tour to America for the first time in years, starting after Christmas 1947. Once he arrived back in London after New York, he was living in his suite every weekday and working down in his office, as usual. On 12 September 1948, a quiet Sunday, he died in his bedroom from a stroke brought on by his hemiplegia, aged seventy-one, in front of Bridget.[3] This left Bridget's only close family now as Lady Dorothy, who she did not see from one year to the next. She was on her own.

A few days later, Bridget made the journey from Paddington to Coleton Fishacre with her father's ashes. Around her, the Harrods undertakers and a coterie of her father's former staff arranged themselves at the tables of the private railway carriage for the five-hour journey. At the other end, a cortège of gleaming black Daimlers took Bridget and her retinue from Totnes Station to the idyll that she had come to dread now that she had no family left. On the narrow, winding lane she passed all the familiar sights: the cherry trees and horse chestnuts, the empty tennis courts, the unruly orchard, and her father's garage, lined with Bentleys. The cortège swept in through the stone pillars by the house and on to the dark granite drive.

Whatever her ambivalent feelings towards them, it must have struck her as poignant to see her parents' garden becoming so overgrown – its fruit putrid, its flowers in disarray, the view of the cover becoming obscured by unkempt trees. The gardening staff had been pruned down from six to one during the war, but there was evidence of their former labours everywhere – their wheelbarrows and rusting tools, their tucked-away sheds, and their greenhouses. Inside the potting shed her parents' planting notebooks, documenting hours of planning, would remain curling at the edges and gathering dust for decades to come.

Bridget, the undertakers and the mourners set off down the slate terrace steps. The long path to the sea through the garden was bordered by herbaceous plants and roses that created a fragrant pastel patchwork even as autumn was closing in. To the right was the Bowling Green Lawn, a myrtle-edged terrace where Bridget and Michael used to play, and to the left the open-ended loggia where Rupert and Dorothy entertained in the summer. The flower beds were aflame, as ever, with the bright salvias and ginger lilies that Rupert had strategically planted where he could see them from his bedroom window.

The house disappeared from sight as the gathering walked down through a series of glades. The sheltered path descended through denser woodland before opening up at the wisteria-covered gazebo that framed an expanse of sea. The only immediate interruption to the endless water was the stubby outcrop of the Eastern Black Rock. Further in the distance on the horizon was the Mewstone, a jagged little island favoured by resting seals, to which the family and their guests had often sailed. Directly below was the quarry, stone from which the house had been built, its scars now covered up with agapanthus and New Zealand flax. Closer to the sea, right on the rocks, was the old bathing pavilion, sunbathing deck and tidal swimming pool, where they had spent so many long afternoons.

The mourners snaked along single file to the far edge of Pudcombe Cove. Rupert had commissioned a mural for the library wall up at the house that showed the bird's eye view of this headland, with annotations for the villages and notable houses. Just visible, like a *Where's Wally?* character, there was a minute depiction of Rupert himself on the map, walking by the sea with his Dalmatians. It was here he came when seeking solace, and it was here that Bridget scattered his ashes.

More than twenty years had now passed since she had turned eighteen and her parents had set life out for her. She was to marry well, to stay at home and raise a family. None of it had worked out. Instead, Bridget was, by no design or desire of her own, one of the most powerful, independent women in the country. It was, in her words, a 'grave and serious moment'.[4] Newspapers speculated that she would stay in Devon, leaving all of the responsibilities to her father's executors and administrators. But she did not stay out of the way. Bridget, by now a slight, solitary forty-year-old, returned to London to take the reins. A frustrated reporter, nosing around the hotel a week after Rupert's death, found that Bridget was 'keeping closely to her own suite of rooms'.[5] 'Many people are anxious to see and talk to her,' the reporter wrote, 'but Miss D'Oyly Carte is avoiding all of them and keeping her own counsel'.[6] On deciding to take her father's place, she became the most important personality in the empire.[7] From reading the minutes of the shareholders' meetings, she sounded almost monarchical. Hardly a meeting went by without obsequious references to her being D'Oyly's granddaughter in the company directors' speeches.

Her first public engagement was Rupert's memorial service at the Savoy Chapel. As at D'Oyly's, the Opera Company sang ballads from the Savoy Operas, and he had Sullivan's hymn, 'Onward, Christian soldiers'. Many of the Chapel's stained-glass windows were destroyed when bombs rained down all around in the Blitz, but one survived entirely unbroken. Depicting a procession of angelic musicians, it was dedicated to the memory of D'Oyly, and Rupert's name was now added alongside it.

Private as he had been, Rupert D'Oyly Carte was never too far from the fans.[8] He had carried on his father's encouragement of those who wanted to try their hand at performing the operas themselves, which resulted in hundreds of amateur productions every year. He had gladly rented out music, scripts and costumes, and fostered connections with fan clubs and operatic societies from Plymouth to Philadelphia. Dr C. H. Budd, a Cambridge physics tutor who had been a regular at the professional performances for the past forty years and spent one whole summer in America following the tour, was in attendance, as were the heads of the largest Gilbert and Sullivan societies. Although, as his *Times* obituary reflected, Rupert D'Oyly Carte's name was a 'household word', as a person he was scarcely known beyond a very small trusted circle.[9]

Bridget smiled tentatively for the press assembled outside the Savoy Chapel. Many accompanying headlines went straight into details of her inheritance, speculating what would become of the hotels and the theatre with only the 'back up' to take over. She was 'triple heir of opera, hotel and fame', trilled one. After a wartime knock to the hotel shares's value, her inherited wealth of £288,500 (£11m)[10] in 1948, came at a time when inherited wealth was in overall decline. In the nineteenth and early twentieth century, Britain's wealthy had been able to pass on vast riches. The economic destruction and inflation of the world wars had undermined many families' amassed assets and investments. Bridget was a rarity in having a windfall at all in 1948, let alone on such a scale.

After Rupert died, Bridget would work on the family archive, some of which ended up at the British Library and some at the Victoria & Albert Museum – when she was not disposing of it in skips or having it burned. She, perhaps jokingly or perhaps not, said that she did not want anyone else to do it in case illegitimate children made an appearance. The Savoy board dismissed any offers for a family biography for fear it would not reflect well on the hotels. The rumours about the Laundry and its contents continued.

Bridget was not confident enough to accept her father's chairmanship of the hotels and she had not really been groomed for it. She became president and vice-chairman, with Wontner as chairman and managing director. They were an indivisible unit for decades. She was also the major shareholder of the hotels, both directly in her own name and indirectly through a set of offshore and onshore trusts, and sole owner of the Opera Company and Theatre and a few smaller companies. One benefit of controlling so many was that she could follow her personal interests. She was not active in the Strand Electricity Company, for example, but she took the chairmanship of the royal florists Edward Goodyear, and of furnishing company James Edwards, in which she had inherited interests.

Bridget's first big set-piece celebration at the hotel, after Princess Elizabeth's wedding had been handled just before her father died, was Elizabeth's coronation in June 1953. When the Conservative MP Henry Channon noted in his diary that there was a 'Gilbert and Sullivan atmosphere' about the pomp and circumstance of the Coronation, it appeared as if the high Victorian aesthetic of the Savoy Operas was now so ingrained in the public imagination that life was imitating art.[11]

Even with rationing still in place, post-war privations did not get in the way of a decadent party. London's biggest hotels – Claridge's, Park Lane, Grosvenor House and the Dorchester – sprang into action. Of all the celebrations that night, the Savoy Coronation Ball was the most expensive. Most hotels were charging seven guineas (£192). The Savoy was asking twelve (£329), with the profit going to charity.[12] For Bridget's ball committee, she called on Laurence Olivier and Vivien Leigh, now fifteen years into their difficult marriage, Noël Coward, and photographer Cecil Beaton. Coward and Olivier presided over the cabaret, while Beaton and Leigh advised on the decorations, with the theme of a 'New Elizabethan era'.

The 1,400 tickets were offered by invitation only. Despite being double the price of any other ball, there was an extensive waiting list. Guests Prince and Princess Takeda of Japan, twelve Indian princes, Prince Axel of Denmark and the Prime Minister of Australia, Sir Robert Menzies, had been to the Westminster Abbey service itself – as had the Beefeaters who lined the riverside entrance to the hotel to welcome them. Churchill turned up arm-in-arm with the Pasha of Marrakech, whom he had met on holiday, as his guest. A newspaper gushed the next day, 'The Savoy was the centre of the world last night.'[13]

Its floodlit white riverside façade was decorated with garlands, ribbons and flags. Inside, every public room was given a Tudor makeover. Gathered white velvet curtains were made to look like ermine using black felt tails. The Restaurant housed a domed marquee of 4,000 yards of pink, grey and turquoise silk and muslin. There were historic standards lining the halls, 200 Prince of Wales ostrich feather plumes behind the lights, 300 bay and camellia trees and 2.5 tonnes of box hedging.

It took twenty men thirty-six hours to assemble. Guests were showered with thousands of Tudor-style hats, ruffs, jester sticks and whistles at dinner.[14]

Head chef Laplanche's starter was 'Le Zephyr de Foie Gras au Clicquot', with a main course of 'La Noisette d'Agneau Coronation with la Pomme Comtesse', before puddings with the bonus ration of 1lb of sugar and 4oz margarine, made available for the occasion by the Ministry of Food. The guests would need sustenance, as the first cabaret did not start until midnight, with the second at 2 a.m. The cabaret was led by Coward, Olivier, Bing Crosby, and French singer Maurice Chevalier. By the early hours, guests had collectively worked their way through 5,000 bottles of Perrier-Jouët champagne, followed by Bordeaux, Burgundy, sherry and port. When it was finally time to roll into bed, a suite overlooking the river cost £7 and 7 shillings (£192).[15]

The most surprising seal of approval for the night came from Marie Ritz, César's elderly widow. She came on her last visit to London to reminisce with the oldest employees. Finding herself in similarly isolated circumstances to Bridget, she had been living at The Ritz in Paris for the past forty years. By now she was eighty-seven and remained entirely glamorous and poised. She posed for group photographs with kitchen staff in her pearl choker, floor-length black dress, and white fur shrug, sitting next to Laplanche.

The Savoy board threw a dinner party for her in Pinafore, Churchill's favourite. It was a gathering of widows of a venerable vintage, with Lady Reeves-Smith and Madame Schwenter, whose husband had been an assistant manager at the Savoy and most recently manager of the Hotel Meurice in Paris. Marie was moved to see two members of staff again from the first years of the hotel.[16] Harry Williams and James Townsend had started as pageboys when they were teenagers. Townsend was now head of the Gentleman's Cloakrooms and prided himself on knowing regulars well enough not to issue tickets. Williams was still working at the hotel when he celebrated his eightieth birthday. After a while, like a couple celebrating too many wedding anniversaries, the management ran out of gifts to celebrate the milestones of long-standing careers. Harry Williams enjoyed various company shares, champagne, flowers, and honorary dinners in various combinations as one decade after another went by.

Far from retiring to Coleton Fishacre, Bridget barely ventured there on her own and sold it, to a car salesman from Hampstead. She bought a new hideaway in Buckinghamshire that was closer to work. As at Coleton, it was hidden, accessible only through a densely forested drive. Set in a clearing, Shrubs Wood was a modernist house of pure white lines and minimal decoration. Its architecture was alien to 1940s Buckinghamshire, but it suited Bridget. Unadorned on the outside and spartan inside, it was a very literal clean slate. As one of only two residential properties that designers Erich Mendelsohn and Serge Chermayeff built in Britain, it was a design connoisseur's choice. Although it did not have its own expansive headland, as in Devon, there was the same air of being a remote world of its own. Its acres of grounds allowed her to pursue her love of gardening in solitude, for which she remained formally dressed, often in work outfits that were beyond repair. She would do the weeding in one of her threadbare woollen skirts and a frayed silk blouse. Rather than hosting flashy philanthropy at the Savoy, she organised summer parties and Easter-egg hunts for disadvantaged children in her garden.

She did not enjoy her father's money in the way that he had enjoyed his own father's money. Rupert had no hang-ups about spending on fast cars, fine art, antiques, holidays or yachts. By contrast, Bridget seemed far less comfortable, perhaps because the reason that she inherited so much was the early death of her brother. It caused her to live far below her means, to work to the point of exhaustion, and gave her a recurring impulse to do good in some nebulous way. Charitable and hard-working as they could be, Rupert, and of course D'Oyly, had not been encumbered with this Lenten streak. No one on either side of her family was restrained in pursuing all of the pleasure that money could offer. Into old age she still referred to her wealth as her 'father's money', and she felt compelled to spend it on what she could justify.

This is not to say that Bridget was living in any aesthetic hardship. In keeping with her character, the hints of wealth at home were subtle, including the built-in buttons under the tables to summon her live-in housekeeper and gardener, Frances and Fred, whom she brought from Devon. Her parents' belongings, which arrived from the house, would mainly stay in their boxes until they were opened by her own beneficiaries.

At work she pushed herself and expected high standards from the staff, with plenty of structure, formality and tradition. She stuck rigidly to surnames, shied away from any emotional conversation topics, and appreciated plain speaking. Not that she would have wanted to hear it, but the staff felt sorry for her, perceiving her as anxious and lonely. Behind her occasional imperiousness and sharp tongue, they recognised that there was a warm heart and plenty of thoughtfulness. Unprompted, she used to cut flowers from her garden to give to staff in the office, and when a visitor expressed admiration for a belonging of hers, as with Rupert, it often elicited a brisk insistence that they should have it.

Much as she liked to relax in her caravan tucked at the back of her immense garden, far from the Savoy, she made full use of the hotel's myriad services. On the weekend she would call out its handymen to Shrubs Wood. Floor plans of her house were kept in their office, so that they were familiar with the layout before arrival. She would get the Opera Company wardrobe mistress to make her clothes, which were then repaired by its seamstresses. Her office uniform was a skirt suit made from fabric that she bought in Covent Garden with a silk shirt underneath. Even though she was modest in many ways, her lack of domesticity was one of the signs of the privileged life that she had always led. Since birth she had had a retinue of people to look after her. She could not boil an egg or sew a button, because she had never had to, and she had no interest in finding out how.

Having finished work on a Friday, Frederic Lloyd, a general manager of the Opera Company, would give her a lift to Marylebone Station on his way home to St John's Wood. At the other end in Buckinghamshire, Fred would collect her from the station. Unlike the party house that her parents presided over at Coleton Fishacre, invitations to Shrubs Wood were few. They tended to be for friends whom she met through work, including the furniture designer Luciano Ercolini of Ercol, Eleanor Evans, who performed in the Opera Company chorus, and prime minister Harold Wilson, whom she invited to become a trustee of the Opera Company as he was such a fan.

During the working week, Bridget inhabited her father's old rooms. Around her the hotel was full of life and making a record profit, but at the heart of it was a shy middle-aged divorcée who rarely left her suite. Night after night, the Ballroom, Grill and Restaurant downstairs were bustling with guests falling in and out of love, and Bridget was up in her room. As she was so eligible and yet unmarried for so long, there was almost inevitable speculation that she was a lesbian. A few hopeful women were disappointed to discover that this was not the case. Bridget would never be a wife again, but she was a mistress for some years, leaving her the classic mistress's fate of being alone most of the time, in particular on weekends and holidays. Bridget's friends know with whom she had an affair, but say that she would not want it to be public knowledge. Staff tended to assume that she just never had anyone. As one of Wontner's sons put it, 'one knew not to ask'.[17]

In 1953, Bridget engaged a director of productions at the Opera Company, who was a little younger than her, Robert Gibson. She had a 'sparkle in her eye' when she talked about him and the attraction did not go unnoticed around the office.[18] He had worked for Rupert before, but she persuaded him to return from his post as the first British stage manager of Radio City Hall in New York. Gibson directed a revival of *Princess Ida*, based on a Victorian Gothic conception, at the Savoy Theatre, and it involved the two of them working closely together, spending hours discussing costumes, sets and casting. Wontner worried that they were too friendly. In 1956, as one Opera Company member put it, Gibson 'left as mysteriously as he arrived'.[19] No sooner had he headed home for America than Bridget flew out for a visit. Wontner was panicked enough to fly out there in order to retrieve her, fearing that she was planning to ditch her fiefdom on the Strand for Gibson. Wontner need not have worried, it seemed. Gibson became a parish priest in North Carolina, and died, having never married, in a home for retired priests in Texas.

Many of the staff felt, and still feel, protective towards Bridget and disliked the amount of control that Wontner appeared to have over her, and regarding that incident in particular. On balance, one of the Opera Company's general managers, Peter Riley, believed that, 'demanding' as Wontner was with her, he respected and loved her. Supremely well-connected as Wontner was, Riley could not imagine him having a friend as such. In so far as Wontner did, it sounded as though that was Bridget. It is no surprise, given that they built their working and social lives around each other. As Wontner's granddaughter reflected, 'the hotel was his life'.[20] During the week, Bridget lived at the Savoy and Wontner lived at Claridge's, and at the weekends they were just as close, as their houses were only ten minutes' drive apart. In the 1970s, she would become all the more withdrawn in her spare time as the tenant of semi-ruined Barscobe Castle, a small seventeenth-century fortified keep in south-west Scotland, which Wontner owned and she restored for him. As with Reeves-Smith before him, he accumulated a great deal of personal wealth, affording estates and houses in London, Buckinghamshire and Scotland.

Wontner and Bridget had a profound dedication in common that seeped into their social life and their free time. They were two veteran defenders of a unique grand hotel: two romantics fixated on an ideal. A ruthless, urbane fixer, Wontner was grand and courtly in his manner, and fastidious. He was William Cecil to Bridget's Elizabeth I. Bridget cherished his strategising, and gift for understanding her taste and pre-empting her wants. He knew when to impress her with a plan and when to alleviate work by making her laugh. His critics loathed his seemingly unshakeable sense of superiority, regarding both himself and the hotels.

His parents, Arthur and Rose Wontner, had been actors, and his father's best-known role was as Sherlock Holmes for the BBC. He valued his upbringing, which he believed set him up well for managing the Savoy. From a young age he was taught to lift his hat to women, to stand bolt upright and to speak the Queen's English with clear diction. His vocal training meant that when he said 'very' it rhymed with 'beret'. Bridget spoke in a similarly measured, deliberate way.

He was a naturally sociable man. As with Ritz before him, both men were in their element when hobnobbing. When Wontner was at the 'emerging from the chrysalis stage', as he described his adolescence, he thought that he might like to be a diplomat. His reasoning reveals what he loved about being an hotelier: 'I had a picture of gliding about over a parquet floor, and saying "hello madame so-and-so, how nice to see you". I hadn't the foggiest idea what diplomacy was actually about but it seemed like a nice life.'[21] Diplomacy's loss was hospitality's gain. He loved the kudos of the place. As he said about himself and other staff in a rare modest moment: 'there's a certain amount of glamour, which everybody knows, and those of us within the company know it even better because most of us are nobodies and we all become somebodies'.[22]

Wontner had such an imaginative way of speaking that, when asked in an interview about his age, his answer was: 'I was born under the sign of Libra in the Edwardian era. Queen Victoria had died seven years before I entered this life and therefore Edward VII was on the throne and there were six years yet before Europe was involved in the Great War, so it was in, what I imagine, was a relatively happy and stable period of time in England.' The interviewer thinks for a moment on the recording, and ventures 'so that would be 1908?'.[23]

He had not performed well at his boarding school, Oundle, having found it too intellectual. After a stint learning French and working at the London Chamber of Commerce, he remained unsure what to do. He happened to see a job advertised for the general secretary of the Hotels and Restaurants Association of Great Britain and fancied the salary. He wrote in brown ink – 'a quirk of mine' – to Reeves-Smith, who was chairman of the association at the time, as well as being the Savoy managing director.

When the association placed the advertisement, 835 applicants threw their top hats in the ring, Wontner's brown ink application among them. After a long wait, he was called in to meet Reeves-Smith. The older man asked, 'Have you ever thought what a strange thing chance is?' Wontner said that he had not, and asked why the question. To save time, Reeves-Smith had all the applications sent to a law firm to be whittled down first. They selected fifty applications and Wontner's was not among them. Reeves-Smith started ploughing through the pile and found them all 'rather tedious'. He grew so bored that he asked his secretary to start from scratch with reading the rejected applications. Miss Barnett picked out Wontner's, and two interviews later he was given the job. 'If I were you,' said Reeves-Smith, 'I should send her flowers.' Wontner did, and Miss Barnett spent the rest of her career working for him.

Unfortunately for Bridget, at the Opera Company there was no Wontner, but she at least had inherited Rupert's long-serving private secretary. On taking charge, she wrote, 'I did not feel in the least qualified to sustain the responsibility with which I was faced. That I was able to carry on [. . .] was largely due to the staff that surrounded me; particularly my father's private secretary, Stanley Parker, affectionately known to us as "Pickwick", on account of his jovial and portly figure, who gave me the most heart-warming and highly dictatorial support and in so doing the strength to grapple with problems that were new to me.'[24] The 'dictatorial support' that she mentioned was a familiar theme with her inherited staff. Even if she was doubtful of her own abilities, she proved dedicated. As with her father and grandfather, she was both a diligent day-to-day manager for whom no detail was too small and a figurehead who inspired loyalty.

She oversaw the theatrical and hotel operations every day from Rupert's old office, surrounded by furniture that no longer passed muster in the main hotel. As his office, it had been neat and contemporary; as her office, it became a jumble of re-covered armchairs, of scuffed desks and armoires. It looked increasingly dated as Rupert's decoration was not replaced. The only new personal touch was the framed photograph of him looming down from the wall behind the desk. Just at the end of the corridor was one of the most opulent hotels in the world. In its offices, there was no carpet but plenty of dust. With the windows open, they were noisy in the afternoon as the sound of the band rehearsing in the Restaurant drifted up and the clattering of washing-up and cooking came from the kitchens. Bridget's staff in next-door rooms found themselves seated on cast-off padded white brocade chairs from the private dining rooms.

Other decommissioned hotel furniture would end up in the annual spring sale, which offered staff the chance to shop for £1 per item. As there were three separate china services of tens of thousands of pieces, the sale would have been well-stocked from crockery alone. Wedgwood was commissioned for room service, Royal Doulton for the Restaurant, and Royal Worcester for the private dining rooms. The Royal Worcester was of most interest, as it had four designs that depicted different Savoy Operas: *The Mikado, Iolanthe, Pinafore* and *The Gondoliers*.[25] Along the corridor from Bridget, the boardroom was a little smarter than the offices, but so resolutely old-fashioned that, when microphones were introduced for meetings, they were strategically hidden behind voluminous flower arrangements to avoid any technological intrusion.

Upstairs from her unassuming office, during the week Bridget was resident in her father's rooms, 318–9, which had views across the Thames to the new National Theatre, with room 317 as her private study. A few doors down, 312, was Oscar-winning actor Gregory Peck's favourite room, and above was 412, Humphrey Bogart's favourite, and previously that of Coco Chanel. While 312 and 412, and all of the other suites around Bridget's, were fussed over and updated, hers was left unmodernised, and she insisted on paying rent, unlike her fellow company directors, who enjoyed permanent free suites. After breakfast in bed with *The Times*, and ablutions in her antiquated bathroom, Bridget would go for a stroll early in the morning around Covent Garden in her fur coat for her first cigarettes of the day – the beginning of eighty before bedtime. Her father and grandfather had smoked cigars, cigarettes or pipes for different occasions, but she did not deviate. She smoked Du Maurier cigarettes religiously. As they were launched in 1930 by Savoy regular Gerald Du Maurier, they had been fashionable for a twenty-two-year-old to smoke at the time, and she remained loyal to that brand of her youth.

Her cigarettes were a constant feature and the boardroom was thick with smoke after she had been in. Every so often, there was a senior management meeting at Claridge's, and one nearly every day at the Savoy. Under the boardroom table a wastepaper basket was always tactfully positioned by her chair. Into it went the contents of her ashtray, her cigarette boxes and the elaborate origami creations that she folded from the boxes and then discarded. These meetings gave her plenty of time to perfect her technique. One castle that she fashioned from the torn packets, with a file paper moat, was so precise that the person tidying up found it a shame to throw it away.

Whether the working week or the weekend, she was always conservatively dressed, her hair neatly curled, and her face made up with a little red lipstick and a dusting of loose powder. She carried a silk scarf, which she would fidget with, moving it from around her neck to a buttonhole, to the handle of her handbag, through the day. It acted as a scaled-down comfort blanket that she would twist when nervous. If it was not the scarf, she would be fiddling with her rings. Her beaded necklaces had to be restrung whenever she had agitated them until they broke. Even in the late evenings in her suite, she remained smartly dressed, smoking by the window overlooking the river. To relax she would read *Punch* magazine, the *Times Literary Supplement* or occasionally the works of Carl Jung, and drink whiskey and stayed in her suit until bedtime.

As a breather away from her office in the bowels of the hotel, in the daytime Bridget would take elevenses and high tea up in her suite, picking at the broken biscuits that were not presentable for the guests, and smoking, of course. Towards the end of the working day, she would stay to talk in the offices, but never sitting down, just standing in the doorway, swinging her handbag behind her back, before going up to her room.

EIGHTEEN

Static in the swinging sixties

'Fashion changes, but style endures'
Coco Chanel

With Bridget and Wontner at the helm, there was no acknow-ledgement in the hotel interiors, the food, or the drink that London was the 'swinging city' of the world in the 1960s. Unlike D'Oyly and Rupert, Bridget was a person preserved in aspic. Although she was shy conversationally around many people, she was sure enough of her own taste not to adapt to anyone else's. One of her secretaries reminisced that she was like a cross between Miss Marple and the Queen.

Accordingly, the strict Restaurant dress code and French haute cuisine were immovable features. Escoffier's obituary in *The Times* remarked that he had 'made history' at the Savoy.[1] At the Savoy itself, Escoffier did not feel like history at all – even sixty years after his tenure, his influence pervaded. Rupert's last major appointment had been Laplanche, the head chef from 1946 to 1965. While Latry had been an admirer of Escoffier and they had become friends, Laplanche had actually worked for him, making Escoffier's influence keenly felt into the 1960s. London, by this time, was more of a bastion of

French classical cooking than France itself, where times had moved on. Apprentice cooks, of any nationality, who were interested in Escoffier-style cuisine, were coming to London to learn its methods.[2]

James Walsh joined the Savoy as a nineteen-year-old commis chef in 1965. When he arrived he found the formal atmosphere in the kitchen 'intimidating' and stifling. As he explained: 'Everything had to be done by the book. The guests knew how to eat. They would order things that had to be looked up in the repertoire to know what they were.'[3] As with the Opera Company, it would be easy to criticise a lack of innovation with the 'by the book' approach. But when fans were so attached to the status quo, it was tempting not to change – and when you wrote 'the book' in any case, it made even more sense.

Although they are often lumped together, there were, in fact, two kitchens – one for the Restaurant, and one for the Grill Room, which was the floor below. The Restaurant kitchen was the more prestigious, as it provided for the banquets and expensive cabaret dinners. When Laplanche retired, the chef of the Grill, Silvino Trompetto, was promoted to the Restaurant. He had not been the first choice. A French chef had been brought in but had a heart attack within weeks. Trompetto was hastily drafted in from the Grill, and managed to stay put.

In Trompetto, the Savoy had its first British-born head chef and first native English speaker, but French was so entrenched in the kitchen, it remained the lingua franca nevertheless.[4] At the Grill the menu was still the comforting British food of a Victorian gentlemen's club, which meant plenty of roast beef and Yorkshire pudding, bread-and-butter pudding, and endless sponges. At the Restaurant, the fare remained fussily French, with the odd nod to other exotic cuisines.

The kitchens themselves had scarcely seen any modifications since Escoffier's 1890s specifications either. Even his copper pots and pans were kept on display. As D'Oyly had wanted, the acrimony between them was never alluded to and Escoffier's achievements were claimed as the Savoy's own. Walsh, the new commis chef, recalled that the kitchens were 'huge, cavernous and very noisy [. . .] some of the stoves were still run on coal and the place was always very hot. It was like the engine room of the *Titanic* that we see in the pictures.'[5] As with the other head chefs before him, Trompetto had a cubbyhole of an office, which looked out over vast banks of ovens. If Trompetto was receiving visitors, he would often take them to his office for a glass of champagne to cool down and chat in relative calm, with one eye on his chefs through the window.

Responsible for roughly 2,000 meals a day, Trompetto would drive in for the lunch service from his house in St John's Wood and go home for a rest in the afternoon, then be back in again for dinner preparations from 5 p.m. When a young Prue Leith came to London in 1960, looking for work as a chef, she found that smart hotels and restaurants never hired women. She recalled the rejection from Trompetto above all others: 'Over my dead body. They will distract the young men. And they cannot lift a stock-pot.' Then the killer blow: 'At a certain time of the month, they will curdle the mayonnaise.'[6]

Front of house, one of the last great managers of the post-war years was Beverley Griffin, who followed on from Hofflin. Front-hall staff recalled that Griffin created a little tension whenever he walked in: they found themselves standing a little straighter. He wore a tailcoat and starched collar for work every day, which was standard attire for all front-desk staff. Those on the day shift would be in morning suits from 9 a.m. Then, on the evening shift, it would be dinner jackets from

5.30 p.m. until 11 p.m. The only deviation would be white tie for an occasion such as a royal wedding or New Year's Eve.

Griffin oversaw 1,300 staff, including the cabaret at the Restaurant, the ever popular Grill, and the American Bar. To please the demanding clientele called for a well-oiled operation. He was hospitable but serious-minded. He did not enjoy drinking himself, which could be tricky. Whenever he was called upon to have a drink with a guest, he would ask his secretary to order a 'Dubonnet' ahead at the American Bar. It was, in fact, cold tea.

The slick, traditional set-up kept the regulars coming back. Agatha Christie, then in her sixties, held court at the Restaurant on trips to London from Devon, and threw parties there for the opening nights of her plays in the West End. As it happened, her home, Greenway, was just a few miles further inland on the River Dart from Coleton Fishacre, with a familiar sweep of woods down to the water. In 1958, Christie had been in the Restaurant with a thousand guests to celebrate *The Mousetrap*, which is still going, becoming the longest-running play in British history. In the tradition of the hotel's well-publicised press events, a hunched but redoubtable Dame Agatha can be seen in photographs wielding a dangerous-looking knife to cut the cake that weighed half a tonne, surrounded by reporters. Running the length of a small dining table, the cake was embedded with roses and ferns along the sides, with sugar mice and a huge icing trap on top.[7] Outlandish cakes were a speciality. When it came to the premiere for Elizabeth Taylor and Richard Burton's *Cleopatra* in 1963, the pyramid-shaped confection was so spectacular that it merited description in the *Encyclopaedia Britannica*.

Charlie Chaplin, who stayed annually from 1952 until he died in 1977, moved in for three months when he felt unwelcome in America, his adoptive home, because of the

Un-American Activities Committee. Due to the Committee's heavy-handed search for communists working in Hollywood, Chaplin would have been questioned had he returned. So he, his wife Oona, and their four children lived at the hotel while they arranged to move to Switzerland. As female guests were not allowed into the Bar, Oona was often seen waiting around for Charlie outside while he had a few martinis before dinner.

A note from Field-Marshal Montgomery in February 1962, to a Miss Baird, showed that he knew the form well. Montgomery wrote to her: 'I am all "set" for the dinner at the Savoy Hotel on Tuesday March 13 next'. He asks Miss Baird to let him know further details: '1. Time I should arrive? 2. Do I use Embankment Entrance? 3. Dress: dinner jacket I presume?'[8] Montgomery presumed right. There was no relaxation to the dress code until the late 1960s, when women were allowed to wear smart trousers – as long as they were not tight.

As it happened, such strictures did no harm. Despite resolutely not moving with the times, the Savoy attracted the new sixties 'popocracy' of actors, models and musicians all the same. In the way that it had hosted opera singers and stage actors in D'Oyly's day, in Bridget's, it was pop stars and Hollywood actresses. The most fashionable figures of the day made an appearance, apparently unworried that it still was Tournedos Rossini and duck à l'orange on the menu, and that the Thames Foyer was decorated with wingback chairs, *trompe l'œil* screens and walnut side tables. The Beatles, Rolling Stones and Bob Dylan stayed alongside Hollywood royalty Katherine Hepburn, Marlon Brando, Cary Grant and Jane Fonda. Audrey Hepburn was in town for the premiere of *My Fair Lady*, and Ronald Reagan, then an actor a long way from the White House, came for film festivals. Judy Garland, who had been staying since she was a child star, returned with her own children for family holidays. Set in its ways as it was, the hotel was buzzing.

Taking the lead from Rupert, the hotel did not advertise directly, but the in-house press office kept the name in the news through its contacts with journalists. All mentions in newspapers and magazines were assiduously kept in leather-bound cuttings books. As the head of publicity optimistically explained to a new recruit: 'The mother who reads that the Duchess of So-and-So has chosen the Savoy for her daughter's coming-out ball may very well come to us for her own daughter's party. The American who reads that businessmen, stars and politicians from the States have stayed at the Savoy may cable us for a booking too.'[9] So, on the publicity work went.

With the Lancaster Ballroom, the hotel was primed for the all-important American stars to make it their one-stop shop for promoting plays and films with press conferences, junkets, interviews and premieres. When Marilyn Monroe gave her first conference in Britain for *The Prince and the Showgirl*, the journalists from Fleet Street went into overdrive. She was photographed drinking tea wearing a dress with a transparent midriff, considered extremely daring for the time. As a recognisable backdrop, celebrities were often happy to pose around the hotel to signal their arrival in town, which created an exhibition's worth of important people of the day. The hotel's largely black-and-white collection is reminiscent of fashion photographer David Bailey's *Box of Pin Ups* for its famous faces. As the 1960s was the boom decade of nascent celebrity culture, much of that is in evidence in the picture archives.

A number of big-hitting authors held the British leg of international book tours there, awaiting interviews and photo shoots in the private dining rooms. Muhammed Ali held a packed press conference in the Ballroom for his autobiography.

Dr Martin Luther King Junior came to discuss his book on the Civil Rights Movement, *Why We Can't Wait*. Harold Robbins, largely forgotten now but the EL James of his day, had all his interviews organised by the hotel press office. By the time that Robbins arrived to push his latest racy novel after a stroke, he was not easily able to leave his suite, so conducted most promotion work from there. Dependent on an oxygen bottle because of his emphysema, he kept it hidden under the bed covers during interviews. He continued writing to fund his lifestyle, and it was for that he hauled himself from California to the Savoy to sell yet another bonkbuster.

The hotel's theatrical connections meant that it hosted a whirl of opening-night parties and awards ceremonies, which by the 1960s were becoming bigger business than the debutante balls. The Savoy scored a coup in hosting the first Baftas in the Ballroom, which, unlike today's marathon ceremonies, conferred only seven awards and kept the programme snappy, leaving the dinner as a much larger feature than the speeches.

As the banqueting department was a powerhouse of 3,000 private events a year, the range of guests passing through was immense.[10] As with many of the staff, for Walsh, the commis chef, one of many sources of pride and excitement was the guests. As he reminisced: 'the list of famous people who stayed is mind boggling'.[11] At the Restaurant that Walsh was cooking for, the year-round programme of entertainment was drawing in big names too. Patricia Kirkwood became the first woman to host her own BBC show, having caught attention in the cabaret. She had just enjoyed a sold-out three-month acclaimed residency at the Desert Inn in Las Vegas when the Savoy offered her the chance to replicate her success in London. Before that, as an eighteen-year-old, she had first found fame in wartime, for singing Cole Porter's *My Heart Belongs to Daddy*. Not only did diners want to enjoy her singing in the cabaret, no doubt many could not resist coming to see for themselves the soubrette who had inspired such fury in the late George VI. It was rumoured that Prince Philip, then not long married to the Princess Elizabeth, had a fling with Kirkwood, after he was introduced in her dressing room. Rumours persisted for many years and Kirkwood complained that the Prince was not doing enough to quell them: 'A lady is not normally expected to defend her honour publicly. It is the gentleman who should do that,' she complained.[12] She denied any impropriety, but did say: 'He was so full of life and energy. I suspect he felt trapped and rarely got a chance to be himself. I think I got off on the right foot because I made him laugh.'[13]

The Opera Company did sterling work in booking singers for the hotel cabaret at the height of their fame. Petula Clark was in residence for a month, having recently had a number one with 'Downtown'. The soigné singer Françoise Hardy had just released 'Tous Les Garçons et Les Filles' when she arrived to find a white grand piano waiting in her private living room, so that she could practise in seclusion. Dionne Warwick had her hits 'Do You Know The Way to San José?' and 'Walk on By' when she performed there in 1965. As the management was adamant that the dress code should apply to all guests, however famous they were, Warwick had to threaten to pull the plug on the whole show to get her friends in. She had invited The Beatles to 'come on over and hang out', only to find that the maître d' would not allow them in on the grounds that they were 'not properly dressed'. Warwick lost her temper: 'I went a little bit on the ballistic side. I said, "Well, guess what. These are my friends. If they're not allowed in, I'm not going on." They got front-row seats [. . .] Everybody was looking at them a little peculiarly, but, hey, they were The Beatles, come on!'[14]

As well as established stars, the cabaret booked the occasional newcomer. Brian Epstein, the manager whom twenty-three-year-old Cilla Black shared with The Beatles, secured three weeks for her in 1968, the last show of which was televised.[15] She appeared in a tiny floral minidress and an elfin haircut in *Cilla at the Savoy*. Harking back to the mass appeal of the Savoy Orpheans broadcasts of the 1920s, it achieved one of the largest audiences of the decade. Although Black had two number-one singles, it seemed as though Epstein's hunch that she would be an even bigger star on television was right. After the cabaret, she was offered her own BBC series, which ran for eight years.

Comparing guests' outfits and poses in just a decade, the difference is striking. In the 1950s, the hotel's pictures are of Ava Gardner and Ingrid Bergman looking composed and demure in calf-length, long-sleeved dresses, and Margot Fonteyn in her pearls and sensible ballerina bun. By 1965, Sophia Loren, in town to promote a film with Charlie Chaplin, was posing for pictures smoking and drinking in a sheer mesh top, made-up with sweeps of black eyeliner, and Bond girl Ursula Andress made an entrance in a sequined mini dress with a plunging neckline, with photographers thronging outside with their bulky flashbulb cameras. When Mae West 'sailed in like a galleon, blazing with jewels, a thick bracelet shackled to her wrist' to keep this impact up for her stay her luggage included '150 dresses and 60 pairs of shoes with six-inch wedge heels'.[16] Completely uncourted, the sexual revolution had even hit the Savoy. Paolo Contarini, the head of banqueting, complained in a company meeting that the hotel should not change for 'the debauchees of the permissive society' – but they came to stay anyway. The women's hemlines were getting shorter and shorter, and the men's hair was getting longer and longer. Bob Dylan was pictured smoking in his sunglasses, slumped against a radiator, looking so dishevelled that no one would have a hope of getting him into a dinner jacket. He immortalised an unlikely corner by filming the 'Subterranean Homesick Blues' video in the alleyway by the kitchens. Despite the influx of 'debauchees', the dress code for the Restaurant stayed in place. Dylan was turned away for not wearing a tie, and the Rolling Stones had the same short shrift.

In direct contrast were the fashion shows, held a decade apart, by designers Christian Dior and Valentino in the Ballroom. A popular success in 1950 had been Dior's British catwalk debut, when more than 4,000 fashion connoisseurs applied for the 500 tickets. The show was so well-received that the Queen Mother requested a private viewing the next morning for the rest of the Royal Family. Her daughter, Princess Margaret, became a lifelong fan. The show gave Dior the confidence to open his business up in London two years later. With him there was barely a calf, let alone a thigh on show, and the man himself turned up in a crisp suit.

In the 1960s, a young Valentino caused a similar stir with his debut at the hotel. By then the trend for tiny hemlines was clear, and Valentino posed with the *de rigeur* cigarette of a 1960s celebrity, luxuriant hair down to his shoulders, wearing a swirly silk scarf and a patterned velvet jacket. The two shows and how the designers themselves were dressed was a neat demonstration of how times had changed, and quite how quickly.

A brand-new post-war crowd to arrive were the Greek shipping tycoons. They had made their money when they started buying up American military freight boats at discounted prices. They were banking on oil transportation by sea becoming a growth business, and they were right. By the late 1960s, when a military dictatorship ran Greece, they were its titans. The richest of them all, Costas Lemos, who left his children £1 billion, preferred to stay at Claridge's over the Savoy, as a 'home from home for low-profile aristocrats and publicity-shy multimillionaires'.[17] He kept a permanent suite there, alongside his houses in New York and Athens. Lemos was overshadowed, however, by two others.

For all Lemos' fortune, Aristotle Onassis and Stavros Niarchos made a greater impression in London. They competed over the size of their fleets, the beauty of their women and the lavishness of their lives. They engaged in one alpha male stand-off after another, one of which regarded whose patch the Savoy was. Onassis had been staying since he was twenty-five, when he spent six months living at the hotel while doing an apprenticeship with another Greek shipowner in London. Niarchos was a more recent arrival. Rivalry between the two men reached such a pitch that, when Onassis' biographer broached the necessary subject of Niarchos for their book, Onassis left the room, slamming the door so hard that the author expected never to see him again.

Onassis could often be seen in a better mood at the Savoy in his dinner jacket, smoking cigars with his friend Winston Churchill. They had met in the south of France when Winston's son, Randolph, who used to stay on Onassis' yacht *Christina*, introduced them. Then both Randolph and Winston would stay with Onassis, not always harmoniously. Winston's secretary, Anthony Montague Browne, recorded an incident on board in 1963, in which Randolph 'erupted like Stromboli', shouting abuse at his aged father. Randolph accused him of having connived with his first wife, Pamela, to whom Winston was very close, to conceal her affair with Averell Harriman, 48th Governor of New York. Browne wrote: 'I had previously discounted the tales I had heard of Randolph. Now I believed them all.'[18] Winston, too old to argue back, was shaking with rage, so much so that it was feared he might have another stroke. He made it clear that he wanted his son off the yacht. Onassis diplomatically got rid of Randolph by arranging an interview with the King of Greece, to assist Randolph's fledgling journalism career. As they grew ever fonder of each other, Winston invited Onassis, one of very few outside the Establishment, to join the Other Club. The other members were extremely surprised.

For Onassis, being a member of such a select British club was a considerable thrill. He was aware that he was richer than Croesus but short on refinement. As he told his biographer with a rueful smile, 'they say I have no class'. He reflected: 'fortunately even the most powerful people in the world are now willing to overlook this flaw because I am very rich. I learnt early in life that you can't buy class, but you can buy tolerance for its absence. I've been buying that tolerance nearly all my life.'[19]

Not only did attending the Other Club at the Savoy ease Onassis' insecurities, it had the supreme benefit of encroaching on his nemesis's turf. Onassis grew up reading Greek myths, to which he attributed his love of revenge. To a lesser extent his target was Robert Kennedy, brother of President Kennedy, whom he believed had scuppered a deal that he wanted in Saudi Arabia, and he never forgot it. To a much larger extent he rounded on Stavros Niarchos. Niarchos loved the Savoy and Claridge's, and his untouchable level of wealth made him an ideal, tame large shareholder for Bridget and Wontner, and he had been duly invited. They were looking for fans who were far too rich to fuss about dividends or encourage changes. Onassis had his Other Club membership, Niarchos had his say, if largely unexercised, on how the whole place was run.

It would have been awkward for Churchill to be friendly with Niarchos, despite moving in the same circles, not only because of the Onassis rivalry but because of Randolph. At the start of the Second World War, Randolph had been on a proposal binge. Winston and his wife Clementine had hoped that marriage would steady their drunken, womanising, impetuous son. One of the women, Pamela, had agreed on their first date. Despite Randolph reading aloud excerpts from Edward Gibbon's *Decline and Fall of the Roman Empire* on their wedding night, she became pregnant with his only child, Winston. As he intended, he had secured an heir before he left for military service in Egypt.

It was not long before Randolph and Pamela were each having multiple affairs, and divorce became the looming conclusion. One of her first ports of call was Claridge's, where she found William Paley, the owner of the American network CBS. Lady Mary Dunn, a mutual friend of both Pamela's and Randolph's, who was attracted to Paley herself, found a visit to his suite while Pamela was there in 1944 awkward. Lady Mary noted Pamela's 'very proprietary' manner towards Paley. 'I was filled with jealousy,' recalled Lady Mary, who left the couple feeling 'sour as a bit of old rhubarb'.[20] Pamela later stopped off at Claridge's to get acquainted with Paley's head of European news, Edward Murrow, who became a news anchor familiar to millions of Americans. During the war he had coined the catchphrase 'goodnight and good luck', when ending his reports of the Blitz. By the time of the Yalta peace conference to negotiate the end of the war in 1945, three of the delegates were writing Pamela love letters.

Setting her sights on the post-war playboys of Europe, next up for Pamela was Niarchos. They kept everything separate in public, as he was married. He stayed at Claridge's and she stayed in her flat around the corner on Grosvenor Square. Even so, the affair became an open secret. As the actress Anita Colby, who did not even know either of them personally, remarked: 'Niarchos embarrassed her. One heard he didn't treat her with respect.'[21] Onassis was fond of needling enemies by embedding himself in their friends and family. Given Onassis' previous form, he may have partly wanted to befriend Randolph to side against Niarchos and Pamela.

The Onassis–Niarchos antipathy intensified when Niarchos' wife, Eugenia, was found dead at forty-three. Eugenia was the sister of Onassis' first wife, Athina, from whom he was now divorced. Onassis, and many others, were not convinced that it was a drug overdose. A year later, in 1971, in a move that few could understand, Athina then married Niarchos, her sister's widower, herself. After three years of marriage, she died in circumstances that again were not fully explained. Initially, it was thought that, like her sister, she had overdosed, although it later transpired the cause was a swelling of the lung. As with Eugenia, the overdose explanation and the postmortem did not sit easily.

Onassis famously, or maybe even infamously, had already moved on from Athina to Jacqueline Kennedy. He had previously engaged in an affair with Jacqueline's sister, Lee Radziwiłł, who was married into a Polish princely family. In his classic move of needling enemies, this time he was getting close to Robert Kennedy's family, after Kennedy had stood in his way in Saudi Arabia. Onassis wound Robert up about his Lee Radziwiłł conquest: 'you and Jack fuck your movie queen [Marilyn Monroe] and I'll fuck my princess', he rang to gloat. The Radziwiłł family had been coming to the Savoy since at least 1911, when they celebrated George V's coronation alongside the Churchills. The closeness of all these families gave plenty of scope for uncomfortable moments in the corridors.

NINETEEN

Pickwick and co.

When not tending to hotel business with Wontner, Bridget was busy running her other unique family institution, the Opera Company, from the same desk. As a company that had had no fresh material to perform since the 1890s, that it was able to keep going decade after decade was remarkable. Other than the Royal Shakespeare Company, it is hard to think of another enduring success with such a limited repertoire, and even the RSC has more material to work with. However, for all its longevity, the D'Oyly Carte Opera Company was a creaking organisation with burgeoning problems. Bridget's copyright ran out in 1961, turning off a tap that had been flowing into the family coffers since 1875. At that point she lost her inherited rights of exclusive professional performance. She could no longer insist that stage directions be precisely followed in all amateur productions, nor that their programmes should be sent to her in advance to be checked. Until 1962, Britain saw only D'Oyly Carte-approved productions performed in the D'Oyly Carte manner. Thereafter it was a free-for-all.

Bridget donated £150,000 (£4m) worth of her own assets to the Opera Company.[1] Upon the lapse of copyright, it seemed right to Bridget that she should only continue if ticket sales, or her own money, supported the Opera Company, not that of the public. Because she did not want any special favours, Bridget dissociated herself from a petition, presented to parliament by Lawrence Turner, MP, in 1959, asking for her to be granted copyright in perpetuity. It was signed by 500,000 people but did not succeed.[2] It was a quirky suggestion because the concern was not that Gilbert and Sullivan would no longer be performed but that it could be performed by anyone. As *The Economist* put it: 'the heritage in question is national; and what is supposed to threaten it is not loss but possible defilement. Once the copyright for Gilbert's words has lapsed [. . .] anything is possible'.[3]

Instead of the petition's premise which was to effectively entrench Bridget's monopoly, in 1960, she reorganised the company, expecting to need to compete with other professional opera companies. She established the charity, the D'Oyly Carte Opera Trust, to which she donated the company's other rights and properties, stage sets, costumes, band parts, contracts and recording, film and television rights, and a further £30,000 (£822,000) in cash.[4] At the same time she formed Bridget D'Oyly Carte Ltd, with herself as chairman and managing director, to present the operas.

On a roll with her donations, she created another charitable trust, to support the arts, the environment and medicine, including a D'Oyly Carte chair in Medicine at King's College London, chosen as it was Gilbert's alma mater and right next to the Savoy. She was nervous when the copyright expired, braced for a box office dip as other professionals could now use her repertoire for the first time. However, the winter seasons of 1961–2 sold well for fifteen weeks at the Savoy, followed by an American tour.

The threat proved minimal, but touring became increasingly uneconomic. The Company had always travelled by train with reserved carriages for the cast, with trucks supplied for free by the railway for scenery and costumes. Gradually these perks were cut back and the costs went up. Each touring company had its own carpenters plus the local staff. Altogether a group of eight to ten people worked to assemble a set in every venue when they arrived. The tight schedule meant that a show would finish at 10.30 p.m. and, by 2 a.m., they were driving through the night to the next city. It had always been gruelling, but morale was not the same as the old close-knit touring wound down. Performers no longer travelled en masse by train and shared the spare rooms of elderly theatre landladies who took in actors.

Bridget joined the increasing number of American tours, including one marking the seventy-fifth anniversary of the company's first visit, and a festival season at Central City, Colorado. She generally started American trips by taking the Queen Elizabeth II liner from Southampton to New York, where she never missed a first night. There the Opera Company was based at the Century Theatre on Seventh Avenue. Closer to home, she appeared for a royal command performance of *HMS Pinafore* at Windsor Castle, reminiscent of D'Oyly and Queen Victoria with *The Gondoliers* almost a century before. It was held in the same room at Windsor, the Waterloo Chamber. This time it was Bridget and the Queen. Bridget was so nervous that she was sick before it started.[5]

Letters from one of her friends, the costume designer Grace Lovat Fraser, suggested that Bridget found the balancing act of the hotels and Opera Company demanding, and staff noticed it too. After describing the Opera Company work, Fraser was always hoping, in her letters, that Bridget was feeling better after she had managed a holiday. How tired and busy Bridget must be was a recurring theme in Fraser's correspondence, particularly when preparing new tours. Whenever Fraser wanted to meet up, she contacted Pickwick to check Bridget's diary. While Bridget was on tour, he would write a holding response until she returned to London – the manual, post-war equivalent of an out-of-office email. Bridget offered to sign blank cheques for when she was away as well. As Rupert had done, she kept access and understanding of her life restricted to a trusted core of friends and employees, and those within it were notably loyal. Bridget would surely be gratified to know that, in an era long before non-disclosure agreements, her Opera Company staff remained discreet of their own accord. One secretary pointed out that no one who worked there was well-paid, and that, really, they were there out of love for the place and for Bridget.

She would audition countless cast members in person, usually at the Savoy Theatre. Bridget had consistent taste: an aversion to anyone overweight, and in women her preference was for petite brunettes. Any auditionee needed an ability to manage her eccentric line of questioning. Audition notes would be added to the filing system so that, whenever a performer dropped out, a replacement could be found quickly. Notes were succinct and blunt. A Miss Louie Pounds was dismissed with a mere 'rather poor vocally', Agnes Fraser was 'very beautiful – married' and Mr Evett's disagreeable personality was observed: 'very silent – never spoke to anybody'.[6]

However, it could be hard to wrest Bridget's attention for the Opera Company from the hotels. As one Opera Company general manager noticed, she was a 'worrier', who was 'trying to think about everything', and necessarily her mind 'flitted about'.[7] There was plenty of overlap in her mind between her businesses and, where possible, staff doubled up. So Wontner was also a director of the theatre, and Alfred Nightingale, an Opera Company general manager, also ran the hotel's entertainment programme from 1946, until Bridget reluctantly had to let him go because of his incessant drinking. Pageboys from the hotel reception sometimes doubled as child actors for small parts in the operas. Other Savoy services blurred together too. The Laundry continued to clean stage costumes alongside the linen bed sheets, and the printing press made theatre programmes as well as restaurant menus.[8]

As a venerable family business, hotel staff at every level by the post-war period had been there for decades, and there were just as many contenders for the longest-serving Opera Company member. Conductor Isidore Godfrey was at the rostrum for forty-two years, but he was outdone by the wardrobe mistress, Cecile Blain, who retired after forty-nine. Bridget had an early misstep in appointments when she chose Eleanor Evans for the vital role of Director of Productions. As the wife of one of the leading principal actors and a close friend of Bridget's, the choice was a highly unpopular one. One of the most important stars to leave as a result was Martyn Green. To him, it smacked of favouritism. Protest at Evans' appointment prompted the largest exodus of performers in the Company's history. Twenty-two cast members left, which was unheard of. The Company had been characterised by a low turnover since it started, making the departures even more embarrassing. Green explained that, when he warned Bridget, his view 'made no impression on Miss Carte'.[9] Having spent years in the chorus, Evans was not considered at all qualified for such an influential job.

Despite often being perceived as self-effacing, Bridget could dig in. She did not demote her friend, however many complaints rolled in, although Evans did quietly retire after three years. If Bridget did not like a piece of the set, she would make the dismissive comment that it was 'ghastly' and off it would go. Wontner, however, from the hotel side, at least did know how to change her mind. He was self-described as knowing 'how people ticked'.[10] He went to the heart of any disagreement with Bridget by saying 'your father would never have done that'.[11] It often worked.

There was something of the Virgin Queen about Bridget, as her courtiers danced around, by turns flattering and manipulating, and she could easily have adopted Elizabeth I's motto *'semper eadem'* ('always the same'). Her attitude was similarly cautious while she instructed men unused to taking orders from a woman, and relied on favourites to steer her through. At the Opera Company she had two particularly close employees, her manager Frederic Lloyd, whose monocle and chunky cigars made him instantly recognisable around the office, and her highly-strung secretary, Albert Truelove, who took over from Pickwick. Truelove shared an office down the corridor from Bridget, with Margaret Jones from accounts. They bickered frequently in the confined space. Although Bridget often cursed Truelove, she never had the heart to sack him. He had threatened to 'do what his father had done', a reference to his father's suicide, if she ever did.[12] Fussy and devoted, Truelove took his duty to keep her topped up with whisky and cigarettes seriously. Bridget generally picked at food, while drinking and smoking were a much bigger feature. She would go into his office and leave her empty whisky bottle on his desk as his cue to buy another. There was a story, possibly apocryphal, that he kept such an eye on her that when he spotted her making a donation of a five-pound note to a lifeboat charity at a performance of *The Pirates of Penzance*, he fished it back out again and chided her for being overly generous. He seems to have guarded her in much the same way that Wontner did, fussing over her and filtering communications and access as he saw fit.[13]

When Bridget did attend social events for work, it would generally be D'Oyly Carte Trust or Gilbert and Sullivan Society functions in Britain. Abroad it would be a reception at the local consulate or embassy. On an American tour, when the Opera Company was honoured at the British Embassy in Washington, DC, the senior staff stayed at the Hay Adams, the capital's most venerable hotel. Bridget was going to stay in a standard single room, as she usually would, thanks to Truelove's parsimonious bookings. On that occasion an Opera Company manager intervened and chose her a suite instead. As she seldom went abroad on holiday, and would never ask for more than the cheapest accommodation, she was childishly excited to be in a smart room of a smart hotel that was not her home.[14]

The centenary of the first D'Oyly Carte opera, *Trial by Jury*, was celebrated with a triumphant season at the Savoy Theatre in 1975. Every Gilbert and Sullivan work was presented in chronological order to fans from around the world. It was the only time that *Utopia (Limited)* and *The Grand Duke* had been revived professionally, for the sake of completeness. To her initial embarrassment, Bridget was made a Dame to celebrate the International Year of Women. Initially she did not want to accept the honour, as she could not face the fuss and said that it was only a title for 'wrinklies', but she was eventually persuaded to. This fitted with her embarrassment at any unsolicited attention. She would protest at staff attempts to celebrate her birthday, and avoided the front entrances of the theatres in case fans wanted to talk to her and she would not know what to say. She had no interest in being famous. As *The Times* city pages once described her, she was 'powerful but discreet'.[15]

Even in the midst of the centenary celebrations, when Harold Wilson made a speech declaring the D'Oyly Carte 'part of our national birthright', its future was in grave doubt.[16] Despite selling out tours worldwide, and having lucrative American tours to subsidise the uneconomic British ones, she was increasingly out of pocket with paying for performers, orchestra, sets, accommodation and travel.

It was known by this time that Bridget's mother, Dorothy, was gravely ill. Having spent the war and the first few years of her second marriage luxuriating in expat island life, she had more soberly involved herself in local government by 1951, winning a council seat as one of only five women out of 273 candidates in Trinidad and Tobago, when they were contested for the first time. She had also been Chairman of the Plymouth Village Council 'for longer than she could remember', according to a local newspaper interview that she gave when she was eighty-three. It is noticeable in that interview that she says she 'sorely misses' her late son, but makes no mention of Bridget.

Dorothy's political responsibilities still did not curb her gambling much.[17] She would get in touch with Bridget every so often when it created problems. A panicked message would be relayed to Bridget, along the lines of 'your mother is in terrible trouble – please go over'.[18] The terrible trouble was generally financial. In such instances, Bridget sent money, but did not go over. She was always keen to dispatch the money as quickly as possible. She would send someone from the Savoy along to Coutts, her bank on the Strand, immediately.

Staff remember Dorothy visiting Bridget once on a trip to London, and that Bridget seemed 'rattled' by having seen her. Dorothy had considered moving back when her second husband died in the 1960s. Presumably she realised that this was not a welcome suggestion to her only remaining child and thought better of it. She died in February 1977. Bridget told the switchboard that, if the call came through in the night, she did not wish to be disturbed. Dorothy was buried in Tobago next to a friend, Edith Cook, under a tree that they liked.[19] Bridget did not go to her funeral.

TWENTY

Bridget hangs on

'If we want things to stay as they are,
things will have to change.'

Tancredi Falconeri in *The Leopard*
by Giuseppe Tomasi di Lampedusa

On the surface, the Savoy Hotel appeared to guests serene and immovable. Back of house, energetic plotting in the boardroom was keeping the D'Oyly Carte show on the road. Collectively the hotels were making thrilling, if unreliable, profits, but this was attracting unwelcome attention. Profits, coupled with the group's grand dame status and prime London properties, were proving a temptation for would-be buyers.

From 1956 there was the additional incentive of owning the Connaught in Mayfair, for which Bridget had great affection, alongside the other hotels. Wontner had encouraged Rupert to buy it during the war, but his suggestion had tactfully been quashed. Rupert had responded by saying that, when the existing hotels were 'perfect', then they could have a fourth – in other words, as Wontner understood, no. He had more luck with Bridget. And, on the occasions that she did socialise at her own hotels, she often chose the Connaught. Although, for her business dinners, it was usually the Savoy Restaurant, a two-minute walk from the boardroom. She rarely went to Claridge's unless she needed to, after her ill-fated wedding. The Connaught, on the other hand, was an emotional blank canvas for her. A few streets south of Claridge's, it was established in 1815 as the Prince of Saxe-Coburg Hotel. Until 1917 it had been known as the Coburg, until, like the Royal Family, it became too Germanic-sounding for the political climate. It was patriotically renamed after Queen Victoria's son, Arthur, Duke of Connaught. Just as Claridge's had begun, it was a hotchpotch of houses acquired one by one and pieced together.

The Berkeley was now paid attention more or less for the first time since D'Oyly had bought it in 1900. In the 1960s, its current home in Knightsbridge was built from scratch, which involved Wontner engaging in arms-length dealings with the Kray brothers. To secure the plot on the corner of Wilton Place, overlooking Hyde Park, the hotel needed to buy and demolish the Krays' gambling and sex club, Esmerelda's Barn. Wontner was wily enough to realise that if he let on that the land was for the Berkeley, the owners of the various properties that they needed would have put the sale prices up, so it was conducted through associates, and his wife. The land was bought from the twins just before they were finally imprisoned for long stretches in 1969.

The modern Berkeley in Knightsbridge opened three years later. Built from scratch, it was a limestone neo-Georgian block on the outside. The interior was a mixture of materials salvaged from the site's demolished buildings, and panelling and marble fireplaces from the old Berkeley on Piccadilly. Its Grill Room by Lutyens, commissioned by Rupert in 1913, was fully reinstated.

After Bridget took over, it was not so much running the hotels that was a challenge as hanging on to them. She spent her time at the helm looking over her shoulder, as a series of battles tested the ingenuity of her board in the ungentlemanly new era of hostile takeovers. They craftily fended off Conrad Hilton, and property developers Sir Charles Clore and Harold Samuel, among many others. Hostile takeovers, in which owners were forcibly, often secretly, bought out, became a feature of the post-war economy. So it fell to Bridget and her board to keep control. They came up with two ruses that had never been tried before. Wontner was not interested in the theory, as he said, he was only concerned to do whatever was necessary to safeguard the hotels. None of it would have been possible without his strength of personality. Even if he was not interested in theory, the Savoy stratagems are in textbooks to this day as early case studies in how to defeat takeover bids.

Trouble had started in 1953, when the hotels made a record combined profit of £654,438 (£18m).[1] Charles Clore and Harold Samuel purchased millions of pounds of shares in separate attempts to gain a controlling interest. Churchill, who had such fond memories of the Savoy over the decades, was prime minister once again. He still celebrated his birthdays there with roast beef and soufflé, and had his Other Club dinners in Pinafore, and could be in one part of the hotel or another as many as three times a week.[2] Worried that his beloved Savoy was going to be taken over, he instructed his President of the Board of Trade to stop Clore, who made the first attempt, and Bank of England governor Lord Cobbold urged insurance companies to stop lending to anyone 'connected with these take-over operations'.[3] Cobbold was sympathetic to the D'Oyly Carte cause too, viewing it as a matter of 'nice people' potentially losing their business to 'nasty people'.[4] However much Churchill, the City and Cobbold were inclined to come to the rescue, official government policy remained one of reluctant non-interference, so the Savoy was largely left to make its own defence plans. Clore had recently executed a highly controversial but successful bid for Britain's biggest retailer, J. Sears & Co, that had left its shell-shocked departing chairman to sign off: 'We never thought anything like this would happen to us'.[5] Bridget and Wontner were scrambling to avoid the same fate. Their premise, as ever, was that the Savoy should maintain its standards regardless of cost, because there were always enough people to pay for the best. They were worried that any prospective owner would not share their ethos. Clore, indeed, had the mirror-opposite approach. The D'Oyly Cartes, and their protégé, Wontner, enjoyed what money could bring – whether luxury, adventure, power, or solitude in Bridget's case – but profits were a distant second to having the hotels exactly as they wanted them. As Savoy guest Marilyn Monroe liked to say: 'I'm not interested in money. I just want to be wonderful', and they had a similar attitude. Clore, on the other hand, did not see money as a means to an end. To him its pursuit was a driving passion in itself – and he wanted to see the hotels generating far more of it.

After Clore's bid was roundly rejected by the Savoy board, in an informal arrangement he sold his shares to Samuel, with whom he shared an accountant, so the latter could have a go. Clore and Samuel were among the first businessmen to attempt hostile takeover bids anywhere in the world, although they were seen off by the Savoy in turn. Never tried before in the City, the Savoy transferred the Berkeley into a newly formed trust, until Samuel withdrew, to keep it out of his way, as he wanted to make it into a block of flats and offices. This sneaky sidestep caused a sensation, questions were asked in parliament, and it featured in many contemporary legal textbooks, in the *Harvard Law Review*, and the *Cambridge Law Journal*.

The Economist proclaimed it 'outrageous' at the time: 'On

grounds of principle, it is difficult to find condemnation too severe for what the Savoy Hotel board have done. They have taken, without the consent of their shareholders, a valuable property in which the shareholders have an equity and of which the best use is open to dispute. They have made it impossible for the shareholders [. . .] to exert any control in future over the disposition of that property.'[6] By the time it attracted a Board of Trade inquiry, requested by Samuel, the board had beaten off his takeover. Once the coast was clear, the freehold of the Berkeley was transferred back from the trust to the Savoy.

The inquiry that Samuel requested found the directors had acted in the best interests of their shareholders, but that the action was an 'invalid use of the powers of management'.[7] This judgment was of little use to Samuel, who had bowed out long ago. Still, Wontner had bought up all of his shares, giving Samuel a profit of £1.3 million (£36m), so he did not come out of the attempt too badly.[8] Wontner never explained where the money came from to buy them up, beyond 'the directors and their friends'.[9] Even if Wontner himself was coy, Cobbold wrote in his diary that Sir Anthony Tuke, the chairman of the Savoy's bankers, Barclays, who was a Gilbert and Sullivan fan and later an opera company trustee, came to him to look for help on the Savoy's behalf: 'Barclays are anxious to help their old customers and they think that the Savoy are on the side of the angels in this controversy'.[10] Tuke had to do without Cobbold's help, but told him a few weeks later that Barclays had 'fixed up the Savoy business'.[11] Of all those who would seek to acquire the hotels, the board stayed on friendly terms with Samuel, who came to get his hair cut at the Savoy and held his celebrations at Claridge's. There was deep-seated animosity with the others.

The second, permanent Savoy sidestep to avoid a re-run of

the close calls with Clore and Samuel was to create an A and B two-tier voting system in order to protect itself. It turned out to be a vital measure. Bridget, Wontner and their friends on the board created a small number of very expensive, exclusive 'B' shares. They were worth forty times as many votes each as the ordinary 'A' shares. The idea was to make it almost impossible to mount a takeover bid unless you owned the new shares. This structure concentrated power with Bridget's clique of 'B' shareholders, and was put in place without consulting existing shareholders. Sure enough, as long as Bridget and Wontner and their friends held on to their shares, the group was virtually impregnable to bids. Those owning the 'A' shares, and 98 per cent of the company, now had only half of the voting rights. The 'B' shares were, as hoped, rarely traded, and stayed for decade after decade in the hands of D'Oyly Carte loyalists. They included Emile Wolf, who managed the Hotel Lancaster off the Champs Élysées in Paris, Niarchos and Sir Antony Hornby of Cazenove, the Savoy's stockbrokers, who had a free suite at Claridge's. Hornby was an archetypal Bridget favourite: formal, smooth-talking and a perfectionist. His golden rule at Cazenove was that none of his brokers could visit their merchant bank clients without wearing a bowler hat. Whenever the ethics of allowing 'B' shareholding directors to have free suites were questioned, the answer came that they needed to sample the services to assure appropriate standards.

Packing the board with friends and family had been the approach since the very beginning, starting with Sullivan, Hwfa Williams and Michael Gunn. For Rupert, new board members included Daphne du Maurier's husband and the Queen's treasurer, Sir Frederick Browning,[12] and Rupert's stockbroker friend Claude Serocold, who served for over thirty years until he died in 1959. Like Rupert, during the First World

War, Serocold had taken part in intelligence work, as assistant to Reginald 'Blinker' Hall, director of naval codebreaking at the Admiralty. Wealthy and a long-standing friend, Serocold would have no trouble turning down any apparently unfit owners for the benefit of the family.

Tight-knit as ever, a large proportion of the 'A' share-holders were Savoy staff in any case, which goes some way to accounting for their docility over the years, and many of them were pleased by how much extra money investing in their employer had made them. There was a tradition from the outset of offering shares to staff. From 1948 onwards, a particularly large number were shareholders, as they had been given £10 (£400) worth of shares each in gratitude for not joining the royal wedding strike led by Frank Piazza.

As long as Bridget's clique of 'B' shareholders stuck together, they could cheerfully ignore the 98 per cent of 'A' shareholders, and with it the normal strain on a publicly traded company to offer a competitive return every year. In time-honoured extravagance, the management were free to continue in their own way – motivated by attachment to their perks, disdain towards any pretenders to the throne, and by love of their craft. As one of the directors phrased his attitude, for him maintaining generosity should extend 'down to the amount of butter you are given at breakfast'.[13] It was a public company, which spent other people's money, but the D'Oyly Cartes always managed to operate within their own rules. As with the Opera Company, for Bridget, it was about preserving something cherished, whether there was money in it or not. The *Financial Times*, in an echo of *The Economist*, was not impressed with the unique set-up. They complained that the Savoy directors had set a precedent that made the way 'open to the destruction of the whole company system', as directors should not be allowed such control without consultation.

The other board members were a formidable bunch all-round. Sir Alan Herbert, a *Punch* columnist and lawyer, had been the pioneering MP behind the 1937 Matrimonial Causes Act, which relaxed divorce criteria – although that had come a little too late for Bridget. Like Serocold, solicitor Miles Thornewill, having started in Rupert's time, stayed on the board until he died. In Thornewill's case, this happened at the Savoy in 1974, after fifty years of service. Other lawyers on the Board were Major Frank Goldsmith, father of tycoon Sir James Goldsmith and Sir Hartley Shawcross, who was the lead British prosecutor at Nuremberg. Experience of the press was provided by John Hannay, who oversaw the bustling Savoy press office, and became a director in 1948.

By 1960, two of the Savoy's rejected bidders had teamed up for a rival venture. Clore had been on a run of acquisitions, until the Savoy failure, and soon after bought the Mappin & Webb jewellery group, Selfridges and William Hill bookmakers. Still angry that he had been rejected, using his property company he spent eight years buying up land near Park Lane and obtaining permission for a skyscraper hotel. When it was all pieced together, he signed the prime spot over to Texan hotelier Conrad Hilton to build the eyesore that stands there now. At twenty-eight storeys, the Hilton Park Lane was London's tallest building in 1963.[14] Hilton had been another unwelcome, but less persistent, Savoy bidder in the 1950s. His son Nicky had spent part of his honeymoon with his first wife, Elizabeth Taylor, there in May 1950, at the start of their eight-month marriage. After Conrad stayed himself in 1956, he fancied adding it to his 188 hotels, but did not stick at it for long.

The attempted takeovers flared up again in the 1970s. The most prominent were from self-made London-born tycoons

Lord Victor Matthews, chairman of the *Express* newspapers, and Sir Maxwell Joseph, founder of the Grand Metropolitan hotel group. Each time interlopers were seen off using the idiosyncratic share structure. Even so, there was one last battle to be fought. Charles Forte would prove the most obsessive in a long line of suitors. His bid to take over was a big-money drama that ran on and off for fifteen years and cost at least £1 million (£2.4m) in legal fees on the Savoy side alone.[15] Forte had made most of his wealth from Travelodge, a no-frills chain of motels with attached restaurants and petrol stations, but the Savoy had been in his sights for decades.

Forte, Wontner and Bridget were all born within a year of each other. The tussle between them dominated the end of their lives. People from Ciociaria, the area south of Rome where Forte was born, had been settling in Scotland since the 1880s. At the age of four, he came to join his father, Rocco, in a town outside Edinburgh,[16] where Rocco had opened a small café. It laid claim to the first American soda fountain and first Italian espresso coffee-machine in Clackmannanshire. At seventeen, Carmine, soon anglicised to Charles, joined the family business, which grew to become a chain of ice-cream parlours and cafés in Scotland and along the south coast of England. With £500 of savings (£25,000) and £3,000 (£150,000) from his father and another backer, Charles then opened the Meadow Milk Bar in 1935, on Upper Regent Street in London.[17] His offering was a novelty drink called a milkshake, but business was slow. To attract customers, Forte decided to spend more on the premises by making cuts to the staff. He sacked three of them and extended into a neighbouring shop.

By the outbreak of the Second World War, his stringent approach enabled him to add nine more milk bars to make a chain. He saved on costs by supplying all of them from one premises that made cakes, sandwiches and fruit syrups.

Having calculated how to produce cheap food in bulk in the 1950s, Forte was granted concessions at a number of newly developed airports, including Heathrow and Gatwick, won contracts to provide in-flight food, and accumulated service station concessions on the burgeoning motorway system. His approach both to hotels and restaurants was based on saving money in the minutiae of housekeeping, buying and portion control. This was anathema to the Savoy.

Quite reasonably for any conventional business, Forte's driving force was increasing profit. His shareholders were grateful for his record of tight spending and ever larger profits, while detractors complained of his establishments' dispiriting uniformity and mediocrity. His view was that his Little Chef and Happy Eater diners and his Travelodges were reliable and affordable. He claimed for himself that he had 'transformed the hotel and catering industry of this country'.[18] The Savoy board may have agreed, but not that it was for the better.

In 1959, Labour leader Hugh Gaitskell offered to put Forte's name forward for a peerage. Forte's allergy to socialism, and trade unions above all, led him to decline. He later accepted the honour from a politician about whom he could have no such ideological qualms, Margaret Thatcher. Ever the buccaneering entrepreneur, he had moved into a completely different league of wealth and prestige in 1970, when he bought three hotels in Paris – the George V, Plaza Athénée and the Trémoille – followed by The Ritz in Madrid. More pragmatically, back in Britain, he agreed a merger to form Trust Houses Forte. The merger was a commercially logical but personally gruelling decision, as it turned out. Trust Houses, which owned more than 200 hotels, was run by Lord Crowther, a former editor of *The Economist*, who became chairman of the new group. He and Forte clashed immediately and Crowther treated him with open hostility. Crowther and

Forte were getting on so badly that Forte believed he was being spied on and having his papers rifled through at work.[19] After a year, Crowther encouraged a takeover bid from a brewing conglomerate, Allied Breweries. Forte, beyond outraged, had a close shave when he had to borrow £2 million (£28m) to buy up shares to block it.[20] He put his own fortune on the line to hang on and the bid failed in 1972. Having fought so hard to gain full control of his own company, he then started a relentless bid for someone else's.

For his acquisition of the Savoy, he began with charm. In 1980 he had Wontner over for dinner at home. In Wontner's characteristic flowery style, he wrote effusively to thank Forte for the 'rare enrichments' of his table.[21] When Forte's charm disappeared, Wontner likened this early phase to when Hitler befriended the Austrian Chancellor Dollfuss,[22] Hitler made friendly overtures while Dollfuss was useful, then swiftly had him assassinated when he had served his purpose.

A year later, the hotels were struggling financially, with losses of £460,000 (£1.8m), hurt by the decline in foreign tourists to Britain.[23] Forte seized the opportunity and embarked on one of the most ferocious takeover battles in the City's history. There were to be no more rare enrichments from his table. The fur was flying straight away. On both sides, pride and strongly held emotion were at stake. Wontner did all of the upfront fighting, but behind the scenes Bridget hated 'all of this Forte business', and he irked her as well.[24] She found it difficult to ever think about the Savoy at all 'unemotionally' – after all it was both her livelihood and her home.[25] The idea that the Savoy was going to become one of 800 hotels in the Forte group was an over-my-dead-body proposition, and so it proved. The next few years became a battle of attrition between Forte's upstart brashness and the Savoy's old-world hauteur. Forte had dreamed of owning the Savoy since he had opened his first milk bar in 1935. He now had the requisite wealth to match that ambition, and there were only a handful of people in his way.

As sentimental and determined as Bridget and Wontner were, so was Forte. Having been interred on the Isle of Man in 1940 because of his Italian heritage, but without any other grounds, it was not long until he was released. Afterwards, during the dark days of the Second World War in 1942, he had chosen the Savoy to propose to his wife, and had come back there on his honeymoon.[26] He resented the idea that he was not worthy of being its owner when the hotel meant so much to him. He acknowledged criticisms that he wished to acquire the Savoy 'out of vanity, as a climax to my own career' by responding 'what hotel man would not be proud to possess them!'[27]

He launched a £58 million (£225m) hostile bid, declaring the hotels to be run down. When he had sounded out Wontner in 1980 about planning to make the bid, Wontner had not even asked how much he was willing to pay, he had just told Forte not to bother. Forte found this indifference to money extraordinary. Still he pressed ahead. His takeover tactic was to rubbish the management. Wontner, in turn, would publicly rubbish Forte. Wontner revelled in being almost a foot taller than his diminutive adversary and made frequent reference to how 'little' he was. As Wontner put it so patronisingly, 'I've known little Forte since he ran his milk bar', and liked to refer to him as a 'very clever little man'.[28] Little Forte took it on the chin, describing himself as 'the shortest knight of the year' when he received his knighthood.[29]

Most cuttingly, Wontner accused Forte of '*folie de grandeur*'. Responding to the Savoy's 'vicious campaign', Forte sniped that its profits were nowhere near high enough. He insisted that his bid was not a matter of vain ambition, but that he could not bear to see such exquisite hotels run so badly, which was, of course, deeply insulting to Bridget and Wontner. 'I hope we are not stuffy people,' blustered Wontner, 'but there is a limit.'[30] The bid failed. Pushing on, Forte ploughed more money into buying up more and more shares. Whenever he tried to approach the board, offering what he said was a fair price, he was 'always given the complete brush-off, as everyone else was'.[31]

In private as well as in the press, the sniping continued. Never forgetting how Forte had made his fortune, Wontner did not even consider him an hotelier, he said. In the meantime, it is clear from Forte's autobiography that he was preoccupied with plotting against Wontner personally. He asked one of the Opera Company staff if they could dig up any dirt for him. He was particularly interested to know if Wontner had a mistress and wanted any incriminating details.

Forte hit on two criticisms that demonstrated how at odds he was with the Savoy board. He accused them of clinging to 'old glamour', and of not making enough money,[32] when old glamour and freedom from making money were exactly what they held dear. One of their decadent decisions, dismissed by Forte as 'disgusting',[33] was to sell off the portion of the Savoy building facing the Strand, which they found the least attractive part of the complex, for development as flats – not for profit, but on the grounds that it was easier to run a luxury hotel with fewer rooms. This was a hotel that commissioned its own design of taps, bed linen, basins, coffee blend and cutlery, and still made its own mattresses. As Wontner grandly told one shareholders' meeting, 'we are not satisfied with a standardised product'.[34] In defence of this spending, Wontner said, 'it is not our experience that these things pass unnoticed', but Forte found their extravagance beyond eccentric.[35]

Just as in the early days, with D'Oyly telling shareholders that the wine cellar should take precedence over their dividends, the family had an unusual dominance. Their drive from the outset was satisfying themselves, the board and the prestigious clientele at more or less any cost. In any bad year, the message from the management to the shareholders was that spending would continue. In 1974, when Sir Antony Hornby took the meeting on Wontner's behalf, he was on-message too. Having listed the horrors of inflation, Americans travelling less, a go-slow on the railways, a miners' strike, the OPEC crisis of oil supply, the Arab–Israeli War and a shortage of lavatory paper in London that proved 'a disaster' for the hotel, he went on to say: 'I can't pretend we're optimistic but we have seen this sort of thing before [. . .] We shall not stop spending, which would be a short-sighted policy.'[36] This was part of what made the place so special, and therefore so unsuitable to be taken over by anyone who did not share the ethos.

The Savoy's eccentricity and extravagance was part of its mythology, and it caused bemusement in the City. One incredulous analyst told a journalist: 'They don't own a deep freeze, no microwaves, no central buying of food, they've a team of lady embroiderers sewing 100,000 Savoy crests a year. The company report seemed proud of off-loading £290,000 (£870,000) of Chablis about to go past its best. What were they doing with £290,000 of Chablis?'[37]

Thirty-eight million pounds later (£150m), Forte had acquired nearly 70 per cent of the Savoy shares.[38] He felt that he must be close to his holy grail, but for all that money, it bought him only 42 per cent of the voting rights, because of his inability to get hold of those gold-dust 'B' shares. He was infuriated by the board's refusal to negotiate. The directors were too rich and loyal to show interest in any sum of money or in negotiating a sale, as Forte noticed. To him this loyalty was a 'nightmare', but, as he conceded, it was 'flattering' to Bridget and Wontner.[39]

Forte carried on brooding. He looked into one of the charitable foundations, the Fondation pour la Formation Hôtelière, that owned some of the 'B' shares. He claimed that it was controlled by Bridget, Wontner and their associates. Wontner, ever unable to resist a chance to wind Forte up, responded, 'They are accusing me of fraud, the worst thing apart from murder,' adding mischievously, 'only they haven't found the corpse yet'.[40] To Forte's renewed frustration, the Savoy's shareholders did not vote to investigate his claim. He then tried to cancel the Swiss block of 'B' shares, but the legal route did not work either. If there was a proverbial corpse, it remained buried.

Bridget and the management were defensive about these trusts, right back from when they were formed in the 1970s. The Savoy's official, prickly response to a small piece in *The Spectator* hinted at some sensitive points. Considering *The Spectator* piece was essentially flattering, expressed the hope that no takeover attempt would be successful, and referred to them as 'London's best hotels', it was quite a slap down:

> Sir, In your City diary on August 12, you refer to the charitable trust, which Miss Bridget D'Oyly Carte recently established, by the gift to it of Savoy shares.
>
> In the course of your commentary, you say as a basis for your comments: (1) 'The Chairman of the Savoy group, which includes Claridge's and The Connaught, is Sir Hugh Wontner, who is reported to be pleased with Miss D'Oyly Carte's gift . . .'
>
> In fact, Sir Hugh Wontner is away on holiday and has made no statement of any kind about Miss D'Oyly Carte's gift. The alleged 'report' is, therefore, entirely surmise.

(2) You say the gift 'will help the Savoy management to stifle criticism. Of course, it will not do so, could not do so, and is not intended to do so.

(3) You say that 'Some of his (Sir Hugh's alleged) relief is possibly connected with the use he has of Claridge's penthouse suite. Miss D'Oyly Carte's gift has no connection whatever with the occupation of rooms at Claridge's by Sir Hugh Wontner or anyone else.

(4) You add that 'Claridge's penthouse suite . . . is reported to be so magnificent (to the chagrin of Claridge's guests like Stavros Niarchos) . . .'
A reference to 'Claridge's penthouse suite,' as though there was only one, is in itself entirely misleading, and the alleged 'chagrin' of Mr Niarchos and others is wholly an invention.

(5) You further state that 'newspaper photographers are forbidden entry so that small shareholders do not become disaffected and want bigger dividends.'
Newspaper photographers have never been permitted by the management to take photographs inside Claridge's . . . and to give the impression that this is a prohibition confined to one apartment in one hotel, and for the reason stated, is wholly mischievous and misleading. This long established rule, going back certainly at least seventy years, has no connection whatever with shareholdings, large or small, nor has it, or could it have, any bearing whatever upon the dividend.

F. C. Sawford Secretary The Savoy Hotel Limited, Secretary's Office, 1 Savoy Hill, Embankment Gardens, London WC2[41]

The battles with Forte revealed the extent to which the Savoy saw itself as outside the normal rules. Bridget and her cabal felt it was their individuality versus any would-be owner's deadening standardisation. Their lack of commercial competitiveness and their consistency ensured the hotel's charm, and no one else seemed to understand that. Staying in power, as though in some embattled citadel, they kept its timeless quality, deliberately separating it from modern life, which was always pressing at its polished doors.

TWENTY-ONE

Curtain down

At the end of a sold-out season on 27 February 1982, the curtain came down on the D'Oyly Carte Opera Company. Bridget had been running it at a personal loss of £2,000 (£6,100) a week since the late 1970s.[1] It continued to stage the operas until 1982, but by then the productions, with their synchronised fan flicks and regulation semi-circular chorus formations, had become quaint to the point of staleness – according to its detractors. The Arts Council did not see the artistic validity of its staunchly traditional productions, which they criticised as 'tired', and did not offer a grant to save it.[2] Rather cruelly, given Bridget's advancing years, it likened her Opera Company to a 'graceful old lady off to her grave'.[3]

By 1982, many heavily darned costumes were thirty years old, and new cast members were earning £125 (£456) a week, below the actors' union minimum. As with the hotels, most staff were working there because they actively wanted to, despite the relatively meagre pay. D'Oyly's success had partly come from how opulent and fresh his productions were. There was no more money or energy left from Bridget by the 1980s to offer that herself.

Although the Opera Company had initially transformed the family fortunes, and its shows were still selling at 90 per cent capacity, in the end it was draining money at a greater rate than any spending for pleasure that Bridget did.[4] Only she, Truelove and Frederic Lloyd saw the financial statements every week, but the trouble was clear even from the outside. As part of Forte's 1981 bid, he had told Bridget that he was prepared to listen to any request for help with her Opera Company, regardless of whether he was able to take over the hotels. Wontner said that this had been a lie, and that Forte had offered to help on the condition that she sold her hotel shares. Forte denied dropping the rescue offer when she would not.[5]

Bridget agreed to take audience donations at performances, but felt guilty when they flooded in. When children started sending money, she decided that it should stop and she wanted to send the donations back. Under pressure from the trustees, she admitted that it could no longer be sustained and the mounting losses led to its closure in its 107th year. Advertised as one of the most important collections in world theatre, Christie's auctioned off 1,500 of its costumes – from the embroidered kimonos of *The Mikado* to the frilly net skirts of the fairies in *Iolanthe*.[6] Enthusiasts from San Francisco, Boston and New York flew to London to purchase their part of theatre history.

At the last performance, Bridget rose from her box unprompted to acknowledge all the cheers and applause and to thank the public for their support for her family over three generations. Knowing her fear of public events, and how exhausted she was from fending off Forte, making that speech must have taken all her wherewithal. *The Times* lamented that, although Gilbert and Sullivan would surely be performed in the future, it would not have 'the charm, authenticity or sheer old-fashioned Englishness of the D'Oyly Carte'. After that last night at the theatre, Bridget was not seen for a month at work, which had never happened before.

In the same year, Coleton Fishacre passed to the National Trust. Bereft of its furnishings, and with Gilbert and Sullivan relatively unloved at the time, the National Trust bought it only for its gardens and its dramatic stretch of coastline. The house was only later thought worth restoring and opening to the public.

Bridget was far from a disaster, but she did not know how to overcome the difficulties that faced her. The burden of touring at a time of soaring costs, with no public funding help, killed the Opera Company. For all her spending on propping it up for years, she remained one of Britain's wealthiest, most powerful women until she died. However, without an heir there was no one around whom to build up loyalty for the next generation. In the way that Forte was able to gear up with his own empire to hand over to his son, Bridget had no one: it was a family business, in the end, with no family.

March 1985 marked the centenary of *The Mikado*, but there was precious little to celebrate. Having passed out in Marylebone Station, Bridget was told at the hospital near Shrubs Woods that she had advanced lung cancer, and that nothing could be done for her. Her illness was kept private so that it would not impact the Savoy share price. When staff and friends came to visit her in hospital, she sent them away, telling them not to make a fuss. Eventually she was 'sent home to die', as she told them.[7] She disposed of her personal papers and smaller possessions on a bonfire in the garden.

Bridget died at Shrubs Wood, with her housekeeper, Frances, by her side, on 2 May 1985. Her £17 million (£52m) was divided up among charities, employees and friends. As with D'Oyly and Rupert, Bridget's death was marked at the

Savoy Chapel with ballads from the D'Oyly Carte operas. Wontner was choked up as he gave her eulogy, having lost his friend and ally of fifty years.

In three generations the D'Oyly Cartes had pioneered the luxury hotel and the modern theatre, propelled Gilbert and Sullivan to lasting stardom, made Oscar Wilde a transatlantic celebrity, inspired a P. G. Wodehouse series, and popularised early jazz, electric lights and Art Deco. Their modus operandi remained essentially unchanging in uncertain times, which their fans found immensely comforting. Whether wayward performers, cruel reviewers, petulant guests or rival entrepreneurs – the family had navigated them all. Their accomplishments and happiness, however, rarely matched up. They had still found themselves in emotional turmoil in the beautiful surroundings that they made for themselves. Thirteen original Gilbert and Sullivan operas, five luxury hotels, at least three affairs, and three untimely deaths later, with Bridget the last one standing, their line, and their century of success, ended.

POSTSCRIPT

Claridge's Restaurant, July 1990

A few years after Bridget died, the historian A. N. Wilson went to interview bespectacled eighty-two-year-old Wontner over lunch at Claridge's. Wontner had carried on holding the fort, and talked about Bridget and the Savoy all the time. Carrying on from Bridget, he was president of the theatre and of the hotels until he died. Forte, for his part, was 'prepared to wait' to make the Savoy part of his hotel group, and he had his son lined up to continue the battle.[1] In the end, they would not succeed – instead they were pushed out of their own business in a hostile bid, and lost their treasured stake in the Savoy with it.

'You know,' said Wontner wistfully, across the mono-grammed crockery and expanse of tablecloth, 'it is a strange fact that all the people who ever tried to take over the Savoy have ended up with either a peerage or a knighthood: Lord Forte, Lord Thorneycroft, Lord Samuel, Sir Charles Clore.' He lit a cigar at the table. As he laughed to himself, smoke emanated from his nostrils. 'They've all ended up with titles, but they haven't . . .' the historian saw where his thought was going. They said in unison: 'they haven't ended up with the Savoy'.[2]

Note on Money

To find a modern equivalent to historical values, I used software developer Kate Rose Morley's inflation calculator. Data for 1949 onwards for Morley's calculator comes from the Office for National Statistics' Retail Price Index: *All Items: Percentage change over 12 months*. Data up to 1948 comes from *Consumer Price Inflation Since 1750* (*Economic Trends* No. 604, pp. 38–46) by Jim O'Donoghue, Louise Goulding and Grahame Allen.

There are myriad ways of calculating old values that produce myriad results. On Wikipedia it estimates Richard D'Oyly Carte's estate to have been worth £100m in today's money on his death in 1901, while the calculator that I used worked it out as £28m. For consistency, I used the calculator throughout. The modern values are intended as an approximate, hopefully helpful, guide.

NOTES

NB: The D'Oyly Carte Archive at the Victoria & Albert Department of Theatre and Performance starts with THM.

Preface

1 Bennett, Arnold, *Imperial Palace* (London: Cassell & Co, 1930), p. 84.
2 Rose, Andrew, *The Prince, the Princess, and the Perfect Murder* (London: Coronet, 2013), p. 128.
3 Ibid., p. 132.
4 Bennett, *Imperial Palace*, p. 292.
5 Powell, Ted, *King Edward VIII: An American Life* (Oxford: Oxford University Press, 2018), p. 85.
6 Clark Kerr was the likely bearer of letters, from deductions in Rose, *The Prince*, p. 186.
7 Rose, *The Prince*, p. 154.
8 Nash, Michael L., *The History and Politics of Exhumation: Royal Bodies and Lesser Mortals* (London: Palgrave Macmillan, 2019), p. 286.
9 Ibid.
10 Rose, *The Prince*, p. 311.

ACT ONE: RICHARD

One – Curtain Up

1 John Stow, quoted in Denby, Elaine, *Grand Hotels: Reality and Illusion* (London: Reaktion Books, 2002), p. 143.
2 John Stow, quoted in Fuller, Thomas, *The Church History of Britain* (London: Thomas Tegg, 1842), vol. ii, p. 276.
3 *The Romance of a famous London theatre* (souvenir booklet), THM/73/8/6.

4 Stedman, Jane W., *W. S. Gilbert: A Classic Victorian & His Theatre* (New York: Oxford University Press, 1996), p. 170.

5 Richard D'Oyly Carte, letter to Arthur Sullivan, quoted in Ainger, Michael, *Gilbert and Sullivan: A Dual Biography* (Oxford: Oxford University Press, 2002), p. 248.

6 Quoted in Cannadine, David, 'Three Who Made a Revolution', *New York Review of Books*, 7 March 1991.

7 Hampshire Record Office, quoted in Seeley, Paul, *Richard D'Oyly Carte* (London: Routledge, 2019), p. 9.

8 Masson, David (ed.), *The Collected Writings of Thomas De Quincey* (London: A&C Black, 1897), vol. iii, p. 350, quoted in Sheppard, F. H. W. (ed.), 'Soho Square Area: Portland Estate, Nos. 27–28 Soho Square, Nascreno House', *Survey of London: Volumes 33 and 34, St Anne Soho* (London: London County Council, 1966), pp. 106–7.

9 Richard and Eliza's house was on the site of the current 27 Soho Square, according to Jones, Brian, *Helen D'Oyly Carte: Gilbert and Sullivan's 4th Partner* (London: Basingstoke Books Ltd, 2011), p. 30. The House of St Barnabas is now a private members' club that uses its profits to help homeless people.

10 Nightingale, Rev. Joseph, *London and Middlesex* (1815), vol. iii, part II, pp. 657–8.

11 Jacob, Arthur, 'Carte, Richard D'Oyly (1844–1901)', *Oxford Dictionary of National Biography* (Oxford: Oxford University Press, 2004).

12 *The Musical World* (London: G. Purkess, 1845), vol. xx, p. 357.

13 Burgess, Michael, 'Richard D'Oyly Carte', *The Savoyard*, January 1975, pp. 7–11.

14 *The Times*, 16 December 1954, p. 1.

15 Lizzie Carte, quoted in THM/73/9/2/4.

16 Joseph, Tony, *D'Oyly Carte Opera Company, 1875–1982: An Unofficial History* (Bristol: Bunthorne Books, 1994), p. 8.

17 Thomas Arnold, quoted in Crilly, A. J., *Arthur Cayley: Mathematician Laureate of the Victorian Age* (Baltimore, MD: Johns Hopkins University Press, 2006), p. 18.

18 Lizzie Carte, quoted in THM/73/9/2/4.

19 Matriculation results in *The Morning Post*, 1 February 1861.

20 *Lloyd's Weekly Newspaper*, 13 November 1864.

21 'Opera Comique (Last Night)', *The Era*, 27 August 1871, p. 13.

22 Quoted in Seeley, *Richard D'Oyly Carte*, p. 15.

23 Advertisement in *The Era*, 8 September 1872.

24 'Signor Mario's Farewell', *Bath Chronicle and Weekly Gazette*, 8 September 1870.

25 Beale, Willert, *The Light of Other Days: Seen Through the Wrong End of an Opera Glass* (London: Richard Bentley and Son, 1890), volume ii, p. 123.

26 Classified advertisement in *The Era*, 27 December 1874, p. 1.

27 Frank Desprez, quoted in Jones, *Helen D'Oyly Carte*, p. 20.

28 A few secondary sources have the marriage as an elopement, but a timeline accompanying the family tree describes it as 'arranged', THM/73/9/2/4.

29 Certificate viewable online at the Gilbert and Sullivan Archive: https://gsarchive.net/carte/census/index.html.

30 Jones, *Helen D'Oyly Carte*, p. 33.

31 *Morning Advertiser*, quoted in Allen, Reginald, *The First Night Gilbert and Sullivan*, centennial edition (London: Chappell & Co, 1975), p. 5.

Two – 'Entertainment of a higher order'

1 Description in Barrington, Rutland, *Rutland Barrington by Himself* (London: Grant Richards, 1908), p. 29.

2 *The Observer*, 23 August 1874, p. 3.

3 Cannadine, David, 'Three Who Made a Revolution', *New York Review of Books*, 7 March 1991.

4 'Our Representative Man', *Punch*, 10 October 1874, p. 151.

5 Cannadine, 'Three Who Made a Revolution'.

6 'Prosperous partnership, the Gilbert and Sullivan collaboration; Mr R. D'Oyly Carte gives some interesting details', *The Umpire*, 2 February 1890, p. 7.

7 Quoted in Baily, Leslie, *Gilbert & Sullivan and their world* (London: Thames & Hudson, 1973), p. 42.

8 'Prince's Theatre', *The Observer*, 30 March 1884, p. 6.

9 Read, Michael, 'Hawtrey, Sir Charles Henry (1858–1923)', *Oxford Dictionary of National Biography* (Oxford: Oxford University Press, 2004).

10 *Pall Mall Gazette*, 1 February 1875, p. 11.

11 *Pall Mall Gazette*, 3 November 1877, p. 13.

12 Allen, Reginald, *Sir Arthur Sullivan: Composer & Personage* (New York: The Pierpont Morgan Library, 1975), p. iii.

13 Richard D'Oyly Carte, letter addressed to W. S. Gilbert and Arthur Sullivan, 8 April 1880, quoted in Joseph, Tony, *D'Oyly Carte Opera Company, 1875–1982: An Unofficial History* (London: Bunthorne Books, 1994), p. 11.

14 Quoted in Ainger, *Gilbert and Sullivan*, p. 192.

15 Herman Klein, quoted in Jacobs, Arthur, *Arthur Sullivan: A Victorian Musician* (Oxford: Oxford University Press, 1984), p. 113.

16 Jacobs, Arthur, 'Carte, Richard D'Oyly (1844–1901)', *Oxford Dictionary of National Biography* (Oxford: Oxford University Press, 2004).

17 Andrew, Marjorie, and Clissold, Shirley, *The Diaries of John McConnell Black* (Auckland: Hawthornedene, 1986), vol. i, 1875–1886, p. 61.

18 Jacobs, 'Carte, Richard D'Oyly (1844–1901)', *ODNB.*

19 'Prosperous Partnership, the Gilbert and Sullivan collaboration; Mr R. D'Oyly Carte gives some interesting details', *The Umpire*, 2 February 1890, p. 7.

20 Quoted in Stedman, Jane W., *W. S. Gilbert: A Classic Victorian & His Theatre* (New York: Oxford University Press, 1996), p. 149.

21 Seeley, *Richard D'Oyly Carte*, p. 35.

22 Jacobs, *Arthur Sullivan*, p. 111.

23 'Opera Comique', *The Times*, 19 November 1877, p. 6.

24 Comedy Opera Company minutes, quoted in Seeley, *Richard D'Oyly Carte*, p. 38.

25 'London', *The Standard*, 28 June 1878, p. 4.

26 Short, Ernest Henry, and Compton-Rickett, Arthur, *Ring Up the Curtain: Being a Pageant of English Entertainment Covering Half a Century* (London: Herbert Jenkins Limited, 1938), p. 76.

27 Ainger, *Gilbert and Sullivan*, p. 162.

28 *The Era*, 1 September 1897.

29 '100 Electrifying Years', *The Savoyard*, vol. xx, no. 2, D'Oyly Carte Opera Trust, September 1981, pp. 4–6.

30 'Prosperous partnership, the Gilbert and Sullivan collaboration; Mr R. D'Oyly Carte gives some interesting details', *The Umpire*, 2 February 1890, p. 7.

31 Ibid.

32 Rollins, Cyril, and Witts, John, *The D'Oyly Carte Opera Company in Gilbert and Sullivan Operas: A Record of Productions, 1875–1961* (London: Michael Joseph, 1962), pp. 30–31.

33 'The Fracas at the Opera Comique', *The Era*, 10 August 1879, p. 5.

34 *The Graphic*, 11 October 1879.

35 Richard D'Oyly Carte, letter to Arthur Sullivan, quoted in Jacobs, *Arthur Sullivan*, p. 125.

36 Seeley, Paul, *Richard D'Oyly Carte*, p. 46.

37 'Royal Italian Opera, Covent Garden', *London Evening Standard*, 17 April 1876, p. 3.

38 *The Era*, 30 November 1879.

39 Ainger, *Gilbert and Sullivan*, pp. 182–31.

40 Arthur Sullivan, letter to his mother, 31 December 1879, quoted in Jacobs, *Arthur Sullivan*, p. 132.

41 Jones, *Helen D'Oyly Carte*, p. 41.

42 'Supreme Court of Judicature, Aug. 1 – Court of Appeal – Gilbert *v.* The Comedy Opera Company Limited', *The Times*, 2 August 1879, p. 4.

Three – 'Light of the Future'

1 Richard D'Oyly Carte, letter to Arthur Sullivan, February 1882, selected correspondence between D'Oyly Carte, Gilbert and Sullivan, 1880–1885, THM/73/2/4.

2 Ibid.

3 Arthur Sullivan's diary, 11 December 1899, quoted in Canon, John, 'The Suppressed Saga of Two Savoy Sultans', Gilbert and Sullivan archive, gsarchive.net.

4 Richard D'Oyly Carte, letter to W. S. Gilbert, June 1885, quoted in Crowther, Andrew, 'The Carpet Quarrel Explained', https://gsarchive.net/articles/html/quarrel.html.

5 Richard D'Oyly Carte, letters to W. S. Gilbert, 26 April 1890 and 28 April 1890, THM/73/2/6.

6 Richard D'Oyly Carte, letter to Arthur Sullivan, February 1882, selected correspondence between D'Oyly Carte, Gilbert and Sullivan, 1880–1885, THM/73/2/4.

7 'Savoy Theatre Opening Night Programme', 6 October 1881, quoted in Lloyd, Matthew, http://www.arthurlloyd.co.uk/SavoyTheatre.html.

8 *Reynolds's Newspaper*, 16 October 1881.

9 Ibid.

10 'Savoy Theatre Opening Night Programme', 6 October 1881, quoted in Lloyd, Matthew, http://www.arthurlloyd.co.uk/SavoyTheatre.html.

11 Ibid.

12 Jackson, Stanley, *The Savoy: The Romance of a Great Hotel* (London: Frederick Muller Ltd, 1990), p. 19.

13 *The Era*, 1 October 1881.

14 'D'Oyly Carte Opera Company cuttings scrapbooks, 1842–1924', THM/73/30.

15 Ibid.

16 'Correspondence and cutting related to fire safety and electricity at the Savoy buildings, 1881–1900', THM/73/8/3.

17 *The Daily News*, 11 October 1881.

18 *The Times*, 3 October 1891.

19 'The Savoy Theatre', *Reynold's Newspaper*, 16 October 1881.

20 *The Daily News*, 3 October 1881.

21 *The Times*, 11 October 1881.

22 Quoted in Garland Fletcher, Edward, 'Electricity at the Savoy', *Studies in English* (University of Texas Press, 1941), pp. 154–161.

Four – Off on tour

1 *Advertiser* (Adelaide, South Australia), 4 August 1885, cited in Jones, *Helen D'Oyly Carte*, p. 58.

2 *Sporting Times*, quoted in Bradley, Ian (ed.), *The Complete Annotated Gilbert and Sullivan* (Oxford: Oxford University Press, 2001) p. 286.

3 Richard D'Oyly Carte, letter to Helen Carte (*née* Lenoir), 17 December 1881.

4 *Sporting Times*, quoted in Bradley, *The Complete Annotated Gilbert and Sullivan*, p. 286..

5 Mendelssohn, Michèle, *Making Oscar Wilde* (Oxford: Oxford University Press, 2018), p. 21.

6 *Freeman's Journal and Daily Commercial Advertiser* (Dublin, Ireland), 25 January 1882.

7 Ibid.

8 Arthur Sullivan, letter to his mother, 2 January 1880, quoted Jacobs, *Arthur Sullivan*, p. 132.

9 Ibid.

10 Morse, William F., 'American Lectures', *The Writings of Oscar Wilde* (London: A. R. Keller, 1907), vol. xv, p. 93.

11 Oscar Wilde, quoted in 'Wilde about California', *Los Angeles Times*, 5 May 2013.

12 Wilde, Oscar, with Holland, Merlin, and Hart-Davies, Rupert (eds.), *The Complete Letters of Oscar Wilde* (New York: Henry Holt and Company, 2000), letter 126.

13 Ibid., letter 127.

14 Ballantine, William, *The Old World and the New; Being a Continuation of his Experiences* (London: Richard Bentley and Son, 1884), p. 18.

15 Jones, *Helen D'Oyly Carte*, p. 68.

16 Lang, Cecil Y. (ed.), *The Letters of Matthew Arnold*, vol. v, 1879–1884 (Charlottesville and London: The University of Virginia Press, 2001), p. 298.

17 Ibid., pp. 371–2.

18 Ibid., p. 387.

19 Ibid., p. 405.

20 Martin, George Whitney, *Verdi in America: Oberto Through Rigoletto* (Rochester, NY: University of Rochester Press, 2011), p. 226.

21 Arthur Sullivan, letter to W. S. Gilbert, 2 April 1884, quoted in Ainger, *Gilbert and Sullivan*, p. 230.

22 Rutland Barrington, quoted in Traubner, Richard, *Operetta: A Theatrical History* (London: Routledge, 2004), p. 166.

23 Arthur Sullivan, quoted in Tarling, Nicholas, *Orientalism and the Operatic World* (Lanham, MD: Rowman & Littlefield Publishers, 2015), p. 268.

24 W. S. Gilbert, letter to Arthur Sullivan, 19 February 1888, quoted in Sullivan, Herbert, and Flower, Newman, *Sir Arthur Sullivan: His Life, Letters and Diaries* (London: Cassell & Co, 1927), p. 175.

25 'Enthusiasts interviewed. No XVI Mr R. D'Oyly Carte', *The Sunday Times*, 3 May 1885, p. 6.

26 Ibid.

27 Jacobs, 'Carte, Richard D'Oyly (1844–1901)'.

28 Richard D'Oyly Carte, letter to John Stetson, 13 June 1885, THM 1880–1891, f. 407.

29 Ibid., f. 405.

30 Arthur Sullivan's diary, 24 September 1885, Yale University Library.

31 Prestige, Colin, *D'Oyly Carte and the Pirates* (Kansas: University of Kansas Libraries, 1950), p. 135.

32 All Desprez comments from 'The late Mrs D'Oyly Carte', by the editor, *The Era*, 19 May 1913, p. 19.

33 *The Times*, 13 June 1873, quoted in Jones, *Helen D'Oyly Carte*, p. 16.

34 Stedman, Jane W., 'Carte, Helen (1852–1913)', *Oxford Dictionary of National Biography* (Oxford: Oxford University Press, 2004).

35 Ibid.

36 Morse, William F., 'American Lectures', *The Writings of Oscar Wilde* (London: A. R. Keller, 1907), p. 73.

37 Stedman, Jane W., 'Carte, Helen (1852–1913)', *ODNB*.

38 Baily, Leslie, *The Gilbert and Sullivan Book* (London: Cassell & Company Ltd, 1952), p. 163.

39 Waugh, Evelyn, *Brideshead Revisited* (London: Penguin, 2016), p. 185.

40 Lucas D'Oyly Carte's diary, 11 April 1888, quoted in Jones, *Helen D'Oyly Carte*, p. 79.

41 'A Savoy Rehearsal', *The Graphic* 48, 7 October 1893.

42 Lytton, Henry A., *The Secrets of a Savoyard* (London: Jarrold & Sons, 1922), p. 70.

43 'The late Mrs D'Oyly Carte', by the editor, *The Era*, 19 May 1913, p. 19.

44 Barrington, Rutland, *Rutland Barrington by Himself* (London: Grant Richards, 1908), chapter 5, reproduced on Gilbert and Sullivan Archive, gsarchive.net.

Five – 'The Hotel de Luxe of the World'

1 Melba, Nellie, *Memories and Melodies* (Cambridge: Cambridge University Press, 2011), p. 228.
2 'Company Meetings: The Savoy Hotel', *The Times*, 22 April 1932.
3 Savoy Hotel Prospectus 1889, Savoy archives.
4 Veblen, Thorstein, *The Theory of the Leisure Class: An Economic Study of Institutions* (New York: The Modern Library, 1934), p. 36.
5 Savoy Hotel Prospectus 1889, Savoy archives.
6 Ibid.
7 *The Mercury* (Hobart, Tasmania: 1860–1954), 9 January 1933, p. 2.
8 Savoy Hotel Prospectus 1889, Savoy archives.
9 Barr, Luke, *Ritz and Escoffier: The Chef and the Rise of the Leisure Class* (New York: Clarkson Potter, 2018), p. 19.
10 *World*, 31 July 1889.
11 *Morning Advertiser*, 1 August 1889.
12 *Illustrated London News*, 26 October 1889.
13 Ritz, Marie Louise, *César Ritz: Host to the World* (London: George G. Harrap & Co. Ltd, 1938), p. 110.
14 Ibid.
15 Ibid., p. 135.
16 Barr, *Ritz and Escoffier*, p. 8.
17 Stock Exchange, 28 September 1889.
18 Claude Monet, quoted in 'Monet and Architecture review', *Guardian*, 8 April 2018.
19 https://famoushotels.org/hotels/321.
20 Jackson, *The Savoy*, p. 21.
21 Rupert D'Oyly Carte's recollection in *Morning Advertiser*, 13 September 1948.
22 Hugh Wontner, quoted in 'Company Meetings: The Savoy Hotel', *The Times*, 13 April 1964.
23 Savoy Hotel Prospectus 1889, Savoy archives.
24 Ibid.
25 Ibid.
26 *San Francisco Chronicle*, 30 August 1891.
27 Ritz, *César Ritz*, p. 135.
28 R. D. Blumenfeld's diary, 10 November 1890, quoted in victorianlondon.org/houses/savoy.
29 Marie Ritz, quoted in James, Ken, *Escoffier: The King of Chefs* (London: Bloomsbury Continuum, 2006), p. 127.

Six – The carpet quarrel

1 R. D. Blumenfeld's diary, 10 November 1890.
2 W. S. Gilbert, letter to Arthur Sullivan, 21 June 1885, Morgan Library, accession no: 107098.
3 Arthur Sullivan to Richard D'Oyly Carte, in person, at Adelphi Terrace, 29 January 1884, quoted in Crowther, Andrew, *Contradiction Contradicted: The Plays of W S Gilbert* (London: Associated University Presses, 2000), p.140.
4 *The World*, 3 October, 1894.
5 Ibid.
6 Gans, Andrew, 'Andrew Lloyd Webber sells London's Palace Theatre', *Playbill*, 11 April 2012.

Seven – 'Everyone who comes, goes away highly pleased'

1 *Lighthouse*, 4 October 1890.
2 Auguste Escoffier, quoted in 'Sober cooks, tight shoes – how the son of a Swiss peasant became a synonym for luxury', *The Economist*, 12 April 2018.
3 Quoted in 'César Ritz', *Encyclopedia Britannica*, britannica.com.
4 Barr, *Ritz and Escoffier*, p. 54.
5 Newnham-Davis, Lieut.-Col. Nathaniel, *Dinners and Diners: Where and How to Dine in London* (London: Grant Richards, 1901), p. 26.
6 Barr, *Ritz and Escoffier*, p. 120.
7 'Savoy Hotel Limited', *Financial News*, 27 September 1890.
8 Marie Ritz's phrasing in Ritz, Marie Louise, *César Ritz: Host to the World*, p. 153.
9 Louis Echenard, quoted in Newnham-Davis, *Dinners and Diners*, p. 48.
10 Sharland, Elizabeth, *Waiting for Coward: Private Lives Revisited at the Algonquin Hotel* (Bloomington: iUniverse, 2014), p. 10.
11 'The Wares of Autoclycus', *Pall Mall Gazette*, 12 April 1897.
12 Contarini, Paolo, *The Savoy was my Oyster* (London: Robert Hale, 1976), p. 67.
13 Jackson, *The Savoy*, p. 32.
14 Contarini, *The Savoy was my Oyster*, p. 129.
15 First general shareholders' meeting of 26 September 1890, quoted in Barr, *Ritz and Escoffier*, p. 91.
16 'Savoy Hotel Limited', *Financial News*, 27 September 1890.

Eight – Scandals

1 Wodehouse, P. G., *Mike and Psmith* (Auckland: The Floating Press, 2012), p. 6.
2 Wodehouse, P. G., quoted in *The Spectator*, 1 March 1975, p. 234.
3 Douglas, Lord Alfred, *Poems* (Paris: Édition du Mercure de France, 1896), p. 54.
4 Quoted in McKenna, Neil, *The Secret Life of Oscar Wilde* (London: Arrow Books, 2004), p. 209.
5 Wilde, Oscar, with Holland, Merlin, and Hart-Davies, Rupert (eds.), *The Complete Letters of Oscar Wilde* (New York: Henry Holt and Company, 2000), p. 336.
6 Antonio Migge, quoted in McKenna, Neil, *The Secret Life of Oscar Wilde*, p. 297.
7 Auguste Escoffier, quoted in 'Sober cooks, tight shoes – how the son of a Swiss peasant became a synonym for luxury', *The Economist*, 12 April 2018.
8 Figures from Taylor, Derek, 'César Ritz and Auguste Escoffier vs the Savoy Hotel Company', *International Journal of Hospitality Management* (1996), vol. xv, no. 1, pp. 29–39.
9 Quoted in Shaw, Timothy, *The World of Escoffier* (London: Zwemmer, 1994), p. 50.
10 Quoted in Augustin, Andreas, Williamson, Andrew, and Tenison, Rupert, *The Savoy London* (famoushotels.org, 2002), p. 69.

Nine – Fluctuat nec migrator

1 'Under New Management: Startling Changes at The Savoy Hotel', *Daily Mail*, 10 March 1898.
2 Quoted in Augustin, Andreas, 'Kitchen Revolt at The Savoy: 16 fiery cooks took their long knives', famoushotels.org.
3 Ritz, *César Ritz*, p. 206.
4 Ibid., p. 208.
5 Newnham-Davis, *Dinners and Diners*, p. 55.
6 Contarini, *The Savoy was my Oyster*, p. 127.
7 Newnham-Davis, *Dinners and Diners*, p. 57.
8 Letters of R. Coulson, P. Kirkham and J. Mivart, jnr, May 1813, quoted in Sheppard, F. H. W. (ed.), 'Claridge's in Brook Street: South Side', *Survey of London: Volume 40, the Grosvenor Estate in Mayfair, Part 2 (The Buildings)* (London, 1980).
9 *Country Life*, volume 9, 1901.
10 *Caterer and Hotel-Proprietors' Gazette*, vol. xvi, 16 January 1893, p. 3.
11 Ibid.

12 *Evening Herald* (Dublin), 5 April 1894.

13 *Caterer and Hotel-Proprietors' Gazette*, vol. xvii, 1 January 1894, p. 4; 15 October 1894, p. 423.

14 *Caterer and Hotel-Proprietors' Gazette*, vol. xvi, 15 December 1893, p. 512.

15 *The Times*, 24 December 1894, p. 3.

16 Jackson, *The Savoy*, p. 36.

17 Quoted in Jaine, Tom, 'Smith, Sir George Reeves (1863–1941)', *Oxford Dictionary of National Biography* (Oxford: Oxford University Press, 2004).

18 *The Referee*, 14 May 1893.

19 Tillett, Selwyn, 'Jane Annie', *Sullivan Society Journal*, 1993.

20 W. S. Gilbert, letter to the *Sheffield Daily Telegraph*, 21 April 1894, p. 6.

21 Richard D'Oyly Carte, letter to W. S. Gilbert, quoted in Self, Geoffrey, *Light Music in Britain since 1870: A Survey* (London: Routledge, 2017), p. 25.

22 'A Savoy Rehearsal', *The Graphic* 48, 7 October 1893.

23 Ibid.

24 Ibid.

25 Arthur Sullivan's diary, 27 June 1899, quoted on Gilbert and Sullivan Archive, gsarchive.net.

26 Ibid.

27 Ibid., 3 December 1899.

28 Ibid., 10 December 1899.

29 Ibid., 11 December 1899.

30 Ibid.

31 Arthur Sullivan, letter to Helen Carte, 7 November 1900.

32 'The Yeomen of the Savoy', *The Economist*, 24 November 1973, p. 130.

33 W. S. Gilbert, speech at the Hotel Cecil, 30 December 1906, quoted in Dark, Sidney, and Grey, Rowland, *W. S. Gilbert: His Life and Letters* (London: Methuen & Co Ltd, 1923), pp. 193–5.

34 Pearson, Hesketh, *Gilbert and Sullivan: A Biography* (London: House of Stratus, 2001), p. 105.

35 'R. D'OYLY CARTE IS DEAD; The Famous Theatrical Manager Had Long Been an Invalid – He Was Fifty-Six Years Old', *New York Times*, 4 April 1901.

36 Richard D'Oyly Carte, *The Economist*, 11 May 1901.

37 Sullivan had also suffered a grave financial loss when his broker went bankrupt in 1882.

38 For a fuller argument see: Cannadine, David, 'Three Who Made a Revolution', *New York Review of Books*, 7 March 1991.

39 'Patricia Leonard: principal contralto of the D'Oyly Carte opera', *The Times*, 22 February 2010.

40 Quoted in Sherwood, James, 'Richard D'Oyly Carte', henrypoole.com/individual/richard-doyly-carte.

Notes

ACT TWO: RUPERT

Ten – Belle Époque

1 Jones, *Helen D'Oyly Carte*, p. 120.
2 'Lucas D'Oyly Carte, late of the Savoy Hotel' (wills), *The Economist*, 16 March 1907.
3 'Lucas D'Oyly Carte' (obituary), *The Times*, 22 January 1907.
4 Wellcome Collection case notes and photograph of Henry William Carte, 1903, p. 301, L0051774.
5 Seeley, *Richard D'Oyly Carte*, p. 3.
6 'Dame Bridget D'Oyly Carte', *The Times*, 3 May 1985.
7 Barbara Tuchman, *The Proud Tower* (Macmillan Company, New York, 1962) p.283
8 Tuchman, Barbara, *The Proud Tower* (New York: The Macmillan Company, 1962), p. 283.
9 Note to committee members, THM/73/8/5.
10 £300,000 of the amount needed came from raising debentures, as outlined in 'Savoy Hotel (Limited)', *The Times*, 21 February 1903, p. 15.
11 Jackson, *The Savoy*, p. 39.
12 Contarini, *The Savoy was my Oyster*, p. 87.
13 Quoted in Nicol, Jean, *Meet Me at the Savoy* (London: Museum Press Ltd, 1952), p. 23.
14 Sheppard, F. H. W. (ed.), 'Claridge's' in 'Brook Street: South Side', *Survey of London: Volume 40, the Grosvenor Estate in Mayfair, Part 2 (The Buildings)* (London, 1980).
15 Ritz, *César Ritz*, p. 291.
16 'Coronation Postponed', *Evening Express*, 24 June 1902.
17 Advertisement quoted in Lohman, Sarah, *Eight Flavours: The Untold Story of American Cuisine* (New York: Simon & Schuster, 2016), p. 95.
18 MacKenzie, Compton, *The Savoy of London* (London: George G. Harrap & Co. Ltd., 1953), p. 73.
19 Five different newspapers covered her retirement in 1926, including *The Daily Express*, who named her the 'world's most famous barmaid'.
20 Letters between Churchill's private secretary and Savoy management, quoted in 'How To Eat, Drink And Smoke Like Winston Churchill' on Londonist.com, 25 July 2019, from Stelzer, Cita, *Dinner with Churchill: Policy-Making at the Dinner Table* (London: Short Books Ltd, 2011).
21 These were suffragist colours in 1906; the suffragette colours of purple, green and white would come in 1908. Suffragettes and suffragists were

still part of the same movement at this stage. See LSE History blog: 'Suffragettes at dinner – from gaol to Savoy Hotel', https://blogs.lse.ac.uk/lsehistory/2018/12/05/suffragettes-at-dinner-from-the-to-the-savoy-hotel/.

22   'Suffragettes at dinner – from gaol to Savoy Hotel', LSE, https://blogs.lse. ac.uk/ lsehistory/2018/12/05/suffragettes-at-dinner-from-gaol-to-the-savoy-hotel/.

23   'Rupert D'Oyly Carte' (obituary), *The Times*, 13 September 1948.

Eleven – No sackcloth and ashes

1   Rupert D'Oyly Carte, in conversation with Leslie Baily, quoted on https://gsarchive.net/carte/1919/index.html.

2   Ibid.

3   Wodehouse, P. G., *Something Fresh* (London: Arrow, 2008), p. 55.

4   Note to guests, dated April 1917, printed in *Claridge's* magazine, 25 June 2018, p. 87.

5   'Gilbert & Sullivan Revival: Interview with Mr. R. D'Oyly Carte', *The Observer*, 24 August 1919, p. 10.

6   Ramsey, Guy, 'The two worlds of Rupert D'Oyly Carte', *Daily Mail*, 13 September 1948.

7   Interview with Sir Hugh Wontner, National Sound Archive.

8   Ibid.

9   Mrs Sidney Granville, quoted in *Glasgow Record*, 13 September 1948.

10 Ramsey, Guy, 'The two worlds of Rupert D'Oyly Carte', *Daily Mail*, 13 September 1948.

11 *The Times*, 21 September 1926.

12 Bettany, Clemence, *D'Oyly Carte Centenary*, (London: D'Oyly Carte Opera Company, 1975), p. 75.

13 Contarini, *The Savoy was my Oyster*, p. 76.

14 Sweet, Matthew, *The West End Front* (London: Faber & Faber, 2011) p. 126.

15 Ibid.

16 'Delicious Grouse: Some New Recipes', *The Montrose Review*, 13 August 1926, p. 8.

17 'From Historic Figures Comes Today's Menu', *Kokomo Tribune* (Kokomo, Indiana), 25 December 1926, p. 5.

18 Latry, François, 'To the Editor of *The Times*, The Herring.' *The Times*, 31 January 1935, p. 15.

19 'Children Now May Dine on Imitation Delicacies', *Chronicle Telegram* (Elyria, Ohio), 2 August 1929, p. 12.

Notes

Twelve – Rupert's roaring twenties

1 Cooper, Diana, *The Light of Common Day* (Boston: Houghton Mifflin, 1959), p. 56.
2 'The Savoy Hotel', *The Times*, 27 March 1931, p.22; and 22 April 1932, p.20.
3 Sherry, Norman, *The Life of Graham Greene, Vol. I: 1904–1939* (London: Jonathan Cape, 1989), p. 367.
4 Milne, A. A., *The Birthday Party* (London: Bello, 2017), p. 7.
5 Contarini, *The Savoy was my Oyster*, p. 100.
6 'Company Meetings: The Savoy Hotel Limited', *The Times*, 26 April 1965.
7 '£100-a-week Mayfair Playboy Starts a Man's Life', *Daily Express*, 21 August 1937.
8 Bennett, *Imperial Palace*, p. 84.
9 Contarini, *The Savoy was my Oyster*, p. 120.
10 Ibid.
11 Ibid., p. 150.
12 Hibberd, Stuart, *This is the BBC* (London: Macdonald & Evans, 1950), p. 4.
13 *The Referee*, 7 October 1923.
14 *Radio Times*, Issue 90, p. 538.
15 Contarini, *The Savoy was my Oyster*, p. 71.
16 Quoted in Rijks, Miranda, *The Eccentric Entrepreneur, Sir Julien Cahn, Businessman, Philanthropist, Magician and Cricket-Lover* (Gloucestershire: The History Press, ebook, 2014), p. 74.

Thirteen – 'Curzon Street Baroque'

1 Fitzgerald, F. Scott, quoted in 'On the French Riviera, Fitzgerald found his place in the sun', *New York Times*, 10 May 2015.
2 I found the details for this chapter mainly from visiting Coleton Fishacre, which is open to the public.

Fourteen – A scrum in Mayfair

1 *Sporting and Dramatic News*, 14 October 1926.
2 Blythe, Ronald, *The Times by the Sea: Aldeburgh 1955–1958* (London: Faber & Faber, 2013), p. 72.
3 Ibid., p. 73.
4 Ibid.
5 Conversation with Jo Batterham, summer 2016.

Notes

Fifteen – An heir and a spare

1 'Leading the Past', Savoy brochure, 2009, p.1.
2 'London's Phoenix', *The Economist*, 17 July 1993, p. 84.
3 Green, Martyn, *Here's a how-de-do* (New York: W. W. Norton & Co, 1952), p. 83.
4 Ibid.
5 Contarini, *The Savoy was my Oyster*, p. 150.
6 Ibid.
7 de Verteuil, Anthony, *The De Verteuils of Trinidad, 1797–1997* (Port-of-Spain: The Litho Press, 1997), p. 206.

Sixteen – 'Essence de civilisation'

1 Noël Coward, quoted in 'Noel Coward's Blithe Spirit', *Guardian*, 21 February 2014.
2 Wright, C. Kent, *A. R. P. and all that* (London: Allen & Unwin, 1940), p. 38.
3 Contarini, *The Savoy was my Oyster*, p. 75.
4 Jacobs, Sherelle, 'Spies, bombs and caviar: how accurate is *The Halcyon*, and how were London hotels really affected by the Second World War?', *Daily Telegraph*, 20 January 2017.
5 'New Rations Challenge London's Best Chef', *Wisconsin State Journal* (Madison, Wisconsin), 7 January 1941, p. 18.
6 'London After Dark', CBS Radio, recorded 24 August 1940.
7 Langley, James M., *Fight Another Day* (London: Collins, 1974), p. 126.
8 Contarini, *The Savoy was my Oyster*, p. 138.
9 Sweet, *The West End Front*.
10 'The name's Tricycle, Agent Tricycle', BBC News, 9 May 2002, http://news.bbc.co.uk/1/hi/uk/1973962.stm.
11 Ibid.
12 Sweet, *The West End Front*, p. 49.
13 Bradley, John R., 'Just Wilde about the boys', *Independent*, 25 May 1997.
14 Home Office Advisory Committee, 5 September 1940, HO 45/23695.
15 Interview with Sir Hugh Wontner, National Sound Archive.
16 Ibid.
17 Interview with Sir Hugh Wontner, National Sound Archive.
18 Sweet, *The West End Front*, p. 46.
19 Contarini, *The Savoy was my Oyster*, p. 77.
20 'Requisitioned Hotels', *The Times*, 26 September 1939, p. 5.
21 'Did a London hotel room become part of Yugoslavia?', BBC News, 18 July 2016, https://www.bbc.co.uk/news/magazine-36569675.

Notes

ACT THREE: BRIDGET

Seventeen – Reluctant heiress

1 Philip Murphy, *Alan Lennox-Boyd: A Biography* (London, 1999), p. 74.
2 Contarini, *The Savoy was my Oyster*, p. 96.
3 'Rupert D'Oyly Carte' (obituary), *The Times*, 13 September 1948.
4 Mander, Raymond, and Mitchenson, Joe, *A Picture History of Gilbert and Sullivan* (London: Vista Books, 1962), foreword.
5 *Nottingham Guardian*, 16 September 1948.
6 Ibid.
7 Contarini, *The Savoy was my Oyster*, p. 150.
8 *The Times*, 13 September 1948.
9 Ibid.
10 *Daily Mail*, 5 October 1948.
11 Cannadine, David, 'Three Who Made a Revolution', *New York Review of Books*, 7 March 1991.
12 'Savoy Coronation Ball', *The Times*, 25 November 1952, p. 10.
13 Quoted in Contarini, *The Savoy was my Oyster*, p. 106.
14 'Jubilee hotels – a royal rave-up', *The Caterer*, 1 June 2012.
15 Ibid.
16 Contarini, *The Savoy was my Oyster*, p. 107.
17 Conversation with Julian Wontner, January 2020.
18 Conversation with Peter Riley, August 2016.
19 Ibid.
20 Charlotte Wontner, quoted in 'Savoy to sell off 3000 slices of hotel history', *Daily Telegraph*, 18 December 2007.
21 Interview with Sir Hugh Wontner, National Sound Archive, 1990.
22 Ibid.
23 Ibid.
24 Mander and Mitchenson, *A Picture History of Gilbert and Sullivan*, foreword.
25 Contarini, *The Savoy was my Oyster*, p. 152.

Eighteen – Static in the swinging sixties

1 'A Great Maitre-Chef', *The Times*, 13 February 1935.
2 Described in 'Why Escoffier?', *The Art of Eating*, issue 60.
3 James Walsh blog, jameswalshblog.blogspot.com, March 2009.
4 Contarini, *The Savoy was my Oyster*, p. 159.
5 James Walsh blog.

Notes

6 'Do you have what it takes to be a female chef?', prue-leith.com.

7 Contarini, *The Savoy was my Oyster*, p. 168.

8 Field-Marshall Bernard Montgomery, letter to Miss Baird, 24 February 1962, letter sold on 14 December 2013 at International Autograph Auctions, Nottingham.

9 Nicol, *Meet me at the Savoy*, p. 20.

10 Contarini, *The Savoy was my Oyster*, p. 138.

11 James Walsh blog.

12 *The Express*, 27 December 2007.

13 Patricia Kirkwood, quoted in Ryan, Catherine, *The Queen: The Life and Times of Elizabeth II* (New York: Chartwell Books, 2018), p. 114.

14 Interview with Dionne Warwick, *The Noise Network*, 24 October 2012.

15 *Billboard*, 22 October 1966, p. 48.

16 'How wealthy guests turned the Savoy into the world's most decadent hotel as it shuts for a £100m refit', *Daily Mail*, 17 December 2007.

17 'The Rich List', *The Sunday Times*, 18 May 2014, and Barrow, Andrew, *Animal Magic: A Brother's Story* (London: Jonathan Cape, 2011), p. 160.

18 Montague Browne, Anthony, *Long Sunset: Memoirs of Winston Churchill's Last Private Secretary* (Kent: Podkin Press, 2009,), pp. 299–300.

19 Evans, Peter, 'Aristotle Onassis comes to the London stage', *The Times*, 9 October 2010.

20 Lady Mary Dunn, quoted in Bedell Smith, Sally, *Reflected Glory: The Life of Pamela Churchill Harriman* (New York: Simon & Schuster, 1996), p. 121.

21 Bedell Smith, Sally, *Reflected Glory*, p. 186.

Nineteen – Pickwick and co.

1 'Dame Bridget D'Oyly Carte', *The Times*, 3 May 1985.

2 Ibid.

3 'No prettier property', *The Economist*, 28 March 1959.

4 Ibid.

5 Conversation with Margaret Bowden, October 2016.

6 THM/73/14/9/5.

7 Conversation with Peter Riley, August 2016.

8 Contarini, *The Savoy was my Oyster*, p. 152.

9 Green, Martyn, *Here's a How-de-do* (New York: W. W. Norton & Co., 1952), pp. 236–37.

10 Interview with Sir Hugh Wontner, National Sound Archive, 1990.

11 Conversation with Peter Riley, August 2016.

12 Ibid.

13 Ibid.

Notes

14 Ibid.
15 Business Diary, *The Times*, 17 December 1970.
16 Harold Wilson, quoted in 'Sir Royston Nash' (obituary), *Daily Telegraph*, 24 April 2016.
17 'Lady Dorothy – Grand Dame of Tobago', scan of unnamed local newspaper, 1972.
18 Conversation with Margaret Bowden, November 2016.
19 'Lady Dorothy – Grand Dame of Tobago'.

Twenty – Bridget hangs on

1   Contarini, *The Savoy was my Oyster*, p. 88.
2   Ibid., p. 139.
3   Lord Cobbold, quoted in Kynaston, David, *The City Of London, vol. 4, A Club No More 1945–2000* (London: Chatto & Windus, 2001), p. 65.
4   Ibid., p. 64.
5   Ibid., p. 63.
6   *The Economist*, vol. 169, 12 December 1953, p. 832.
7   Hansard, Savoy Hotel Limited (Report), HC Deb, 6 July 1954, vol. 529.
8   Blakey, George G., *A History of the London Stock Market 1945–2009* (Harriman House, ebook, 2011), p. 25.
9   *The Economist*, 1 May 1954.
10 Kynaston, *The City Of London*, p. 64.
11 Ibid., p. 65.
12 Contarini, *The Savoy was my Oyster*, p. 95.
13 'Sir Anthony Tuke' (obituary), *Daily Telegraph*, 8 March 2001.
14 Wharton, Annabel Jane, *Building the Cold War: Hilton International Hotels and Modern Architecture* (Chicago: University of Chicago Press, 2001), p. 97.
15 'Stomping at the Savoy', *The Economist*, 2 December 1989, p. 108.
16 Forte, Charles, *The Autobiography of Charles Forte* (London: Pan, 1988), p. 2.
17 'Lord Forte' (obituary), *The Times*, 1 March 2007.
18 'Lord Forte' (obituary), *Daily Telegraph*, 1 March 2007.
19 Forte, *The Autobiography*, p. 87.
20 Ibid.
21 Ibid., p. 172.
22 Ibid.
23 'Plans for Charles' wedding', *The Economist*, 9 May 1981, p. 102.
24 Conversation with Jo Batterham, summer 2016.
25 Quoted in 'Sugaring up the Savoy', *The Times*, 6 August 1979.
26 Forte, *The Autobiography*, p. 168.
27 Ibid., p. 178.

28 Sir Hugh Wontner, quoted in Rocco Forte interview, *Observer Food Monthly*, 12 August 2001.
29 'Lord Forte' (obituary), *Daily Telegraph*, 1 March 2007.
30 'If walls could talk', *The Times*, 5 December 2007.
31 'Why there could still be a place for Sir Charles at the Savoy', *The Times*, 18 May 1981.
32 Forte, *The Autobiography*, p. 168.
33 'Why there could still be a place for Sir Charles at the Savoy', *The Times*.
34 'Company Meeting: The Savoy Hotel Limited', *The Times*, 22 April 1963.
35 Ibid.
36 Eighty-fifth annual general meeting, reported in *The Times*, 26 April 1974.
37 'Escoffier was our Forte', *Independent*, 4 August 1994.
38 Kay, John, 'What the Savoy shares with Google founders Page and Brin', *Financial Times*, 29 September 2015.
39 Forte, *The Autobiography*, p. 169.
40 Van Der Weyer, Matrin, 'The Fall of the house of Savoy', *The Spectator*, 10 September 1994, p. 18.
41 'Savoy gift', *The Spectator*, 12 August 1972.

Twenty-one – Curtain down

1 'Outlook for D'Oyly Carte brighter', *The Times*, 11 February 1978.
2 Quoted in Morrell, Roberta, *D'Oyly Carte: The Inside Story* (Leicestershire: Matador, 2016), p. 252.
3 'Gilbert and Sullivan, Take 2', *The Economist*, 21 May 1988.
4 Conversation with Peter Riley, August 2016.
5 'Exit Sir Charles amid acrimony over opera', *The Times*, 20 June 1981.
6 Poster advertising a Christie's auction of items from the company wardrobe department, 1984, 'Materials related to the closure of the D'Oyly Carte Opera Company, 1981–1984', V&A Department of Theatre and Performance, THM/73/6/11.
7 Conversation with Margaret Bowden, November 2016.

Postscript

1 Forte, *The Autobiography*, p. 178.
2 'Savoy Soap Opera', *The Spectator*, 21 July 1990.

INDEX

Index

Index

Index

Index

Index

ACKNOWLEDGEMENTS

Some good-natured people allowed me to interview them for the raw material, and offered me countless cups of tea: Margaret Bowden, Peter Riley, Jonny Gathorne-Hardy, Jo Batterham, Julian Antonia Leech, Christabel Gommer, Louise de Ville Morel, Peter Parker, Susan Scott.

Some caring people nurtured this idea along from my laptop to becoming an actual book: Fiona Crosby, Anna Hervé and Caitlin Raynor at Headline; Annabel Merullo, Laura McNeill and Tim Binding at Peters, Fraser and Dunlop.

Some important people rooted for me to get it over the finishing line: Mary Williams, Owen Williams, Luke McGee, Paul Johnson, Angharad Thain.